The
30
GREATEST
– – Sports – –
Conspiracy
Theories of
All Time

The
30
GREATEST
--Sports--
Conspiracy
Theories of
All Time

Ranking Sports' Most Notorious
Fixes, Cover–ups, and Scandals

Elliott Kalb
with Mark Weinstein

Skyhorse Publishing

Skyhorse Publishing books may be purchased in bulk at special discounts for sales promotion, corporate gifts, fund–raising, or educational purposes. Special editions can also be created to specifications. For details, contact the Special Sales Department, Skyhorse Publishing, 555 Eighth Avenue, Suite 903, New York, NY 10018 or info@skyhorsepublishing.com.

www.skyhorsepublishing.com

10 9 8 7 6 5 4 3 2 1

Library of Congress Cagaloging-in-Publication data is available on file.

ISBN: 978-1-60239-678-4

Printed in the United States of America

CONTENTS

FOREWORD

I had just retired from the Cincinnati Bengals, and was in my rookie season for HBO's *Inside the NFL.* Luckily for me, there was one other rookie on the show that 1990 season, and that was writer/researcher Elliott Kalb. We've been teammates for almost two decades since—not only at HBO Sports but at NBC Sports as well. We've worked live studio shows, taped studio shows, and live college football and NFL games. During football seasons, we spend more time with each other than we do with our wives and families.

It's a damn good thing Elliott never nags me to go anywhere or fix things. He's a great friend, and the fact that he likes Jimmy Buffett as much as I do and loses gracefully in ping–pong are some of the reasons I like having him on my side. Professionally, he gets the big picture. He gets it.

It's no surprise to me that Kalb has written this book. It's right up his alley. Here he presents the stories behind the stories. Everyone celebrates April 15, 1947, as Jackie Robinson Day in baseball, but Kalb wonders about the gentleman's agreement that prevented integration until that fateful day. Yes, the NBA is to be commended for opening its doors to black players—and now international players—more swiftly than other sports and quicker than most of society. But it is Kalb that has talked to many of the first black stars of the NBA and read through all the books, and has come across dozens of printed references to a quota system employed by the League in the 1950s.

I've learned to trust Elliott. He can spot trends, especially in the team sports that he follows so closely. Working so many live events with him, I have always drilled it into his head that we can't read about something that happened in our games the next day. We report what happened, and serve as immediate "first–edition" sources.

I have to admit, I'm not much of a conspiracy theorist. I thought that when Elliott brought this book to me, it would be filled with crazy Roswell UFO type stories. Or worse, that it would serve as a rationale for every underdog that ever lost a big sporting event. I was happy to see that Kalb makes a big distinction. Of course, it's better for the professional leagues and their broadcast partners if certain teams win. But there's no way that they can influence actual game play. The only thing we can be certain of is this: if Elliott and I need a team to win to make our traveling easier, that team will lose. After that, nothing is fixed!

Instead, Kalb focuses on people's lost stories. In the history books, the 1946 NFL Championship Game was marred because two players on the Giants were questioned before the game about offers they received from gamblers. Kalb goes back and discovers what the people were talking about at the time. Did Giants backs Philcock and Hapes accept money from gamblers? Why didn't they report the bribes to their coach? Should the game have been postponed?

What this book is to me, then, is history. It is history forgotten, and it is history from a different perspective. It's not that Kalb is saying "Super Bowl III was fixed." He's saying, "Here is a theory that has been talked about for years. Here is what I agree with. Here's what I find crazy, and here's what I believe."

It makes for interesting reading, even if I don't happen to personally agree with everything he says. Elliott has always been there to provide me with instant analysis and witty lines. Now he's written a book that attempts to do even more. He writes to remind, to provoke, to entertain, and to enrage.

—Cris Collinsworth

INTRODUCTION

I am a skeptic. I have always questioned the validity of many things purported to be factual. "Don't believe everything that you hear," I tell my kids. "Don't believe everything your teachers tell you." It is my belief that one has to read—a lot—and get differing points of view. Read a newspaper with a conservative slant, as well as one with a more liberal viewpoint. Keep an open mind. And be aware of the times when people or organizations have reason to lie, or to keep the truth from being told.

I'm not alone, of course. There are many people who love a great conspiracy theory, and refuse to blindly accept what is fed to them by authorities. In the 1997 motion picture *Conspiracy Theory* starring Julia Roberts and Mel Gibson, at one point Gibson's character says, "A good conspiracy is unprovable. I mean, if you can prove it, it means they screwed up somewhere along the line." Exactly.

If you opened the sports section of any major newspaper in February of 2007, you would have read reports of boxer Tommy Morrison's comeback. He hadn't fought in eleven years due to his testing positive (several times) for HIV. But Morrison had never taken his medication, and never believed that he had HIV. Now, he's boxing again—and his recent tests came back without a trace of HIV. I just find it interesting that he "no longer" has HIV, and that he says he was exiled from boxing by the powers that be right before he was set to make $35 million dollars to fight Mike Tyson. In July of 2007, the *New York Times* quoted experts as saying the possibility that Morrison's test results of HIV–antibodies were false positives were fewer than 1 in 100,000. The odds of a conspiracy in the world of boxing are probably much higher than that.

Two months later, in April of 2007, was another interesting story, when two–time NASCAR Nextel Cup champion Tony Stewart accused NASCAR of "playing God." Stewart, after finishing second in a race in Phoenix, used his radio show as a platform to call out NASCAR for four yellow flags caused by debris on the track. He claimed they did that to create a closer race. "It's about the integrity of the sport," he said. "When I feel our own sanctioning body isn't taking care of that, it's hard to support them and feel proud about being a driver in the Nextel Cup Series. I guess NASCAR thinks, 'Hey, wrestling worked, and it was for the most part staged, so I guess it's going to work in racing, too.'" When one of the leading competitors in a sport says, as Stewart did, that "I don't know if they've run a fair race all year," people don't know what to believe.

Conspiracy theories are nothing new. They first began to grace the front pages of newspapers in 1963, after President Kennedy was assassinated. By the late 1960s, the government and politicians had to answer to a growing number of investigative journalists who refused to suppress information. It was no longer enough to know that tragedies had happened; people were clamoring to know why they happened and who was behind them.

Some organizations still think that the best way to deal with a crisis is to cover it up, deny access, and stonewall. The thing about conspiracies is that they aren't always toppling politicians or governments. Sometimes people lie in entertainment, private business, and, yes, sports.

I have been around professional sports for over twenty–five years, and I've seen a lot of things that don't make sense. Sometimes, as the saying goes, if it walks like a duck and talks like a duck, it's just a duck. But sometimes you have to scratch your head and wonder.

Fans always look for motives and reasons beyond what is presented to them. Sometimes it is said that a certain team got screwed by the league. Sometimes, certain teams aren't "wanted" in later rounds of the playoffs, or championship rounds of certain events. In other words, fans of less–popular (or small–market) teams always look for reasons that their team was eliminated. They tend to see a powerful motive behind it, and that motive is usually money. Major League Baseball, the National Football League, and the National Basketball Association get enormous amounts of money from national television contracts. The television networks pay millions (and sometimes billions) of dollars for the rights to secure these contracts because they charge advertisers millions of dollars to promote their products to the millions of people tuning in to their broadcasts. The more people watch, the more advertisers will pay the following year. (Television networks get their money up front, and advertisers pay for projected ratings; sometimes networks will air additional commercials to "give back" to the advertiser, when the rating is somehow much lower than projected.) Therefore, it is always better for baseball when a team like the Yankees makes the World Series than when any other team advances, because the Yankees bring with them the widest possible national viewership. A popular team like the Yankees maximizes the number of viewers and advertising dollars. And because of this, many have speculated that Major League Baseball has a vested interest in seeing the Yankees make the Fall Classic.

The trouble with that is, there is entirely too much evidence proving why teams win and lose games. In the NBA, Michael Jordan's Bulls attracted record audiences in the 1990s. The ratings of the NBA Finals in 1998 were superior to the 1998 World Series, which featured the New York Yankees. Did the League (and then–television partner NBC) want Jordan around for the Finals? Of course it did. But if the League wanted to arrange or fix the Bulls, then they left entirely too much money on the table. Think about it. The Bulls, in their six NBA Championships, never needed a seventh game. The record ratings would have skyrocketed with each Game Seven. In 1998, the deciding Game Six (Jordan's final game with the Bulls) registered an NBA record 22.3 rating with a 38 share. The game was viewed by an estimated seventy–two million Americans. There would have been three days to build up the hype surrounding a Game 7. The game would have been played on a Wednesday night, when most people are home. So it's not a stretch to say the game would have attracted nearly a 30 rating with a 43 share. That's roughly the same number of people that watch the Academy Awards, which is usually the second most watched show in a calendar year, following the Super Bowl.

While it's unlikely that the Bulls could have been extended to a full seven–game series in all six championship series they played in, it certainly could have happened once or twice. But it didn't. All it would have taken was a phone call here, a blown call there. But sometimes you have to believe in the integrity of the game, the commissioner, the coaches, the referees, and the players on the court.

Sometimes, the difference between the winning and losing team in a semifinal series can be monumental in terms of championship game ratings. But I cannot put much stock into any fan thinking that a group of people would jeopardize the integrity of their sport for a few extra ratings points. In the 2002 NBA Western Conference Finals, the Shaquille O'Neal and Kobe Bryant–led Lakers defeated a more or less anonymous Sacramento Kings team in seven games, saving the NBA and NBC from a potentially low–rated finals series. But for every instance in which the leagues got their dream championship match–up, I can point out other examples in which they didn't. Major League Baseball had the Chicago Cubs in the League Championship Series in 2003. Don't you think that everyone wanted to see the Cubbies in the World Series for the first time since 1945? It would have been huge! Instead, the Florida Marlins defeated the Cubs in seven games, and advanced to the Fall Classic.

Which brings us to referees and the trust in which sports fans place on them. Until July of 2007—just before the first edition of this book went to press—the four major sports in the United States (Major League Baseball, National Football League, National Basketball Association, and the National Hockey League) had never had a scandal involving referees fixing games. That changed in late July of 2007, of course, when NBA referee Tim Donaghy came under federal investigation for his involvement in a gambling and point–shaving operation. NBA commissioner David Stern issued a statement, saying, "We would like to assure our fans that no amount of effort, time or personnel is being spared to assist in this investigation, to bring to justice an individual who has betrayed the most sacred trust in professional sports, and to take the necessary steps to protect against this ever happening again." Soccer fans in other parts of the world that I know little about have had referees or officials accused and convicted of fixing games countless times—in places like Israel, Zimbabwe, the Czech Republic, and Italy. It challenges the very integrity of the games. Sports fans that invest their time and money on these games have to believe (outside of isolated incidents that the leagues can't control) the games are contested fairly.

Along these same lines, I have to believe that the voting done by fans to select All–Star Game starters or MVPs is completely legit. In the final few days before fan voting ended for the 2007 All–Star Game, Barry Bonds trailed Chicago's Alfonso Soriano by more than 120,000 votes. If he wasn't elected a starter by the fans, it would have been up to National League manager Tony LaRussa (in conjunction, no doubt, with Commissioner Bud Selig) to decide whether or not to invite Bonds as a reserve in the game played in Bonds' home park in San Francisco. What happened? Bonds was voted in as the starter, sparing baseball a potential embarrassment (or conflict, depending on your point of view). I have to believe that rules were not broken, the ballot boxes were secured, and that the public relations message that the Giants put out effectively elected Bonds.

Not only are there people that believe that leagues want certain teams to lose, there are people who believe that powerful people in sports conspire to protect teams' or players' hidden vulnerabilities. Just as the nation's press protected President Kennedy (by looking the other way and not reporting or investigating his infidelities) the press has similarly protected sports stars of the past, including the immensely popular Babe Ruth. Ruth, it was reported, missed half of the 1925 season because of a bellyache. When players were drunk, or lewd, or contracted sexually–transmitted diseases, the media colluded and covered up those stories.

The conspiracy theories that I have chosen for this book—my personal subjective choices, by the way—have more historical significance than a few extra bucks that a ratings point or two could mean. This is a book about factually important or histori-cally significant conspiracy theories—not about which players might have been gay.

Are we supposed to believe that every baseball team prior to 1947 made an individual decision not to sign a black player? That there wasn't a single maverick owner willing to risk alienating his fan–base or southern players—despite the potential reward of winning championships and creating whole new revenue streams? Did the NBA have a quota system in the 1950s and early 1960s that limited the number of black players per team? It sure seems that way, although nothing of the sort was ever talked about or written down at the time.

Not all of the secretive stuff was done by conspiring owners, however. Some of the conspiracies were perpetrated by players against their owners. Sometimes gamblers conspired with athletes to fix games—even championship games. Sometimes boxers lost fights on purpose. And sometimes the owners and players conspired together. In the case of amphetamines, owners looked the other way for over four decades as "speed" was ingested in baseball clubhouses. It wasn't until very recently that baseball instituted a policy against amphetamines.

Did baseball executives conspire with the players to look the other way as a certain percentage of the players artificially bulked up? When Jason Giambi signed a free-agent contract to join the Yankees following the 2001 season, lawyers writing up the contract specifically took out any references to the word "steroids." Of course, that was before baseball had any steroid policy, and the Yanks felt they were protected by even broader contractual language. Giambi's contract reportedly banned the slugger from using "*illegal* drugs" and from "chemical use and dependency." Of course, in any negotiation, lawyers dicker over words. But it is funny in retrospect that the ballclub may have signed him despite suspecting (at least) he had taken steroids.

So, sometimes the conspiracy is to stick one's head in the sand, while other times either real or moral crimes are committed. And sometimes, it just looks like a conspiracy. Sometimes, players and executives and owners and the media are just naive.

All of these conspiracy theories are just that—theories. When strange circumstances are observed, skeptics look for answers. They look for motives. They look for suspects. They look for evidence.

Everyone loves a good conspiracy theory, especially me. Here are my top 30 conspiracy theories in sports history.

*Editor's note: Conspiracy theories #26–30 were written by Mark Weinstein.

The

30

GREATEST
− − Sports − −
Conspiracy
Theories of
All Time

KEY TO LIKELIHOOD OF CONSPIRACIES

5 Oswalds: There was a high–powered conspiracy committing people to silence, which in time was proven. (100% likelihood)

4 Oswalds: I believe there is highly credible evidence to support a conspiracy theory. (75% likelihood)

3 Oswalds: Many people have valid reasons to believe this conspiracy theory, although others can point to equally good reasons not to believe it. (50% likelihood)

2 Oswalds: There is plenty of motive, and plenty of opportunity for co–conspirators to flourish, and even I'm skeptical. (25% likelihood).

1 Oswald: There is not much real evidence, and primarily less–credible people believe the conspiracy theory (1% likelihood).

Baseball avoided integration in the 1930s and 1940s by an unwritten agreement

On April 15, 1947, the Brooklyn Dodgers penciled Jackie Robinson into their lineup and single-handedly integrated Major League Baseball. Robinson's dignity, courage, and talent is well-known by sports fans and non-sports fans alike, as is the story of how the Dodgers' General Manager Branch Rickey signed him. But the question remains: why wasn't Major League Baseball and its affiliated Minor Leagues integrated sooner?

In 1947, baseball was the most popular professional sport in the United States by an incalculably wide margin. When organized baseball finally did integrate, critics warned that in segregated southern cities, there would be opposition and a loss of fans.

"Ballplayers on the road live close together. It won't work," said Rogers Hornsby, a retired baseball star, when asked about integration in 1947.

According to Arthur Ashe's 1988 book, *A Hard Road to Glory: A History of the African-American Athlete, 1919–1945*, even an outstanding war record could not help African Americans break into the Major Leagues in 1919. "Rube Foster, owner of the Chicago

American Giants, the most dominant force in black baseball, had challenged the organizers of the white Federal League in 1915 to integrate, but he was turned down," Ashe wrote. "Race riots in the 'Red Summer of 1919' had further reinforced the gentleman's agreement among Major League owners that integrated baseball was not a good idea."

In his 1982 book, *1947: When All Hell Broke Loose in Baseball*, legendary broadcaster Red Barber wrote that organized baseball had its own legal structure, separate from the laws of the land. "Baseball did not want or intend to have Negroes in it," Barber wrote.

It was a white man's game except for an occasional Indian or a Cuban. Whenever some writer would press Commissioner Landis as to when a Negro would be allowed to play in organized baseball—and rest assured that in the Negro Leagues there were some wonderful black players fully capable of playing in the Major Leagues—the Judge would say, "There is nothing in the laws of baseball that prevents a Negro from playing in it." And he would change the subject or walk away, or both.

Commissioner Kenesaw Mountain Landis (so named because his father, a Union surgeon, was crippled during the battle on that Georgia mountain in the Civil War) was in absolute authority over baseball from 1920 till his death on November 25, 1944. The first—and maybe most famous—action that Landis took was to give lifetime bans to eight members of the 1919 Chicago White Sox. But Landis also banned a common practice in the 1920s: He banned Major Leaguers from barnstorming in the off-season and playing against Negro League teams.

Of course, there can't be a conspiracy of just one man. And it would be unfair to assign sole responsibility for segregation in base-ball to Landis. But the commissioner sure didn't help to advance matters. Despite saying words that said otherwise, Commissioner Landis did everything he could to keep the color line unbroken.

Landis wasn't alone in his thinking, either. Alvin Gardner, president of the Texas League (a vital Minor League which fed into the majors in the 1920s), was quoted as saying, "I'm positive that you'll never see any Negro player on any of the teams in organized baseball in the South as long as the Jim Crow laws are in force."

You can see why the conspiracy had to be unwritten: It was morally wrong. But there are reasons why so many people clung to it. One of the unintended consequences of integration would be that many white ballplayers would lose their jobs to better black players. Another reason to keep from integrating was that the white owners would lose a stream of revenue, as they rented out their ballparks for Negro League games. With integration, that income would vanish.

The Negro Leagues were separate, but they were hardly equal. Contracts weren't worth anything, and players jumped from team to team all the time, in search of a few extra dollars. Even the star players were paid relatively little. It wasn't uncommon for fans in the stands to pass a hat around, taking up a collection for the players. Negro League players slept on busses and traveled great distances, and needed to play year-round just to earn a living.

There was no way that the nation would have been able to handle integration in the 1920s, anyway, as the Ku Klux Klan wielded considerable influence throughout the country. According to the 1920 census, the population of white males eighteen years and older was about thirty-one million, and though many of these men would have been ineligible for membership in the Klan because they were immigrants, Jews, or Roman Catholics, Klan membership peaked at between four and five million in the early 1920s. Any way you slice it, a big percentage of American men were members of the KKK. Some of these men are enshrined in Baseball's Hall of Fame, including Tris Speaker. Speaker, born in 1888 in Texas, grew up in a time and place where local KKK members were considered heroes, and lynchings were common. Speaker, who played between 1907 and 1928, would never have played with black teammates (although in his later years as a coach he is reported to have accepted integration). Ty Cobb, another proud Southerner and Hall of Fame ballplayer, came from a similar background. And these are just a few examples.

By the 1930s, however, society appeared to start acceping black sports heroes—especially after the 1936 Olympics, when runner Jesse Owens became famous for winning four gold medals. To find out more about the conspiracy that kept baseball segregated at that time, I spoke with ninety-six-year-old Lester Rodney, a champion of racial integration in sports. Beginning in 1936, he served as sports editor and columnist for the influential newspaper, the *Daily Worker*. He began a movement, a crusade—devoting hundreds of columns to this issue.

EK: Were you a Communist, or a journalist who happened to be working for the Communist paper, the *Daily Worker*?

LR: My father was a Republican. The stock market crash in 1929 changed everything, not only for me but for a lot of people. We lost our house. Anyway, if you were around in the 1930s and didn't question capitalism, you were brain-dead, in my opinion. I joined the Communist Party in 1936, when I joined the *Daily Worker*. It was nothing remarkable, or way out.

EK: Can you tell me a little about your newspaper, the *Daily Worker*?

LR: We had a very low budget, which is why we were only an eight-page paper. If we were getting gold from Moscow, as was long whispered, we would have been larger, and more effective. I used to do the fund-drive, which depended on readers contributing $10 or $20, [which was] pretty significant in those days.

The *Daily Worker* was published in New York, and it was a national paper until similar papers appeared in Chicago and Los Angeles. I believe in L.A. it was called *People's World*. The later papers had their own columnists, but we exchanged, so my columns, for instance, were read in other cities. At our peak, circulation was 125,000 during the late 1930s, and our Sunday paper even exceeded that.

EK: My conspiracy theory starts at the top of the baseball establishment. Tell me what kind of a man Judge Landis was?

LR: He was a racist. It was barely disguised. The owners of that period couldn't have picked a more appropriate choice to carry on with Jim Crow baseball. I would write stories that screamed things like *"Can You Read, Judge Landis?"* and *"Can You Hear, Judge Landis?"* When we went to Judge Landis, when we began our campaign to publicize what was going on, Landis told us that there was no ban, that all we had to do was just talk to the owners. I'm intrigued by your calling this a conspiracy theory. I have to mull this over.

EK: Talk a little bit about National League President (and later Commissioner) Ford Frick.

LR: We asked Ford Frick in 1936 if there was a ban, when we began our daily sports section. Frick also said there was no written ban, and that each owner was free to do as he pleased. So, I suppose he was in on the conspiracy.

EK: There had to be some owners that wanted to win badly enough to shake up the system. Did you run across any owners in the 1930s that you thought might be strong enough to sign a black player to a Major League team?

LR: I would periodically ask managers, whenever they came into New York, and players to shoot down the conventional wisdom that players and managers wouldn't stand for integration. There was one owner that I asked, "Would you be willing to hire a qualified black player?" that answered favorably. Pittsburgh Pirates owner Bill Benswanger told me, "If the question of admitting colored baseball players came into issue, then I would be in favor of it." That was in 1939. Later, he agreed to try out—which my newspaper endorsed—a young catcher named Roy Campanella. The tryout never happened. I have no hard evidence, but to me it is obvious that pressure was put on Benswanger then. If you don't believe me, the late sportswriter Dick Young wrote about the proposed tryout in his 1951 book on Campanella.

EK: This might be a silly question, but how did you gain access to the players and press boxes? Knowing, for instance, the anti-Communist stance that Branch Rickey took.

LR: Rickey, had he wanted to, couldn't [have kept] me from the Brooklyn press box. I was credentialed and a member of the Baseball Writers of America . . . so I was accredited in all ballparks across America. By the way, Rickey acted properly to me. He just asked me not to be political with Jackie Robinson, at least for the first year.

EK: Were the other newspapers—New York had eleven major dailies at the time—in on the conspiracy before 1947?

LR: In the 1930s, when we began our campaign, check all the major newspapers, including the *New York Times*, the paper of record. There was not a word about their being a ban on blacks, not one editorial. There were no queries put to Judge Landis.

Shirley Povich wrote some things (in the Washington Post), but that would came later. Around 1942, there was a shift. It happened because World War II was taking place, and blacks were asked to die for their country. It was absurd that they couldn't participate in the Major Leagues.

EK: You covered the great Negro League players, and the Negro League owners of the 1930s. Did any of them want the white Major League owners to continue their Jim Crow policy?

LR: Effa Manley, owner of the Newark Black Eagles, told me bitterly, "You know what you people are doing, you're going to put out of business one of the most successful black-run business in the country." Only later did she agree that you had to open the game to all black players. She was very bitter about it, but I can understand that. All the owners of Negro League teams were concerned with the bottom line.

EK: I found a significant news story in July of 1942, when you may have been in the service to this country, but your paper was still fighting this conspiracy. The headline I found was this: LANDIS CLARIFIES COLOR LINE ISSUE. And the article said, "There is no rule in organized ball banning Negroes." Judge Landis made his statement after a story in the *Daily Worker* had been brought to his attention. The story attributed to Leo Durocher, manager of the Brooklyn Dodgers, a remark to the effect that "a grapevine understanding or subterranean rule barred Negroes from play." Landis said he summoned Durocher to his office and that the Dodgers manager denied he had said this, or that Landis himself would not permit Negroes to play in organized ball.

"Negroes have not been barred from baseball . . . and never have been during the twenty-one years I have served as commissioner," Landis said. "If Durocher, any other manager, or all of them want to sign one or twenty-five Negroes, it's all right with me. The business of the commissioner is to interpret the rules of baseball and enforce them."

LR: I thought that Leo said that earlier, and Landis had just waited and waited until he made him recant and that story came out. By 1942, as I said, there was a shift. Landis, at the Winter Meetings, addressed the issue by telling reporters that there was no rule against integrating, and that is when Paul Robeson made his remarks to the baseball owners, calling for the end of segregation. But Leo told me, a few years earlier, "Hell yes, I would use a colored player in a minute."

EK: What role do you believe that you had in exposing this conspiracy of silence, this gentleman's agreement?

LR: The main thing was that we made known the existence of the great Negro players, by featuring players who were good enough to play in the majors. I recall that in 1937 I spoke with Burleigh Grimes, who was the manager of Brooklyn. His team was in seventh place in an eight team league. He said to me, "Well, I could use a little more hitting and pitching . . ." I said to him, "What if you signed Satchell Paige and Josh Gibson?" He acted as if I'd hit him over the head with a two-by-four. He said it would never happen, because teams travel on trains, and spring training takes place in the South. Grimes was a baseball guy, and knew how good those players were. We let *everyone* know how good those players were, not just baseball people. Of course, Grimes told me not to write what he'd told me in the paper. He wasn't willing to stick his neck out. Would you have considered him a co-conspiracist?

EK: I've asked you about commissioners, league presidents, managers, and other sportswriters. How about the majority of the players? Were they ready to accept integration earlier?

LR: That's very difficult to answer. One of the things we did was shoot down the idea that most players wouldn't stand for it. There were players, like Carl Furillo and Bobby Bragen, that went on the record saying that they were against integration. After the war, though, I'd say many were ready. There were players like Pee Wee Reese, coming back from the Pacific, freely admitting to having mixed feelings. Yet, Reese played a positive role in Robinson's years with the Dodgers.

EK: When Rickey and Robinson integrated baseball, that didn't put an end to racism, of course. I found an editorial in a mainstream paper from May 16, 1949. Apparently, there had been an argument in a game between Dodgers manager Leo Durocher and a fan. And you must have written that you weren't going to pre-judge either side, not knowing what precipitated the disagreement. But in this smart-alecky wire service story, it was written, "Rodney forgot that, as a good Communist, he must always assume that in any dispute involving the race angle, the Negro is always right and the White man is always wrong. And the fan involved in this case is a Puerto Rican Negro."

LR: And what was so wrong about not wanting to pre-judge a fan who heckled a manager? And what was wrong about rooting for the black man?

EK: Nothing, of course. I just wanted to point out what baseball fans were accustomed to reading in the mainstream press at the time you were writing.

LR: The most interesting concept you have brought up is the newspapers of the time.

Newspapers [certainly] had a conspiracy of silence . . . they never told their readers there was a ban. The pretense was that it wasn't anyone's fault. There was no ban, but the owners and fans and players would never stand for it . . . so the newspapers never did anything about it. The newspapers just kept it out of the news. The Daily Worker stirred it up a bit, but I can't take too much credit. After World War II, it became preposterous for a country to ask guys to go into a war and possibly die when they weren't allowed to play in our national pastime. It was a final push to the campaign, which by then was a growing movement.

* * * * *

It is remarkable that baseball wasn't integrated a decade earlier than it was. It's not that there weren't innovative and open minds among baseball team owners—including maverick owner Bill Veeck in the 1930s. It's not that teams weren't playing in cities with large black fan bases (Philadelphia, Washington, and Brooklyn, to name three), or that the country wasn't embracing black sports heroes. Joe Louis was a beloved heavyweight boxing champion, and there were many black college football stars, including the young Jackie Robinson at UCLA.

By the end of World War II, the conspirators—which included the commissioner and the owners—were facing problems far beyond what liberal Communist papers or black newspapers were calling for. Quite simply, their talent pool had been diminishing. I found a column by legendary sportswriter Grantland Rice from February of 1945, concerning his conversations with college football coaches about finding football talent for the National Football League. "For one reason, the supply of young stars that the colleges once turned out is running thin—almost running out," Rice wrote. "They will have no such supply as they formerly had to draw on. In the second place, there will be returning stars—but quite a number of them won't return, and many of those who do will be too incapacitated from wounds or too battle-worn to help a lot. As kids turn eighteen now, they are headed for active war service . . ."

Baseball not only faced the same problems as the NFL, but baseball was also facing competition from other sports for the first time. And baseball risked losing some of the best young athletic talent to football, if it held on to its antiquated color line.

Once Judge Landis passed away in late 1944, some of the own-ers—especially Landis foe Branch Rickey of the Dodgers—seized the moment. Until a new commissioner was named, Landis' administrative aide Leslie O'Connor, along with the League Presidents, formed a Baseball Council to run the game. Prominent black journalists wrote to the Council, urging that action be taken. A committee was formed to explore ways that integration could take place. In the spring of 1945, Happy Chandler was named Baseball Commissioner. Red Barber's book, *1947: When All Hell Broke Loose in Baseball* quotes extensively from a 1971 *Sports Illustrated* interview that Chandler had given to sportswriter John Underwood. "Jackie Robinson came into baseball in 1947 as the first black Major-Leaguer in modern times," Chandler told Underwood.

> Many of the owners didn't want the change. I wasn't asked for a decision, so I never gave one. The dissenters had to think they were on firm ground because Judge Landis had been in office twenty-four years and never lifted a finger for black players. He always said, "The own-ers have a right to hire whom they please." Obviously, Branch Rickey [owner of the Dodgers] thought so, too. He came to see me at my home in Versailles. He may already have made up his mind by then. He said, "I can't bring Robinson in unless you back me." "Can Robinson play baseball?" I asked. "No question about that," Rickey replied. "Is he a Major Leaguer?" "Yes, sir." "Then bring him on."

Chandler, in the same interview, went on about the long-held conspiracy that prevented blacks from entering the majors. "I do not mean this account of the integration of baseball as a criti-cism of Judge Landis for not having ordered it before. The owners simply didn't want it, and Landis washed his hands," Chandler continued. "If he did nothing to help the Negro, it can be argued that neither did he do much . . . to improve the sorry conditions the umpires worked under in those days or help to introduce a pension or raise players' salaries."

The game was finally integrated in April of 1947. A number of factors led to the inevitable end of segregation. In the 1930s and '40s, the media was in on a conspiracy of silence. The owners were in on the conspiracy. The commissioner was in on the conspiracy. It was shameful.

CONCLUSION:

NBA owners cater to the "white dollar" in the 1950s with a quota system

In the 1930s and 1940s, before there was a National Basketball Association, the best professional black basketball players barnstormed the country as members of the Harlem Globetrotters or the Harlem Renaissance (known as the Rens). One theory advanced by the black press, according to Arthur Ashe's 1985 book, *A Hard Road to Glory: A History of the African-American Athlete from 1919–1945*, was that, "being white, Abe Saperstein made an arrangement with the owners of the white teams to keep blacks out so that his Globetrotters could always have the pick of the best blacks. This would accomplish two ends: ensure that the Globetrotters always had quality black players and, with no black players in the white leagues, the white players would never complain. This was never proven one way or the other. Nevertheless it was believed by many black players and fans."

The NBA was started in 1947, and the League's color barrier wasn't broken until October 31, 1950, by Earl Lloyd of the Washington Capitols, one of three blacks in the League that season. Chuck Cooper of the Boston Celtics and Sweetwater Clifton of the New York Knicks debuted in their teams' season openers the next day. One would think that the National Basketball Association would have been more open to people of all races, and perhaps compared to other sports, it was. In fact, Mr. Lloyd told me a few years ago that he greatly admired Jackie Robinson, as the indignities and slurs that he faced in the NBA were a fraction of what Robinson had to put up with. Lloyd said that that was because most NBA teams were located in the north-east, and most fans in that region were already used to inte-grated college sports teams. But that doesn't mean that a quota system didn't exist. On the contrary, it seems clear that there was an unwritten agreement between the all-white owners that prevented a team from having too many black players on their roster (and even dictated how many black starters each team could employ).

The Hawks, the franchise now playing in Atlanta, entered the League in 1949–1950, playing in three mid-western cities (Moline, Illinois; Rock Island, Illinois; and Davenport, Iowa). At that time, they were known as the Tri-Cities Blackhawks, and Red Auerbach coached the team that first season. After two years as Tri-Cities, and four more permanently situated in Milwaukee, the team moved to St. Louis for the 1955–1956 season. The city was the southernmost in the NBA at the time, and its star frontline players included Bob Pettit and Cliff Hagen, southern men who had played college ball at segregated schools. St. Louis made the Western Conference Finals in 1956, and took the Boston Celtics to the seventh game of the NBA Finals in 1957 (losing Game Seven in Boston, 125–123, in double-overtime). The Hawks lost to the Celtics mainly because of a trade that Auerbach—by then with the Celtics—had made with the Hawks, which had sent center Bill Russell to the Celtics.

In 1958, the Hawks defeated the Celtics in the NBA Finals, becoming the last team in NBA history to win a championship without a black player on its roster. (Well, that's mostly true. The Official NBA Guide, the League's history book, includes the team picture of every NBA champion, and the 1957–1958 champion Hawks team picture features only eleven players. The twelfth member of the team, Worthy Patterson, a black guard from the University of Connecticut, played four games in the regular season for St. Louis but did not appear in the playoffs and was left out of the picture.)

Two years later, the Hawks drafted a black forward with the fifteenth overall selection in the draft. His name was Cal Ramsey. I caught up with Mr. Ramsey recently at Madison Square Garden in April of 2007.

Cal Ramsey: Hell yes, there was a quota system in the NBA, and I was a victim of it. I'll give you an example. I averaged 17.4 rebounds per game in my three years in college, averaging close to 20 rebounds per game the same year that Chamberlain averaged 18 and Elgin Baylor 18.3. You can look it up. I was drafted by the Hawks, so I played behind Hagen and Pettit. I wasn't expecting to start over them. But man, I only played four games with the Hawks before they put me on waivers. [In those four games, Cal scored 17 points and had 19 rebounds in only 35 minutes]. I was claimed off waivers by the Knicks in November of 1959, and was waived two months later. I averaged more than 11 points and 7 rebounds per game (playing only 22 minutes per game) which today would have made me millions. And yet, I couldn't stick with New York. The coach told me he had to cut me. Probably too many blacks, since we already had Willie Naulls and Johnny Green [on the roster].

I was far from the only black player that was good enough for the NBA but didn't make it. When I played in the Eastern League, believe me, I saw lots of guys that were just as good, if not better, than players in the NBA.

Five years after drafting Russell (and trading him) and two years after drafting Ramsey (and waiving him), the Hawks used their 1961 first-round draft pick (eighth overall) on Cleo Hill from Winston–Salem Teachers College.

Ramsey: Hill was not a good college player. He was a *great* college player. He went to the Hawks, and got into some kind of beef with somebody, and essentially was blackballed from the NBA.

Cleo Hill was considered "too flashy" a player, which was just a thinly-veiled euphemism for "too black." He played in only fifty-eight games his rookie season, running into problems with white Hawks stars Hagen, Pettit, and Clyde Lovellette. Like Ramsey remembered, Hill never again played in the League.

Ramsey: I do want to say that Hagen and Pettit, in particular, would work with me after practice and I never had any problem with them. St. Louis, the city, wasn't great. There were restaurants that I was not allowed to eat in. But the team itself, I couldn't complain about. [Black player] Sihugo Green was on the team—he was my idol when he played at Duquesne. I do feel that, for whatever reason, I was held back, and not given a chance, like many others of the time.

*   *   *   *   *

It wasn't just the southern-based teams that made life difficult for black players in the 1950s. Bill Russell was reportedly rebuffed when attempting to buy a home in the Boston suburbs, and according to John Taylor's book *The Rivalry*, Russell had to put up with racial slurs from his hometown Boston fans. Russell, at least, was a superstar, as were most of the black players in the League at the time. If there were only so many slots that owners could use for black players, they wanted the Elgin Baylors and Bill Russells of the world to be filling those slots.

Why did owners feel that they needed a quota system? They felt it was a "white dollar." They felt the majority of ticket-buyers were white, and didn't want to watch black players. Yet, look at the list of Rookies of the Year from 1956 to 1962. Six of the seven were black players, with Boston's Tommy Heinsohn being the lone white Rookie of the Year during that stretch. In *The Rivalry*, Taylor recounts that "Heinsohn had established himself as a terrific player, a defensive rebounder as well as a gunner, but even so, everyone in the League, including Heinsohn himself, knew that Russell, not Heinsohn, had been the key to the Celtics' first-place finish in the regular season. . . . The ostensible reason Russell did not receive the award was because he'd joined the team in mid-season. . . . Russell could not believe that the decision to deny him the award was not motivated by racism. The previous season, Maurice Stokes had become the first black player to be named Rookie of the Year, and it seemed clear to Russell that the owners wanted to assure fans that blacks were not taking over the NBA and so were offering up Tommy Heinsohn, not Bill Russell, as the new face in the League."

Rookies of the Year

1956: Maurice Stokes
1957: Tom Heinsohn
1958: Woody Sauldsberry
1959: Elgin Baylor
1960: Wilt Chamberlain
1961: Oscar Robertson
1962: Walt Bellamy

Al Attles was the thirty-ninth player selected in the 1960 NBA draft, from the virtually unknown school North Carolina A&T. It's amazing that he lasted in the League. Here is his story as told to me in early February of 2007.

Al Attles: I was from Newark, New Jersey, and had some offers from the New York schools like St. Johns and NYU and some others. But I didn't hit the books like I should have, and North

Carolina A&T gave me an offer. I played four years at A&T. At first, it was on a look-see basis. I did well my first two quarters, and was able to play basketball all four years. I eventually made the Honor Roll there, even. The black college had the same problems as society, but it was a really self-sustained school. We didn't have to go into the city that much. I never had to go to a segregated movie theatre, for example, and I really enjoyed those four years. I got drafted by the Warriors, but I never thought I would make the team. I thought I was going to be with the Warriors for one week.

See, I was offered a job teaching junior high school in Newark. I got my homeroom, and was thinking about what I would put up on the walls. But I got a greeting from the Army. I thought it wouldn't be right to start a teaching job that I might have to leave following my Army physical. I went for the physical, and I had a bad back, and was classified "Y," meaning that I could only be called if there were some sort of a breakout. I figured that I would play basketball for the Eastern League, and that I would teach. Then I decided I might as well go through with the Warriors tryout.

Here I am now, nearly forty-seven years later, with the same organization. Let me set this straight. There *was* a quota system. The most number of blacks on a team was four, and no more. That just couldn't be a coincidence. There were what, eleven or twelve players on every team, and every team had four blacks on it. It was never written about, but everybody knew it. No one said anything, though. For instance, in 1960 I was trying out for the Philadelphia Warriors. We had five black players trying out. Then I found out they traded Woody Sauldsberry. I found out from a redcap at the Philadelphia Airport that Sauldsberry was traded. I thought that was crazy. He was Rookie of the Year just two years earlier. That meant that I had made the team, joining Wilt and Guy [Rodgers] and Andy Johnson [as the only black players on the team]."

* * * * *

Even the black NBA superstars acknowledged the quota system, whether or not they were affected. In his 2003 biography, *The Big O: My Life, My Times, My Game*, Oscar Robertson wrote that his brother, Bailey Robertson, never got a chance to play in the NBA. Although Bailey was drafted by Syracuse in the mid-1950s, they still had a quota system in those days, so there was no room for Bailey. Oscar Robertson wrote that the quota system vanished for good with the coming of the American Basketball Association and the explosion of black basketball talent that just couldn't be ignored. In Wilt Chamberlain's 1972 autobiography, *Wilt: Just Like Any Other 7-Foot Black Millionaire Who Lives Next Door*, Chamberlain wrote, "About the time I broke in, the NBA actually had a quota, an unwritten rule—no more than three blacks per team. And those had to be good blacks—starters, stars, not bench-warmers."

In David Wolf's 1971 book on Connie Hawkins, *Foul*, Wolf explains that the quota system was widespread in the early 1960s, not just in the NBA. "Connie was encountering the quota system. It was widespread in professional sports in 1962, and was another reason why countless schoolyard stars never escaped the ghetto," Wolf wrote. "The quota can be a formalized agreement between owners and coach or among the owners themselves. More often, it is an understanding that 'too many' blacks are bad for business, hurts the team's image, and are 'hard to coach.'" Wolf explains that there was evidence of a quota system in the ABL (the forerunner of the ABA) in 1962, and that is why Hawkins' Pittsburgh team restricted the number of blacks on the roster, and on the starting team—and that the coach worked hard to publicize whites instead of blacks.

As recently as 1962, there were only thirty-seven black players in the NBA, less than one-third of the League's players—with no team having more than four black players. The quota seems to have been broken in the 1963–1964 season. The first time that

five blacks were on one NBA team was detailed in K.C. Jones'
1985 autobiography, *Rebound: The Autobiography of K.C. Jones
and an Inside Look at the Champion Boston Celtics.* "Over the
mantelpiece in Willie Naulls' beautiful house is a large painting
of five Celtics with their heads together on the court," Jones
wrote. "There is Russ [Bill Russell], Satch [Sanders], Sam Jones,
Willie, and myself. Five black men. We were the first NBA team
to put five black men on the floor. We are all proud of that; that
'we' includes Red [Auerbach], the spirit of Walter Brown, and I'll
bet everybody that's ever worn a Celtics uniform."

By the time Stu Lantz, now a broadcaster for the Los Angeles
Lakers, entered the NBA in 1968 with the San Diego Rockets, the
quota system had become, by his description, "more subtle. We
still heard the jokes about teams not being able to start more than
two blacks at home, that kind of stuff," Lantz told me recently.

What happened between the early 1960s and the late 1960s?
Did the dominance of the Boston Celtics (eleven championships
in thirteen years, from 1957–1969) create a situation in which
teams attempted to emulate their blueprint for winning?

The ABA came into existence in 1967. This new League
showcased a different brand of basketball, as it featured players
who played above the rim. Connie Hawkins, Julius Erving, and
players like the electrifying Hawkins and Erving found a home
in the ABA, and gravitated to the upstart league for a few reasons. For one thing, unlike the NBA, players were eligible even
if their college class hadn't graduated. (Chamberlain, for one,
had to play a year with the Harlem Globetrotters, as he wasn't
eligible for the NBA draft until his senior year was complete.)
Therefore, players who wanted to leave school early found a
home in the professional ranks of the ABA. The League became
quite good—and quite memorable—and created leverage for
players and real competition for the established NBA. The ABA
featured players like Marvin "Bad News" Barnes, George "Iceman"

Gervin, "Mr. Excitement" Wendell Ladner, and Artis Gilmore, also known as "The A Train."

Before long, NBA teams were featuring all-black starting lineups. By 1972, the Western Conference All-Star squad had only two white players on the team (guards Gail Goodrich and Jerry West, both with the Lakers). The NBA had expanded to seventeen teams by then, and there were close to 250 players who appeared in at least one game that season. Only seventy-seven of those players were white—and many of them were fringe players or seven-foot centers.

Despite the reluctance to integrate its players, the NBA has been progressive—some might say the most progressive—in terms of hiring black coaches and black general managers. In 2007, there are even black team owners.

In John Taylor's *The Rivalry* he writes, "In the early fifties, when there were few black players in the NBA, they were almost all forwards and they would be assigned to guard each other, which in effect meant they canceled each other out, leaving the game to be played by the four white players on each team, who often refused to pass the ball to the black players. By the late fifties, blacks were playing all positions and black representation on teams had increased, but a de facto quota system was in place limiting the number per team."

CONCLUSION:

Baseball owners collude against
free agents in the mid-1980s

Major League Baseball owners have long been used to doing things to their own advantage. Throughout baseball history, owners have held the upper hand against players. In the days before free agency, owners used a reserve clause that bound players to their original teams for the entire length of their career. Ballplayers had no real options if they wanted to play in the majors. They could play for the club that drafted or traded for them, or they could retire and do something else.

The reserve clause was the result of a Supreme Court decision in the 1920s which freed Major League Baseball of anti-trust laws. But in the 1970s, smart men like Players' Union chief Marvin Miller and brave men like St. Louis Cardinals outfielder Curt Flood won the right for baseball players to play out their contracts and sign as free agents with any team they wanted. Players who were born in Cincinnati, for example, were therefore able to negotiate with their hometown team, the Reds. Players stuck behind a superstar at the same position were allowed to play out their existing contract and then sign with a team that could find more at-bats for them. Miller time-released his free agents onto the market, setting up a demand for his growing supply. The owners stumbled and bumbled, signing free agents with the zeal of last-minute Christmas shoppers. They bought everyone in sight, signing starting pitchers with scant track records to ten-year contracts.

Baseball players saw their average salaries quadruple after the introduction of free agency, and by the mid-1980s, the average annual salary for a Major League player was $473,496. Was that progress? Well, when Curt Flood made $90,000 in 1969, he was one of the highest paid players in the game. Only a handful of superstars had six-figure salaries at that time. Owners in the 1980s needed a plan to keep their fellow owners in check, and fiscally responsible. So they made a tacit agreement to "watch" their spending. Following the 1985 season, thirty-five free agents were available on the open market, but only four switched teams. It was obvious that owners were intentionally limiting, if not altogether abstaining from, signing free agents. Even Yankees owner George Steinbrenner, a notorious spendthrift, restrained himself from signing catcher Carlton Fisk, reportedly taking his offer off the table after talking to White Sox owner Jerry Reinsdorf. The Player's Association filed a suit charging collusion, but the owners were feeling quite smug. After all, no one could force them to sign players and increase their payroll, right? And even if an arbitrator ruled against them and fined the owners millions, it would just reduce the amount they would have to pay the next crop of free agents. After the 1986 season, three dozen more players became free agents, and again, it became nearly impossible for any of them to receive legitimate contract offers.

The 1987 American League Red Book, an official record book published by Major League Baseball, states that "For the fourth time in the last five years, the American League set a new, all-time sports league attendance record in 1986. In setting the new record, the League passed the twenty-five million mark for the first time. The 1986 season was the first time ever that all fourteen teams went over the one million mark in attendance. Five teams went over two million fans. The Kansas City Royals won the World Series in 1985, and drew a team record of 2,320,794 fans." In 1985, the Cleveland Indians doubled their attendance. The Texas Rangers had an increase of 600,000 fans passing through their turnstiles from the previous year. The rosy picture was similar in the National League, and baseball's overall profits rose 15%. Under these conditions, a seemingly win-win proposition for owners, players, and fans, would owners really continue to collude to keep players' salaries down?

Yankees' ace Ron Guidry was thirty-six years old in the 1986 season, a free agent looking for a new contract. He had made $975,000 in 1986, a season in which he pitched 192 innings, struck out 140 batters and walked just thirty-eight. That's an average of just 1.7 walks per nine innings, one of the lowest in the Majors. Guidry was just one year removed from a twenty-two-win season in which he placed second in the Cy Young voting, and over the previous three seasons he had posted an impressive 41–29 record with a 3.85 ERA. In 1986, Guidry (who by that point was 163–80 in a Yankee uniform) had a record of only 9–12, yet in his defense the Yanks averaged just 3.8 runs in his thirty starts.

It was reported that he asked the Yankees for a two-year contract worth $850,000 a year. Because he and the Yankees couldn't come to terms on a new contract by January 8 (the Players Association selected that date as the last a player could negotiate with their old club until May 1st), Guidry was unable to negotiate with the Yankees again until a month after the 1987 season began. It seems unfathomable, but no team showed interested in signing "Louisiana Lightning," at that time. One more piece of evidence. The Yankees won ninety games in 1986, finishing five games behind the Boston Red Sox. The Sox had a young superstar at the top of their rotation (Roger Clemens), and two other reliable starters (Bruce Hurst and Al Nipper). But the back end of the Red Sox rotation was in shambles, thanks to an injury to Oil Can Boyd. But instead of signing an ace like Guidry, Boston chose to use journeymen like Jeff Sellers (7–8, 5.28 ERA) and Bob Stanley (4–15, 5.01 and a World Series goat) as their fourth and fifth starters in 1987. It seems odd that they wouldn't therefore make a run at signing Guidry, solidifying the back end of their rotation while taking strength away from their hated rival at the same time. But they didn't, and this non-move reeks of collusion.

After that same 1986 season, forty-two-year-old Steve Carlton was looking for a new team. He won only nine games in 1985 and, despite his impressive career accomplishments, he couldn't attract a single offer. The same was true for forty-two-year-old Tom Seaver, who had won seven games. Compare this to the situation of forty-year-old Greg Maddux who, twenty years later, signed a one-year deal for $10 million to pitch for the San Diego Padres in 2007. And that pales in comparison to what Roger Clemens received from the Yankees in 2007, the summer that he turned forty-five.

It's not just that the owners colluded in the mid-1980s, it's that they did it so badly. The California Angels relied on thirty-seven-year-old Bob Boone to catch for them in 1986. All he did was catch 144 games, win his fourth Gold Glove (of a career seven) for fielding excellence, and then in seven postseason games, bat .455 with a home run. Despite those numbers, Boone was unable to get a contract offer in the off-season, either from his team or any other. Imagine, Boone didn't want to take a cut in pay! As it was, in order to play in 1987, he had to accept the same $850,000 that he had made the year before.

The Red Sox couldn't come to terms with their catcher following the 1986 pennant-winning season, either. Twenty-seven-year-old Rich Gedman had belted sixteen homers and driven in sixty-five runs in 1986, yet he still couldn't get an offer. Choosing to "wait it out," Gedman eventually missed both spring training and the first month of the 1987 season.

Maybe teams didn't want to take a chance on aging pitchers. Maybe teams felt that they could compete without good catchers. But the leading hitter in the National League, Tim Raines, was available, and one of the best leadoff men in history. The twenty-seven-year-old Raines was coming off a season in which he led the National League both in batting average and on-base percentage. He ranked second in OPS (on-base plus slugging average), third in stolen bases, third in triples, and sixth in doubles. He was an electrifying athlete in the prime of his career, certainly among the top talents in the game at the time.

In 1986, Raines had made $1.5 million. He wanted to play for the Dodgers, but would have played for the Padres, who insulted him with an offer of two years and $2.2 million total.

Raines was able to negotiate with his own team, the Expos, on May 1st, and signed immediately. Manager Buck Rodgers put him in the lineup against the Mets, in spite of the fact that Raines had not faced live Major League pitching since the previous season, having missed all of Spring Training. I was in attendance that day, working on NBC's national Game of the Week, and was fortunate to witness Raines turn in one of the greatest individual efforts I have ever seen. He had four hits, including a triple and the game-winning home run. In his first five games, Raines batted .400 with three homers and seven RBI. If that didn't send a message to all the general managers that had passed on him, I don't know what would have caught their attention. The media—and the fans—focused on the storyline of Raines' ability to play without benefit of spring training more than the deeper issue of Raines groveling back to his old team. The feeling was that players made too much money. It might have been wrong what the owners were doing, but Raines and the others were still making good wages.

And then there was Andre Dawson, Raines' teammate on the 1986 Expos. Dawson was thirty-one years old, coming off a season in which he was plagued by chronic knee problems. Dawson had just twenty homers and seventy-eight RBI for the Expos, on the last year of a contract that paid him more than $1 million. His injuries affected his ability to play on turf, and he wanted to switch teams so that he could play most of his games on grass (this was in an era where more than a third of teams played on Astroturf). Dawson felt that he would be a good fit for the Cubs, and hoped they would sign him to a contract. He told Chicago general manager Dallas Green that he would sign a blank contract, and that the Cubs could fill in the amount. On March 9, Dawson signed with the Cubs, allowing himself to take a hefty paycut ($500,000 base and incentives). He would go on to win the 1987 National League MVP award for Chicago, hitting a career-high forty-nine home runs and driving in a whopping 137 runs.

The owners had accomplished their goal. For the first time since the start of free agency, the average Major League salary declined. Free agent salaries went down 16% in 1987, despite the healthy attendance at the ballparks.

THE CONSPIRATORS

Commissioner Peter Ueberroth takes the biggest hit here, but he's an obvious and easy villain. The much beloved successor to Mr. Ueberroth, A. Bartlett Giamatti, was also on the Executive Council in 1985, and is not above suspicion. And then there were the culpable owners, made up of the old guard as well as newcomers to the game. The O'Malley family held ownership of the Los

Angeles Dodgers for decades. The Boston Red Sox were still in the control of the Yawkey family in the 1980s. Tom Yawkey had been the sole owner of the team for forty-four seasons. After his death in 1976, his wife Jean became the general partner and president of the team (the Yawkey estate sold the club in 1978 to an ownership group that included Mrs. Yawkey, Haywood Sullivan, and Buddy LeRoux). Gene Autry had owned the California Angels since their inaugural 1961 season. Bud Selig has been the Milwaukee Brewers' President and CEO since 1970, their first year. There were also new ownership groups replacing the longtime baseball people. In Minnesota, the Twins were sold on September 7, 1984 by the Griffith organization. Cal Griffith and family had been connected with baseball for nearly a century. The Twins were sold to Carl Pohlad, a civic, business, and banking leader in the Twin Cities. Richard and David Jacobs purchased the Cleveland Indians on December 9, 1986.

These owners were in violation of the labor agreement they had signed in 1981, in which they agreed not to conspire to fix salaries. All it would have taken was for one or two renegade owners to crack, and gain a competitive advantage on their opponents by signing some of the free agents to big money contracts. A competitive nut like the Yankees' George Steinbrenner, for example, was likely salivating over the available talent on the marketplace.

My theory is that the owners never would have colluded if journeymen ballplayers like Bob Shirley and Dave Collins, had performed better after signing their free agent deals. In the first free agent classes, Steinbrenner enjoyed instant success, which translated to World Series appearances in 1976, 1977, 1978, and 1981 (and 103 victories and a division title in 1980). Free agent signings of Catfish Hunter and Reggie Jackson gave the Yankees the push they needed to get over the top. Steinbrenner, who had bought into the Yankees in 1973, was the first owner to take real advantage of free agency. His next wave of free agents didn't work out so well. In retrospect, however, the ten-year deal he gave to outfielder Dave Winfield turned out exceedingly well. The $20 million contract was viewed the way modern fans and baseball people think about Alex Rodriguez' contract, which is worth more than $250 million. Winfield didn't come through in the 1981 World Series for Steinbrenner, who labeled him "Mr. May" for doing well in the early part of each season, padding his Hall of Fame statistics. The next year, Steinbrenner signed free agent outfielder Dave Collins from the Cincinnati Reds. Collins was a speedster, an outfielder in his twenties that had stolen seventy-nine bases just two years earlier. In 1982, Collins batted just .253 and had an on-base average of just .315 for the Yankees. He stole just thirteen bases. The next season, Steinbrenner signed Bob Shirley, also from the Cincinnati Reds. Shirley was in his twenties, a left-handed starter, and a supposedly valuable commodity. The Yankees gave him a four-year contract worth more than $2 million. Shirley won only five games with an ERA over 5.00 in his first season as a Yankee, and thirteen total in thirty-eight starts over four seasons in pinstripes.

But what if Collins had done what he was supposed to do and Shirley had proven himself to be a big winner? The Yankees won ninety-one games in 1983, finishing only seven games behind the eventual World Champions, the Baltimore Orioles. Shirley started the second game of the season, and couldn't make it out of the third inning. By June 14, the Yankees were only 29–30, and one of the main reasons was Shirley. He was 2–5, with a bloated earned run average of 5.50. Who is to say the Yankees wouldn't have won the division in 1983 if Shirley had gone 14–8 rather than 2–5?

Steinbrenner took over the team in 1973, and in just five years built them into a powerhouse. Following the 1981 season, he signed some free agents that didn't work out, and became skittish about signing others, especially if they weren't proven superstars. Experiences he had with players like Collins and Shirley let the other owners reel him in on their plans for fiscal responsibility.

At the same time, the Yankees were drawing well, but they were nowhere near the attendance numbers they've enjoyed in the new millennium. They drew more than two million fans to Yankee Stadium in 1982, more than 2.2 million in 1983, then dipped to 1.8 million in 1984. The Yankees didn't lead the League in attendance in the 1980s, but were usually among the top three or four clubs. So it can be argued that Steinbrenner attempted to build up value in his team with free agents, but found that he couldn't depend on signings to either push his team into the postseason, or to increase attendance. So Steinbrenner, following the lead of his fellow owners, steered clear of signing big free agents for a while. At the same time, Steinbrenner wasn't averse to giving away his prized pupils from the Yankee farm system for high-priced commodities such as Rickey Henderson.

I'm still trying to figure out why the Cleveland Indians went along with the conspiracy. In December of 1986, the sale of the Tribe was approved and the Jacobs family assumed control of the team. They bought an Indians team that hadn't been to a World Series since 1954, and that hadn't won the World Series since 1948. However, the 1986 Indians finished 84–78, and led the American League in batting. They had drawn 1.4 million fans into their Municipal Stadium, more than double the number that attended Cleveland home games in 1985 (655,000). Any sane person would have tried to capitalize on the 1986 success, and improve their glaring weakness: pitching.

The Cleveland Indians' top pitcher was knuckleballer Tom Candiotti. Candiotti and forty-seven-year-old knuckleball pitcher Phil Niekro started sixty-six games for the Indians that year, and they desperately needed to bring in some new blood. Yet in the months before the 1987 season, the Indians did not sign a free agent pitcher until April 4—when they signed forty-three-year-old Steve Carlton, five years past his last twenty-win season.

There were other pitchers on the free agent market that winter, of course. They could have gone after Doyle Alexander (who would help the Tigers win the division in 1987 with spectacular pitching down the stretch). They could have gone after John Denny (11–10 with a 4.20 ERA with Cincinnati). They could have gone after the aforementioned Guidry. Instead, they sat and did nothing. Could there be any greater evidence of collusion?

Cleveland wound up regressing to 61–101 in 1987. Candiotti won only seven of his twenty-five decisions. Forty-eight-year-old Phil Niekro started twenty-two games, and won only seven. Carlton was traded to Minnesota in July.

On February 18, 1987, the MLBPA filed their second grievance in two years. The first collusion grievance was decided in favor of the players, as seven of the 1985 free agents were awarded a "new look" free agency, whereby they could offer their services to any team without losing their existing contract. This ruling enabled Kirk Gibson to sign with the Los Angeles Dodgers (three years, $4.5 million). All Gibson did was win the Most Valuable Player award and hit one of the most famous home runs in World Series history, beating Athletics closer Dennis Eckersley in Game One.

In October of 1989, arbitrator George Nicolau ruled against the owners again in the second collusion case and awarded damages of $38 million to the players. That also meant that the Boones, Guidrys, and Gedmans of the world were afforded a second chance at free agency. It doesn't seem a punishment that fit the crime, as many of the players had signed one-year contracts anyway. Plus, many of the players were frustrated by the process. Tim Raines, for example, would have been a new-look free agent, but waived that right after agreeing to a three-year deal with Montreal worth $6.3 million.

The owners weren't through with their little games, either. Following the 1987 season, the owners—defeated in court—said in essence, "You got us. We'll make bids and go after free agents." What they did, however, was cooperate with one another by telling each other what their offers were. As a result, Nicolau ruled a year later that the market must be "free and unencumbered." It really isn't a free agent system if teams can participate and conspire to keep prices down. Why would a team make an outrageous offer to a player, when it knew it didn't have to?

On July 18, 1990, the owners lost their third straight collusion case in court. This time, owners faced damages of $64 million (more than the first two decisions combined). Still, with salaries for hundreds of Major League players stalled and even declining, the $64 million didn't seem too bad a pill for the ownership to swallow. The Players Union is nothing if not dogged, however, and a final settlement was reached in November of 1990. The owners agreed to pay the players $280 million in a lump sum. It was up to the union to evenly distribute it. By paying this sum, the owners essentially admitted that they had stolen that $280 million from their players.

Before the start of the 1989 season, Peter Ueberroth stepped down as Commissioner of Baseball to pursue other interests, such as the purchase of the Pebble Beach golf course with partners

Average Salary of Major League Baseball Players:

Year	Average Salary		Top Salary	
1985	$473,496	top salary:	$2,130,300	(Mike Schmidt)
1990	$483,399	top salary:	$3,200,000	(Robin Yount)
1995	$962,323	top salary:	$9,237,500	(Cecil Fielder)
2000	$1,921,939	top salary:	$15,714,286	(Kevin Brown)
2005	$2,479,125	top salary:	$26,000,000	(Alex Rodriguez)

*Source: MLBPA

Arnold Palmer and Clint Eastwood. The scenic holes on the golf course never asked him for more money, or tried to get a better deal by being transplanted to a golf course in another city.

As for the players, well, they did okay. Ueberroth would have done a fine job as commissioner from the owners' point of view—if they hadn't gotten caught in the conspiracy. Look at how the average salary stayed roughly the same from 1985–1990 and then skyrocketed shortly after. In a legal, free enterprise system, those things can happen in a booming business like baseball.

CONCLUSION:

Did Sonny Liston throw his fights against Muhammad Ali?

There were just too many crazy things going on the world at the time the young, brash Muhammad Ali fought Sonny Liston—twice—in the mid-1960s (the first time fighting under his birth name, Cassius Clay). And all sorts of conspiracy theories have been bandied about over the pair of fights throughout the years. Some have involved mobsters making millions from betting against Liston. Others involved Black Muslims threatening Liston's life. Some have the organized crime figures of Liston's entourage conspiring with the Black Muslims from Ali's camp. But before we can examine these various conspiracy theories, it's important to go back and recognize the time and place that the fights took place.

The first fight was held on February 25, 1964. Sonny Liston was the world heavyweight champion at the time, and had been so since defeating Floyd Patterson in September of 1962. Cassius Clay had won an Olympic gold medal as a light heavyweight for the United States in 1960 and became known as a brash young boxer with a penchant for predicting the outcome of his fights.

According to Jose Torres' 1971 book *Sting like a Bee: The Muhammad Ali Story*, Clay began his string of predictions after watching Gorgeous George, the great wrestler, in a fight. Clay said, "I hear this white fellow say, 'I am the world's greatest wrestler. I cannot be defeated. I am the Greatest. I am the King. . . . When he was in the ring, everybody booed, booed. And I was mad. And I looked around and I saw everybody was mad. I saw 15,000 people coming to see this man get beat. And his talking did it. And, I said, this is a g-o-o-o-o-o-o-d idea!"

Before all of his first fights, Clay would come up with a poetic prediction, a boastful Hallmark-like rhyme like "Jones like to mix, so I'll let it go six. If he talks jive, I'll cut it to five. And if he talks more, I'll cut it to four."

According to Torres, by 1963 Clay had been right twelve times in predicting which round his opponent would fall. When his prediction failed in his fight against Doug Jones, the public screamed that their fight was fixed. The odds had Clay favored 4:1 just a few weeks before the fight with Jones, but the odds dropped to 2:1 by fight time. Clay won the fight, but had to go the distance.

In his next fight, Clay traveled to England and knocked out European Champion Henry Cooper, but not before Cooper floored Clay at the end of the fourth round. A win is a win is a win, however, and Clay was undefeated in his first nineteen fights.

Sonny Liston, on the other hand, was not just the heavyweight champ but by most accounts also a very intimidating person. He had served two different prison sentences and had a string of convictions. Sportswriter Jimmy Cannon wrote in 1962 that "Liston has been a mugger, a cop-slugger, a stickup man, a strong-arm guy, and a bodyguard for the mandarins of the St. Louis mobs. . . . Time spent in penitentiaries helped to form Liston's attitude. He is generally hostile, suspicious, rudely curt, surly, and menacingly indifferent. During the years when he was a fierce muscle guy for the syndicate bosses, his signature on police documents was an X. Since then, Liston has learned to sign his name." According to ESPN's "SportsCentury" biography written by Mike Puma, "Liston had ties to organized crime. In 1952, after serving two years in prison, he was paroled to a team of boxing handlers with ties to John Vitale, a St. Louis underworld figure. Six years later, Frankie Carbo and Blinky Palermo, top Mafia figures in the Northeast, became the majority owner of Liston's contract. Carbo was later indicted on conspiracy charges, multiple counts of undercover management of prizefighters and unlicensed matchmaking. Liston fought twelve fights under Carbo and Palermo's control. In 1960, the man [Liston] who never learned to read testified before a Senate subcommittee probing underworld control of boxing."

Liston won the heavyweight championship by beating Floyd Patterson in 1962. Only one thing could prevent a Clay–Liston fight. Liston had to give Patterson a rematch. That fight took place on July 22, 1963, in Las Vegas, the very first time a heavyweight championship match took place there. This time, the fight lasted all of two minutes, ten seconds. It was little wonder that Clay wanted Liston, who had inflated his record to 35–1 at that point.

The public wanted the Clay–Liston fight, too, but the popular betting choice—and the man that most of America wanted to see win the fight—was Liston. (Of course, white America had rooted—hard—for Floyd Patterson to defeat Liston earlier.) Murray Kempton wrote in *The New Republic* in 1964 that "Liston used to be a hoodlum; now he was our cop; he was the big Negro we pay to keep sassy Negroes in line."

The most popular conspiracy theory regarding the first fight between Liston and Clay goes like this: Liston at the time had a close relationship with a flamboyant underworld figure named Ashe Resnick. Resnick owned the Vegas casino where Liston trained. Did Resnick orchestrate a gambling bonanza by ordering Liston to lose in the middle rounds of the first fight (or the first round in the rematch)? Suspicions aside, to this day no hard evidence (no paper trail, testimony trail, or money trail) has ever surfaced that could prove a fix was in on either fight. Besides, it can be argued that Liston was more valuable to the mob as a champion.

Heading into the first fight, Clay began intentionally agitating Liston. He rented a bus and followed Liston. Written across the top of the bus was, "World's Most Colorful Fighter" and under that "Liston must go in eight."

The twenty-one-year-old Clay was a big underdog and few believed he could win, including the great former heavyweight champion Rocky Marciano, who said, "First, Clay is horribly short of experience to be going against a brute like Liston. Clay may have the basic tools, but he's at least a year away from full maturity, both physically and as a strategist."

It wasn't just that Liston was favored to win the fight, it was that he was favored by so much. All of the experts predicted the champion would prevail. I've read that Liston was a 7–1 favorite. Some sources had it as much as 8–1. To add even more intrigue, the Clay camp was using all its influence to convince the Army not to induct Clay before the match with Liston. Liston was the champion, but Clay was the drawing card, the lightning rod. There were so many characters surrounding both fighters that it would have been surprising if the fight wasn't tampered with in some way. In any case, whoever conspired to fix these fights needed to get to only one person: Sonny Liston.

Convention Hall in Miami held only 8,300 fans. In the first round, Clay ducked most of Liston's punches. He moved backwards, and from side to side. Toward the end of the third round, Clay caught Liston with a flurry of punches, and a cut opened up under the champion's eye.

The most memorable—and most suspicious—round of that fight was the fifth. Between the fourth and fifth rounds, something got into Clay's eyes. Clay came out fighting anyway. With his corner pushing him out toward the champion, Clay began waving his arms at Liston. In a 1971 article for *Life* magazine, Norman Mailer wrote that Clay had a look of "abject horror on his face, as if to say, 'Your younger brother is now an old blind beggar. Do not strike him.' For Clay looked like a ghost with his eyes closed, tears streaming. . . . Liston drew back in doubt, in bewilderment, conceivably in concern for his new great reputation as an ex-bully; yes, Liston reached like a gentleman, and Clay was home free."

Clay destroyed Liston in the sixth round. Incredibly, the champion didn't come out for round seven. Liston claimed that he had an injured shoulder. The question remains: What blinded Clay in that fifth round? The most probable answer is that when Ali opened up a cut on Liston's face in the third round, the champ's corner men put medicine on the cut, and some of this medicine must have gotten on Clay's gloves when he hit Liston in the fourth round. When Clay wiped his forehead, the medicine came off his glove and ran into his eyes. The heavily-favored Liston, needing to lose the fight (possibly to save his life) reacted in bewilderment when Clay was temporarily blinded, and pushed out for the fifth round. He "let up," until Clay's eyes had cleared, and the challenger was able to take control of the fight. At that point, Liston stayed in his corner, unwilling to risk any more fluky outcomes in which he would find himself winning the fight.

Of course, it could certainly be argued that someone paid Liston to put a foreign substance in his glove with the intention of temporarily blinding the challenger.

The next day—the very next day, February 26, 1964, the first day that Cassius Clay spent as Heavyweight Champion—he announced that he had become a member of the Black Muslims, and wanted to become known as Muhammad Ali. At the time, the Black Muslims were an intransigent order of militant, anti-white blacks calling themselves the Nation of Islam. Malcolm X, one of the more visible members of Elijah Muhammad's group, had been a constant presence around Clay's training camp. It's not hard to see why Liston could have been afraid of Malcolm X. (Ali would later reject Malcolm X's offer to join a Muslim splinter group, and instead opted to stay with his guru, Elijah Muhammad. Within a year, Malcolm X was assassinated. No one was ever charged with the crime and Ali never commented on it.)

Assuming that Liston wasn't a quitter (unlikely), what were some of the reasons that could explain the fight's outcome? First, of course, Sonny could have owed his life to underworld figures who needed him to dump the fight in the middle rounds for a big payoff. Liston could have also feared the Black Muslims.

One theory that goes against a conspiracy goes like this: According to the late sportswriter Jim Murray's 1993 autobiography, Ali told him that "That weigh-in won my fight. . . . That man [Liston] is spooked. I learnt that from fighting Archie Moore. . . . Liston in the first round, I put it to him and he back off and get the fear in his eyes."

So maybe Liston didn't lay down and throw the first fight. When Ali came in to the weigh-in like a crazy man, full of rage, it was possibly a great act meant to pysch out the champion. But even if Liston didn't throw the first fight, how does one possibly explain the rematch?

It was hard enough to get Ali and Liston in the ring together for another bout. According to boxing historian Bert Randolph Sugar, in his book *The Sweet Science Goes Sour: How Scandal Brought Boxing to its Knees*, there were problems getting the World Boxing Association to recognize the fight. Many states wouldn't stage the return match because they had banned Liston due to his underworld connections. There were hints of a grand jury investigation after it was revealed that before the fight the previous year, the same promoters had paid Ali $50,000 as an advance on his first title defense. One of the main stockholders in the company was Liston. Once all this had been straightened out, the thirty-one-year-old Liston trained like a madman to regain the title. But just three days before the fight, Ali was rushed to the hospital for a hernia operation.

The two parties agreed to reschedule the rematch for May 25, 1965, in Lewiston, Maine. It's possible that if Liston had been able to fight Ali in November, he would have regained the championship. Imagine training for the fight of your life, only to have the whole thing put on hold, and to be told to gear up again six months later. In any case, Ali was once again the 8–5 underdog to Liston.

This was one of the most controversial fights of all time. Watch the one-round fight on youtube.com, and you'll see why: Ali won the fight, despite landing only two punches. It doesn't seem possible. Where was the knockout punch? This is the famous "phantom" punch that Ali called his "anchor" punch. He would later explain that his punch was so fast, people couldn't see it. That a magazine had timed the punch at 4/100 of a second.

Here's the suspicious part. Ali stood over Liston, waving for him to get up. Referee Jersey Joe Walcott didn't start his count because Ali was running around and not in his corner. As Walcott went to check with the timekeeper, Liston appeared to get up slightly, before falling back. When Liston got up and it appeared that the fight would resume, the fight was stopped as Walcott was told that the timekeeper had reached ten seconds with Liston on the canvas.

Sugar quotes Ali in *The Sweet Science Goes Sour*: "Once he went down, I got excited and forgot the rules. I know I should have gone to a neutral corner. I was having fun."

Come on. Ali was in the ring with an intimidating boxer. Despite being only twenty-three years old, he knew the rules regarding knockouts. Even if he wanted to give people their money's worth, in light of the fact that everyone thought the first fight was fixed, he should have gone to a neutral corner. Walcott, the referee, always maintained that it was no phantom punch, but a short right to the chin. Was the punch capable of ending the bout? That is something that Liston took to the grave.

My opinion is that there had to be a conspiracy. There is no other rational explanation. One popular reason is that Liston over-trained for the aborted rematch. Norman Mailer explained in his 1971 *Life* magazine article:

> The second time Liston trained, he aged as a fighter. He had a sparring partner, Amos Lincoln, who was one of the better heavyweights in the country. They had wars with one another every afternoon in the gym. By the day before the fight, Liston was as relaxed and sleepy and dopey as a man in a steam bath. He had fought his heart out in training. . . . And their fight created a scandal, for Liston ran into a short punch in the first round and was counted out, unable to hear the count. The ref and timekeeper missed signals with one another while Clay stood over the fallen Liston screaming, "Get up and fight!"

Well, now, I haven't seen a phantom punch (or a glancing blow) pack that much strength outside of a Bugs Bunny cartoon, but here are what the conspiracy theorists say about that second fight. One popular theory is that Liston owed a ton of money to organized crime figures, so he bet against himself, and didn't want to risk landing a lucky punch. Another popular theory is that Liston was afraid of the Black Muslims. Torres wrote that Liston, in his estimation, quit in both fights. In the first, because he was completely frustrated; in the second, it was his subconscious mind. Deep down, wrote Torres, "Liston feared Muhammad Ali. And, even more, he feared the Black Muslims."

Many of the greatest boxers of all time believe that at least the second of the two fights was not on the level. Liston's widow

Other boxing matches that were likely fixed:

1947: "Blackjack" Billy Fox beats Jake Lamotta

LaMotta took a dive. It's recounted in *Raging Bull* and is indicative of many of the fights of the era. Fans yelled "Fake, fake!" at Fox's TKO.

1951: Kid Gavilan beats Billy Graham despite dominating the fight

In August of 1951 at Madison Square Garden, Graham did everything but knock out Gavilan, but didn't get the decision. Graham became known as the "Uncrowned Middleweight Champ."

1954: Johnny Saxton beats Kid Gavilan

This was one of the worst decisions in boxing history—and that's saying a lot. Saxton was a Philadelphia fighter controlled by organized crime figures. Twenty of twenty-two ringside reporters thought Gavilan had won. The officials were unanimous that Saxton had won.

1990: Julio Cesar Chavez beats Meldrick Taylor

One of the greatest fights in the last quarter century was marred when ref Richard Steele stopped the fight at 2:58 of the twelfth and final round, preventing Meldrick Taylor from winning a decision over then-undefeated Chavez.

1992: Lennox Lewis and Evander Holyfield fight to controversial draw

Lewis wound up with a draw, in a fight he clearly won. One of the judges, Eugenia Williams, scored a clearly Lewis-dominated fifth round for Holyfield.

1993: Pernell Whitaker whips Julio Cesar Chavez in dubious draw

Sweet Pea Whitaker frustrated Julio Cesar Chavez from beginning to end, but the judges didn't see it like that. Yes, the fight took place in San Antonio, where Chavez had a number of Mexican-Americans on his side, and a clear home-field advantage. But not even that could explain the bizarre scorecards of the officials.

1997: Oscar de la Hoya defeats Pernell Whitaker

In those days Bob Arum held a huge sway over the Las Vegas commission and the judges. This was even more egregious than the Whitaker vs. Chavez match.

believes the second fight was fixed, and that Sonny took that secret to his grave. One thing that's for sure is that the two boxers took different directions in their lives after Walcott raised Ali's hands in Lewiston. Ali's draft status changed, and he became a symbol for a generation. In time, Muhammad Ali would become one of the most famous athletes and beloved figures in the world. Sonny Liston, on the other hand, boxed for a few more years, and then, in the final days of 1970, he was found dead in his home at the age of thirty-eight, in mysterious circumstances. The investigation couldn't prove much, and many people claimed it was an overdose. But others believe that Liston was murdered. The man had many underworld contacts, so it wouldn't have been a total shock if that was the case.

What an amazing pair of stories. Liston, an illiterate hoodlum, rose to become the heavyweight champion of the world. Ali went from being one of the most hated public figures to one of the most beloved. Liston could have taken a dive. Ali could have been in on it. Either or both of their fights could have been fixed.

Certain questions will never be answered. Watching the two-minute rematch, it is amazing that Ali was still the unpopular choice going into the fight. Who would have ever imagined that Ali would become the most beloved athlete in the world in the following four decades?

CONCLUSION:

NBA's first-ever draft lottery delivers Patrick Ewing to New York

I watched the very first NBA draft lottery on television in 1985, and I remember the excitement that resulted from NBA Commissioner David Stern pulling the envelope that gave New York the right to draft Georgtown's Patrick Ewing, the national college player of the year. There have been whispers ever since that this inaugural draft was fixed. But was it?

THE MOTIVE

Make no mistake about it. The success of the NBA has always depended on a strong presence in the New York market. New York is where the League offices are located. New York is where the advertisers are, too, and it's got the largest population of any NBA city, by far. In fact, according to the 1986 U.S. Census, only one other metropolitan area (Los Angeles) had *half* as many people as the New York metropolitan area did at the time.

The NBA rose in popularity when the New York Knicks prospered from the late 1960s to the mid 1970s. The 1969–1970 Knicks not only won the NBA Championship, but they became a team with national appeal. Blue-collar Detroit native Dave DeBusschere, brainy "Dollar" Bill Bradley, and stylish Walt Frazier, dubbed "Clyde" after a popular character in the movie *Bonnie and Clyde*—each represented key parts of a complete and true team, known for their passing and unselfishness.

The Knicks were, for lack of a better word, *cool* in those days, and captured the imagination of the city's sports fans. After winning the NBA Championship in 1970, they lost in the Eastern Conference Finals the following year and then in the NBA Finals the year after that. Then, in 1973, they again won the NBA Championship. In 1974, they were eliminated in the Eastern Confererence Finals by the Boston Celtics in five games.

In the five seasons beginning in 1969–1970, the Knicks averaged more than 19,000 fans per game and sold out every seat in 133 of their 205 regular season home games at Madison Square Garden.

Following the 1974 season, though, Dave DeBusschere, Jerry Lucas, and Willis Reed all retired, and the Knicks became a less competitive team. The 1975 Knicks still featured stars like Earl Monroe, Walt Frazier and Bill Bradley, but the team's victories fell from forty-nine in the previous year to forty. Attendance fell from 19,133 per game and twenty-five sellouts to 18,556 per game and only nineteen sellouts. After 1975, the team's fan attendance slipped much further.

The NBA fell into a league-wide abyss regarding attendance and television ratings, and the drop off from the team in New York was a big contributing factor to that decline. The team that played the most like the Knicks of the early seventies were the Portland Trailblazers, who won the NBA Championship in 1977. The Seattle Supersonics won the Championship two years later. Without trying to sound too east coast biased, teams from Portland and Seattle just didn't move the needle much in the northeast, and attendance and television ratings continued to plummet.

After their impressive run ended, the Knicks simply became a bad team to watch. They not only stopped winning championships, they even stopped winning playoff series. Following the 1974 season, they didn't win a seven-game playoff series again for nineteen years.

It seemed that the franchises in Boston and Los Angeles were able to keep their teams competitive through their superstars' retirements far better than New York could. When legendary Celtics coach Red Auerbach stepped down from the bench and into the front office, respected center Bill Russell became head coach and led Boston to two more championships. When the Knicks coach Red Holzman stepped down following the 1977 season, however, respected center Willis Reed became head coach, but he steered the club through thirty-one victories and fifty-one defeats before having to be replaced by Holzman.

The Celtics always seemed to be able to make a shrewd deal that kept the dynasty intact, while the Knicks couldn't seem to make a good draft pick or trade for a decade. With the fourth overall pick in the 1978 draft, the Knicks chose the talented yet mercurial guard, Michael Ray Richardson, from the University of Montana. Two picks later, the Celtics chose Larry Bird, who still had one year of college eligibility remaining. Although Bird decided to play his final season at Indiana State, the Celtics retained his rights until the next draft. It took almost the full twelve months, but eventually Boston managed to sign the player who would go on to become known as "Larry Legend." Richardson, on the other hand, would create news of his own. He played four seasons with New York, and when asked once about the direction the Knicks were taking, Richardson replied, "The ship be sinking."

Bird was inducted into the Basketball Hall of Fame after leading the Celtics to three championships. Richardson failed several cocaine tests, and, despite his four all-star appearances, was banned from the NBA for life by Commissioner David Stern. He played in Europe for close to fifteen years, and made news again in March of 2007 when, as coach of the CBA's Albany Patroons, he told reporters that he had "big-time Jew lawyers" to help him negotiate a new contract as coach. This from a man who once played for Red Holzman!

The Knicks had other talented players in that fallow era, such as Spencer Haywood. Haywood played with the Knicks for four seasons, beginning in 1976. Haywood was later traded to the Jazz and then to the Lakers, where he was kicked off the team during the 1980 NBA Finals for freebasing cocaine. In later years, he would tell *Sports Illustrated* that "I did drugs, like 80% of the players in 1979 and 1980."

The Knicks averaged just 13,000 fans per game at Madison Square Garden in 1979, selling out the building only three times. By 1982, the Knicks were averaging just 10,000 fans per game, with zero sellouts.

New York began to turn things around in the early 1980s, though. In 1982, the Knicks won thirty-three games. Hubie Brown was hired as head coach, replacing the venerable Holzman. In 1983, they won forty-four games and made the playoffs, losing 4–0 to the eventual NBA champion 76ers in the Eastern Conference Semifinals. In 1984, the Knicks won forty-seven games and again made the playoffs, taking the eventual NBA champion Celtics to seven games in the Eastern Conference semifinals. Even greater than Brown's impact on the Knicks' improvement was the signing of dynamic scorer Bernard King as a free agent just before the 1983 season began. When Golden State matched the Knicks' offer sheet, the Warriors and Knicks worked out a trade that sent King to New York for Richardson.

The ship be afloat.

With King aboard and the team steadily improving under Brown, the Knicks had high hopes going into the 1984–1985 season. The season turned out to be a disappointment, but King established himself as the League's most unstoppable offensive force. He was averaging 32.9 points per game when he suffered a torn anterior cruciate ligament of the right knee in a game in late March. The Knicks' superstar won the scoring title, but was lost for the season. He was also out for the entire next season, and would only play six more games in a Knicks uniform before resurrecting himself and his career in Washington as a free agent.

Losing King was devastating to the Knicks, but a superstar savior loomed on the horizon—Patrick Ewing of Georgetown University. And, giving them their best chance at landing Ewing, the consensus College Player of the Year, the Knicks lost their last seven games of the season, gaining them entrance into the NBA's first-ever draft lottery.

When the NBA instituted its lottery system in 1985, it was designed to prevent teams from "tanking," or losing on purpose. In 1966, the League adopted a policy where the last-place finishers in each of the two conferences would flip a coin to determine which team would have the honor of drafting first. In some seasons, the difference between the top two picks in the draft was negligible. In other years, that coin toss determined future NBA champions.

For instance, the top two picks in the 1969 NBA draft were Kareem Abdul-Jabbar and Neil Walk. Milwaukee won the coin toss against Phoenix, and the Bucks won the 1971 NBA Finals. Phoenix, to this date, has never won an NBA Championship.

The top two picks in the 1974 NBA draft were Bill Walton and Marvin Barnes. Portland won the coin toss against Philadelphia, and drafted Walton. Three years later, the Blazers won the NBA Championship.

In the spring of 1984, the Houston Rockets coveted University of Houston center Hakeem Olajuwon, and there were virtually no scenarios in which it appeared Olajuwon would be available to be drafted without the first overall pick in the draft. The Rockets had finished 14–68 in 1983, had won the coin toss, and used it to draft center Ralph Sampson of the University of Virginia with the first overall pick. Although Houston had improved in Sampson's first year, they still found themselves battling the San Diego Clippers for the worst record in the west. Houston knew that if they lost more than the Clips they would have a 50% chance to draft local hero Olajuwon, and to pair him with Sampson, the 1983–1984 NBA Rookie of the Year.

The Clippers and Rockets met on March 16, 1984 in San Diego, and the Clippers managed a 128–118 victory. If Houston had won that game, their record would have been 27–39, 3.5 games better than the Clippers. They couldn't do that and maintain a reasonable chance at Olajuwon. Instead, Houston lost, and began their push to lose games and "win" Olajuwon. The Rockets finished their season by losing fourteen of their final seventeen games. Of their last ten games, they won only one. Would you say that they tanked? I sure would.

The Clippers, on the other hand, went 5–10 in their last fifteen games after beating the Rockets, which allowed them to gain ground and pass Houston in the standings. The Rockets had won twenty-nine games, the Clippers thirty, and the race for the worst record in the Western Conference came down to the final day of the season. On April 14, the Clippers defeated the Utah Jazz 146–128. The Rockets laid down and lost to the Kansas City Kings, 108–96, guaranteeing their place in the coin toss—in which they "won" the right to draft Olajuwon. With Hakeem in the fold, the Rockets were contenders for the next fifteen years, including back-to-back NBA Championships in 1994 and 1995.

Suspicious of the Rockets' less-than-stellar stretch and acutely aware of the much coveted Ewing, the NBA instituted a lottery system the very next year (1985) in which all seven teams that failed to make the playoffs would have an equal shot at getting the first pick in the draft. In 1985, the Indiana Pacers finished with the worst record in the Eastern Conference and the Golden State Warriors finished with the worst record in the Western Conference. But instead of a coin toss to determine which franchise would ultimately land the seven-foot-tall Ewing, each of the seven non-playoff teams had an equal shot at the first pick.

Prior to 1985, finishing last and winning the coin toss became the fastest way to turn a franchise around whenever a truly great player came along. Anyone who watched college basketball in the early 1980s knew that Patrick Ewing was a special player. He was Bill Russell-type special, schooled and coached by Russell's former backup, John Thompson. Ewing was a defensive presence who could also could score. He had an outside touch with his jumper (rare for a player of his size), in addition to being a tenacious rebounder and shot-blocker, and he was exactly the kind of player Knicks brass believed could help lead the franchise back to glory.

EVIDENCE FOR A CONSPIRACY

League officials had to know that their lottery wouldn't stop teams from tanking games. And it didn't. The 1987 Spurs finished with a record of 28–54, "won" the lottery, and were thus able to pick David Robinson, the National College Player of the Year. To secure a place in the lottery, the Spurs lost eleven of their final thirteen games. The Los Angeles Clippers were an abominable 12–70 that same year, but only managed to draw the fourth overall pick in the draft, which they used to select Ewing's former Georgetown teammate Reggie Williams. Williams played ten seasons in the NBA, but never quite reached his potential, let alone approached the statistics and accomplishments of Robinson, who helped lead San Antonio to two Championships.

Even after the NBA tweaked its lottery to protect the teams with the lowest records, teams still tanked. In 1997, the Spurs lost fifteen of their last nineteen games (and eight of their last nine) as they geared up for a successful run at Wake Forest's Tim Duncan.

Ten years later, in March of 2007, national sportswriters hinted at a conspiracy as teams supposedly tanked games in an attempt to boost their draft position. The Milwaukee Bucks let Andrew Bogut and Charlie Villanueva, two of their top players, sit out the last few weeks with nagging injuries. Celtics head coach Doc Rivers left all five of his starters on the bench as Boston blew an eighteen-point lead to the Charlotte Bobcats late in the season. What did the Bobcats—also fighting for additional odds in the upcoming lottery—do? They sat out two starters a few nights later for their game in New Jersey.

Jeff Van Gundy, then the head coach of the Houston Rockets, was quoted in 2007 as saying that he "never quite understood why losing is rewarded, other than for parity." Well, Jeff, that's the point. The point of the draft is to make sure the best players aren't always signed by the richest and/or most competitive teams.

Van Gundy wanted to take away all the possible conflicts of interest, and give everyone an equal chance at the top pick. That way, Van Gundy told the *Houston Chronicle*, there would be no questions by anybody about anything.

Oh, but there would. All Van Gundy would have to do is set the "Way-Back" machine to May of 1985, when seven teams entered the first draft lottery and all had equal shots at a coveted first prize, to see why.

The seven teams in the 1985 lottery were the Sacramento Kings, the Atlanta Hawks, the Seattle Sonics, the Indiana Pacers, the Golden State Warriors, the Los Angeles Clippers, and the New York Knicks. From the NBA's perspective, there was a lot less money to be made all around if Ewing was delivered to any city other than New York, but it would be especially bad for the League if he went to one of the four west coast teams (the Clippers, the Sonics, the Kings, or the Warriors) in the running.

The lottery was held on Mother's Day, 1985, with the general managers from each of the seven teams gathered like contestants on a game show. Commissioner David Stern drew envelopes for the drafting order, starting with the seventh pick. The late Dave DeBusschere, then the General Manager of the Knicks, made like a winning game show contestant when it became apparent that New York had won the first pick. Rumors immediately began to fly that the proceedings were "fixed." One theory was that there was dry ice in the Knicks' envelope, so the commissioner would know which one to pick. Another theory claimed that it held rocks. Still others talked about a crease in the Knicks envelope which marked it for the commissioner.

The day after the lottery, Sportswriter Randy Galloway offered the following opinion in the *Dallas Morning News*:

> The NBA lottery delivers Patrick Ewing to New York and your nose immediately detects a smell of a rat. . . . The whispers said the right strings would be pulled by league fathers to ensure the right envelope ended up under No. 1 on the lottery board. Why? Got to have a big winner in the Big Apple—it's for the good of the league, don't you know? Hopefully, this is all a coincidence, surely that is the case. But the NBA has put itself in a position where suspicion clouds the lottery situation. Ewing to the Knicks—there's just something too convenient about that arrangement, and there were also too many people inside the NBA privately predicting it was going to happen.

On March 5, 2007, the entire 1985 NBA Draft Lottery—
originally broadcast by CBS Sports and hosted by Pat
O'Brien—wound up on the website youtube.com. Count me
among millions who had not seen the tape of Stern pulling out
those envelopes in more than twenty years. On April 19 of that
year, popular sports columnist Bill Simmons wrote about the
conspiracy in his column for espn.com. He said, "After twenty-two
years, we now have indisputable video evidence that something
fishy happened." That spurred hundreds of thousands to look for
themselves. Within weeks, there were nearly a quarter-million
views of the nine-minute, fifty-eight-second video. The clip also
generated a ton of comments, some claiming that Simmons was
reaching for something, others claiming proof positive of what
had been whispered for years. "At 5:28 you can see an upturned
corner while they are laying at rest in the globe and at 5:31 you
can see that same bent corner for a split second while in David
Stern's hand, but that bend could have happened while rotating
the globe six turns," wrote one viewer of the youtube clip.

After viewing the video many times, a friend of mine who is an
avid conspiracy theorist wrote this:

> Watching that video pretty much cements the theory
> that the lottery was rigged. Watch how the "impartial"
> accountant tosses in that fourth envelope—slamming it
> against the side of the drum. That fourth envelope gets
> dog-eared with that toss against the drum wall, making
> it all the easier for Stern to find it. It begs the question,
> if the envelopes are going to get spun in the drum, why
> put it 'em in one at a time? To count and make sure all
> seven are there? Plus, watch Stern. He takes his time
> with the "lock," then takes that deep breath, giving him
> time to spot the dog-eared envelope. Then watch how
> he grabs that stack of three and takes the bottom one

(the dog-eared one), again being able to look at the whole thing all the while.

This is one conspiracy theory that will not go away. The youtube comments ranged from brilliant to bizarre. Many fans wrote that the Knicks envelope was frozen before it was placed in the drum, so that Stern would be able to tell it by touch. Still, others did not see anything suspicious. Some did, but rationalized that the Knicks didn't win a Championship in the ensuing Ewing-era, so it was much ado about nothing. Without giving any unwanted publicity to the person who posted the video, I must say it's fascinating to go back and stop the tape at different points. I know it's not the same as watching the Zapruder film of the JFK assassination, but for sports fans, it's as close as we're likely to get.

THE RESULT OF EWING WINDING UP WITH THE KNICKS

In the forty-eight hours after the Knicks won the right to draft Ewing, the club received more than 1,000 season ticket requests. The league had one year remaining on CBS' four-year contract to televise the NBA nationally. At the time, the NBA was getting only $22 million per year from the network. Ewing in New York meant millions more in the next television contract.

And how did Ewing respond to playing in New York? In *Garden Glory*, an oral history of the Knicks, historian Dennis D'Agastino quotes then-coach Hubie Brown as saying of Ewing, "The thing that we immediately saw as a coaching staff was that he could score. He was a better scorer than he was a rebounder and shot blocker. He came out of college as a rebounder and shot blocker. Well, for NBA standards he was below average in both of those categories, but he was a prime-time scorer." Despite missing thirty-two games with a knee injury, Ewing won the NBA Rookie of the Year award after the 1985–86 season, averaging twenty points, nine rebounds, and two blocked shots per game. The Knicks failed to make the playoffs in Ewing's first two seasons, due in part to injuries to Ewing (who also missed nineteen games in his second season) and the lingering injury to King. Following that, Ewing led the Knicks to thirteen consecutive playoff appearances—twice leading the Knicks to the NBA Finals. Logic dictates that there would have been more Finals appearances and possible NBA titles, if not for a certain player in Chicago named Michael Jordan.

When, after fifteen years, Patrick Ewing left the Knicks, they had enjoyed a run of 347 consecutive sellouts at Madison Square Garden, one of the longest home sellout streaks in NBA history. In fifteen seasons with Patrick Ewing, the Knicks sold out Madison Square Garden 394 times in the regular season. By contrast, they had only 205 sellouts in their first thirty-nine seasons without Ewing, most of them clustered around their two Championships.

Ewing played in 135 playoff games for the Knicks, and was responsible for millions of dollars of playoff revenue at Madison Square Garden. He concluded his Knicks career as their all-time leader in games (1,039), points (23,665), minutes played (37,586), field goals made (9,260), field goals attempted (18,224), free throws made (5,126), free throws attempted (6,904), rebounds (10,759), blocks (2,758), and steals (1,061). He was selected to eleven NBA All-Star games, and in 1996 was voted one of the Fifty Greatest Players in NBA history.

My Opinion

On the NBA's official website, nba.com, there is a section on the evolution of the draft and the lottery. It seems strange to me that in this section it says "A lucky bounce of the ping-pong balls [in 1985] made the New York Knicks the first draft lottery winner."

It's strange because the ping-pong ball machine wasn't used that year.

I've written many articles and I know that mistakes are made, and not always caught by even the most sharp-eyed editors. But this one seems particularly curious.

Also, the NBA has gone to great pains to ensure that there would be no questions concerning any hanky-panky in subsequent lotteries. But by many accounts the 1985 draft lottery was just a little too perfect.

CONCLUSION:

AFL gains credibility with victory in Super Bowl III

One of the leading sports conspiracists, Brian Tuohy, gives us his version of the conspiracy theory that Super Bowl III was a fixed game. I talked to Brian about his theory and present it here as it was recorded.

Brian Tuohy: In my mind, the two questions one has to ask when talking about the Super Bowl III conspiracy are not "if" and "how could" but "why" and "how easily" it was fixed. In fact, the "why" is barely a question at all.

The AFL was a young league in 1968, not even ten years in existence, when finances forced the two leagues to make the deal to merge. Even though the AFL/NFL merger was a done deal prior to Super Bowl III, questions remained—not only in the fans' minds, but in some of the players' and owners' minds as well—about what kind of competition the AFL really offered the NFL.

EK: By the mid-1960s, the war between the leagues was getting out of hand. According to author and historian Jeff Davis, the stakes were so high for coveted draft picks that the two leagues kept moving their drafts up earlier and earlier, and both leagues employed babysitters to stash away their draftees, often at out-of-the-way locations and incommunicado, to keep them out of contact with the teams from the rival league that had also drafted them. Don Weiss, who worked in the NFL offices in 1965 and who later became the executive director of the league, said "they were dubbed babysitters, but body snatchers would have been just as appropriate." Even though television revenues went up for both leagues, most of the money was being spent on securing good players.

As for the kind of competition the AFL offered, maybe the NFL wolves were only as strong as the Pack (excuse the pun). Even though the Packers won the first two Super Bowls convincingly, the first game was only 14–10 at halftime. The Packers defeated the Raiders by nineteen points in Super Bowl II, but they had also beaten the Los Angeles Rams (11–1–2 during the season) by twenty-one points in the playoffs a few weeks earlier.

Tuohy: To put a modern spin on it, think about what might have happened if the XFL managed to make it through that first year, and then started to sign some of the bigger talent coming out of college, and by doing so, make a name for itself as a true rival league to the NFL. How would modern-day fans have taken to an XFL/NFL merger? Would they have accepted it?

EK: I only wish the XFL had made it past their initial season. I'm all for choice, for opportunity, for additional jobs, and excitement. But a better example, Brian, would be the USFL; a league that actually did compete with the NFL for the top college players in the 1980s. I wonder what would have happened if that league had deeper pockets, or had been awarded millions in their lawsuit against the NFL. I do believe that a certain few teams would likely have merged into the league, with the rest folding—similar to when four ABA teams merged into the NBA in the mid-1970s. I guess what you're saying is that you were afraid that unless the ten AFL teams provided real competition for the sixteen NFL teams, the merger would fall apart, with only some of the teams surviving to join the NFL; and that without competitive championship games, the popularity of the new combined league would wane.

Tuohy: The first Super Bowl (then called the NFL–AFL Championship Game) was really an after-thought of the merger. Even the owners didn't take that first game very seriously. But when Super Bowl II came, with the NFL team again winning big, all the owners came to realize the significance of their proposed 1970 merger. Would the deal they fought so hard to make die in front of football fans every Sunday on national television?

EK: Sorry to disagree, but the fact that the leagues would play a world championship game following the 1966 season was one of the key points of the merger; along with the fact that Pete Rozelle would serve as the commissioner of the combined league, that all existing franchises would remain in place; a common draft would be held; and a single-league schedule would begin in 1970. That said, I will support one thing you said. A third straight blowout in the Super Bowl was of real concern to all NFL and AFL owners. In Pete Rozelle's press conference before Super Bowl III, he announced that the league would consider altering the structure of the postseason tournament after the 1970 merger, so that two NFL teams might meet in the final. Professional leagues always want the two best teams to meet in the finals, so this wasn't shocking. What *was* shocking was the headline the next day in the *New York Times* that read "Rozelle Indicates Tomorrow's Super Bowl Contest Could Be Next to Last."

Tuohy: So with Super Bowl III looming, and the juggernaut Baltimore Colts most likely to be the NFL's representative in it, the owners knew that something had to be done to help legitimize the AFL. The solution? The AFL had to win that game. How to ensure that happens? Fix it.

Was it possible to get all the owners to agree to this? It wouldn't [have been] necessary to do so (like a good CIA plan, only certain people might have been on that "need to know" basis), but I believe it was possible. Their football was also their business, and the owners were businessmen, first and foremost. If you want to get ultra-conspiratorial, two owners—Clint Murchison of the Cowboys and H.L. Hunt, father of Lamar Hunt of the Chiefs—have both been linked to the JFK assassination as financiers. NFL owners who weren't crazy about the merger to begin with realized that they had reached the point of no return by year three. They couldn't un-merge the leagues. The fail-safe point had been passed, and the owners had to not only make the merger work, but also make the expanded league both profitable and competitive.

Look at what might have happened had the Colts won Super Bowl III. Besides the obvious negative fan and media reactions, the new NFL would have faced serious internal strife. There was only one more year left on the existing TV deals that created what had become known as the Super Bowl. This "Super Bowl" might have died before it had a chance to fly. And realignment would have been horrific if teams had to become AFC teams to balance out the two new conferences.

Once motive has been established, you have to figure out how to fix a football game. First off, while the AFL team had to win the game, they didn't have to be told of the plan. That may seem unnatural, but it takes half of the worry out of it. And I truly believe that the Jets didn't know they were going to be given that game. I actually wonder if the Raiders laid down in the AFL Championship Game to let the Jets (the biggest market team in the AFL) with Joe Namath (the biggest star in the AFL) get into the Super Bowl to begin with.

EK: Sorry, Brian. No can do here. I know Al Davis, and I'm sure that he and his small staff at the time would have rather died a gruesome death than lay down and lose for the good of the merger. The Raiders probably were better than the Jets that year. Hell, the Raiders had a better record that year than the Jets, but played the AFL Title game in a cold, raw afternoon in New York because championship games alternated home sites by Eastern and Western champions, not by best records. Even at that, Namath needed to come from behind in the final minutes and did so, finding Don Maynard in the end zone for the game-winner. Trust me, the Raiders would have loved to have been the ones to give the NFL its comeuppance in Super Bowl III.

Tuohy: I don't believe Namath's famous "guarantee" was made with some foreknowledge of the game's outcome. Having the Jets in on the fix would have made for some bad football. Two boxers can dance their way through a fight, but two football teams cannot.

So, the fix has to be made by convincing those on the Colts to lay down. The 1968 version of the team was one of the best in football history. That year, the Colts finished the regular season 13–1, and their average margin of victory was eighteen points. Their lone loss was to the Cleveland Browns. Baltimore got revenge by crushing that same Cleveland squad 34–0 in the NFL Championship Game, however, and were favored from anywhere between seventeen and twenty-two points heading into the Super Bowl with the Jets. Vince Lombardi, the great Packers head coach, called the Jets chances of winning the game "infinitesimal."

EK: Brian's conspiracy theory isn't the only one that I've heard concerning this game. Former Cleveland Browns player Bernie Parrish—one of the organizers of the NFL Players Union in the mid-1960s—wrote a book in 1971 called *They Call it a Game* in which he detailed his theory. "Namath and his teammates' performance secured the two leagues, at the very least, $100 million in future television revenues . . ." But I don't buy Brian's, Parrish's, or even Bubba Smith's claims of a fix, despite the fact that Smith played in the game.

Tuohy: Now, turn to the ownership of the Colts, one Carroll Rosenbloom. Legend has it that Rosenbloom placed a $1 million bet on his own team in the 1958 NFL Championship Game against the New York Giants. In that game, with time running out and the Colts controlling the ball inside the Giants' ten-yard line, Rosenbloom supposedly called down to the sidelines and ordered head coach Weeb Eubank not to kick a game-winning field goal, but instead to push the ball into the end zone so Rosenbloom's Colts could cover the four-point spread.

EK: There was a heated debate at the time about whether Rosenbloom had a large bet on his team to win by four or more. Did he order Ewbank to go for the touchdown? He denied it vehemently. The rumors never went away, however, and Commissioner Rozelle eventually addressed the rumors five years later, claiming that they weren't true. Of course, Rozelle worked for the owners, including Rosenbloom.

Tuohy: On the field, the two best choices to cajole into going along with the fix were the Colts' head coach Don Shula and his starting quarterback, twelve-year veteran journeyman Earl Morrall. How did each perform in Super Bowl III?

Let's look at Morrall first. Despite being the MVP of the season, putting up twenty-six touchdowns and nearly 3,000 yards, Morrall was flat out horrible in Super Bowl III (6–17, 71 yards, 0 TD, 3 INT). The Colts had numerous scoring chances in the first half. The first resulted in a missed field goal (hmmm). One of the best scoring chances was the famous "flea-flicker" play. The flea-flicker was a staple of Morrall's repertoire during his time in New York with the Giants. He was very familiar with the play. Yet when the Colts ran it in the Super Bowl, Morrall, with time and protection, somehow missed his intended receiver—a wide open (and I mean *all alone*, flapping his arms in the air, wide open) Jimmy Orr in the end zone. Instead of the easy touchdown, Morrall opted to throw the ball into coverage over the middle where it ended up in the arms of Jets' strong safety Jim Hudson.

EK: When I talked to former Jets defensive back John Dockery, who played in that game, about why rumors persist about the game being fixed, the only answer he had was Rosenbloom. "There were rumors about him gambling when he lived, and he died a mysterious death," Dockery said. Rosenbloom did have a reputed gambling problem, dating back to the 1950s. An active man and a good swimmer, he was found dead in the ocean in back of his home in early 1979. Foul play was suspected, but eventually his death was ruled an accidental drowning.

So I hear you on Rosenbloom, Brian. This is the strongest part of your conspiracy theory. In his book *The Making of the Super Bowl*, Don Weiss wrote that the Colts were so confident of victory that Rosenbloom threw what looked for all the world like a victory party (at his Florida home where he would be found dead just ten years later) for his coaching staff, eight days before the game was played. If he had been in on a conspiracy, this would have been a perfect move for him to make.

Morrall had a terrific season, true, but this crew-cut Cinderella was fast approaching midnight. It should not have been a shocker that Morrall didn't play well in the Super Bowl. It's not like the Jets were in awe of him. Jets cornerback Johnny Sample, an ex-Colt, told his Jets teammates about what [Johnny] Unitas could do, especially under fire. "I knew we'd be in trouble if he started," Sample said. But he didn't start. Morrall started.

AN INSIDE LOOK AT THE COLTS' FIRST HALF SCORING CHANCES

Colts first possession: First Quarter (10:55 remaining)

On Baltimore's first offensive play, Morrall hit John Mackey for a nineteen-yard completion. Tom Matte ran for ten yards, and another first down. Jerry Hill ran a sweep for seven more. The Colts worked their way to New York's nineteen-yard line. On first down, Morrall's pass was dropped. On second down, Morrall's pass was overthrown, incomplete. On third down, Morrall was lucky to get back to the line of scrimmage, avoiding a rush. On fourth down, Lou Michaels missed a short, twenty-seven-yard field goal attempt.

Colts second possession: First Quarter (3:05 remaining)

Baltimore ran three plays, then punted. The Colts' punt was downed on the Jets' four-yard line.

Colts third possession: First Quarter (0:14 remaining)

The Colts managed to force a turnover, as Lenny Lyles made George Sauer cough up the ball following a reception. Baltimore overtook New York at the twelve-yard line. Hill lost a yard, running off-tackle on first down. On second and eleven, Matte gained seven yards on a sweep. On third and four, Morrall's pass to Mitchell was intercepted by New York corner Randy Beverly in the end zone for a touchback.

Colts fourth possession: Second Quarter: (9:03 remaining, Jets up 7–0)

Morrall found Matte for thirty yards on second and ten, and the Colts had the ball in New York territory. Two more rushes and one incomplete pass later, Lou Michaels missed a forty-six-yard field goal attempt.

Colts fifth possession: Second Quarter: (4:13 remaining, Jets up 7–0)

After a fifty-eight-yard run by Matte, the Colts had a first down at the New York sixteen-yard line. One running play later, Johnny Sample intercepted Morrall at the two-yard line.

Colts sixth possession: Second Quarter
(0:43 remaining, Jets up 7–0)

Baltimore took over at the New York forty-two-yard line. Morrall completed a one-yard pass. And then, the famous "flea-flicker." Matte lateraled back to Morrall, and Earl never saw a wide-open Jimmy Orr. Instead, Morrall was intercepted for a third time. And so ended the first half. Shula always defended Morrall for not seeing Orr in the end zone. He would say repeatedly that the Baltimore Colts' band got out of the stands, was going behind the end zone, and the colors blended in.

It is clear that the Colts' offensive ineptitude killed any chance they had of winning the game. It is puzzling, though, that at halftime Shula could have chosen to make two vital adjustments, but made neither. I truly believe that Shula made the worst coaching decision in Super Bowl history by not starting Johnny Unitas at quarterback. Unitas was out for most of the season with an injured elbow, but was—according to Shula's words at the time—80% healthy. Starting Unitas was debatable, considering the success the team enjoyed with Morrall. But after Morrall threw three interceptions in the second quarter, Shula compounded his poor decision. He *started* Morrall in the second half, despite his problems in the first half. (Shula would learn his lesson, however. Four years later, he started Bob Griese in Super Bowl VII, despite Morrall quarterbacking the Dolphins to eleven consecutive victories following a Griese injury).

The Jets had only scored seven points in the first half, but they'd moved the ball well (179 yards) and had had some missed opportunities of their own (losing a fumble and missing a field goal). The Colts' left defensive end, Bubba Smith, told author Jeff Miller in *Going Long*, his 2003 oral history of the American

Football League: "At halftime, I said, 'Let me get over the center. I can stop Snell from running over there.' Shula said, 'Just play your f—ing position.'"

Tuohy: Somehow, Shula, still in his thirties then, managed to take the most dominant team in the NFL and turn them into a bunch of semi-pro also-rans. Oddly enough, Super Bowl III would be the last game he would ever coach for the Colts before signing a lucrative deal to lead the Dolphins for the rest of his long career.

EK: Bubba Smith told Jeff Miller, "This might sound crazy, but I don't think the game was kosher. In order for the merger to go through, [the Jets] had to win. If you read the terms of the merger, if [the AFL] didn't establish credibility by the end of three years, the terms of the merger were null and void. You're talking the difference of millions and billions of dollars. The line opened at eighteen and went down to fifteen or something like that because a big bet had been placed on the game. And I know where the bet came from. It came from Baltimore, from someone on the team, from what I understand."

Tuohy: So what was the payoff for the Colts? If Shula and Morrall took dives, what did they receive for their efforts? Once the AFL and the Super Bowl were legitimized with an AFL victory in Super Bowl IV (which I believe was also rigged), the NFL could then let Rosenbloom and Morrall reap the rewards of winning Super Bowl V in January of 1971. And as for Shula, he 'coincidentally' then led the Dolphins to the first of two Super Bowl championships in Super Bowls VII and VIII. Payback can be sweet when paid in championship rings.

EK: I only wish Bubba had evidence—*real* evidence—to support this big bet from Baltimore. Was it a Rosenbloom bet? I can't believe that he bet against his own team. He was described as a picture of complete and utter devastation at game's end. Don Weiss wrote, "By the end of the game, Carroll was totally drained of color and just sat there in silence." Plus, Rosenbloom's relationship with Shula soured. In a fix, wouldn't the conspirator/owner have taken care of his co-conspirator/coach? Here is another reason that I believe the game was not fixed: Shula was so perplexed walking off the field at halftime, he remarked to an aide, "Damn it, the flea-flicker is designed especially for Orr. Morrall is supposed to look for him. What in hell is happening?" That is not how Shula would react if he were in on a fix. Not even a great actor could pull that one off.

The truth is that the Jets were a better team than people thought. Their coach, Weeb Ewbank, was not only experienced (first assisting Paul Brown in Cleveland, and then later leading the Colts to a pair of NFL Championships as head coach), but he had been released by the Colts and knew many of their aging stars. Ewbank used an injured Don Maynard as a decoy, and that helped the Jets' offense tremendously. The Jets were confident, with Namath full of swagger. They were bitter, with cornerback Sample upset over his time with the Colts. Namath broke the rhythm of the Colts defense, something the NFL teams had not done. Jets right tackle Dave Herman did a great job on Bubba Smith, and the Jets controlled the clock over thirty-six minutes in the game.

Shula would prove in later Super Bowls that perhaps he wasn't the greatest big-game coach. His Dolphins lost Super Bowl VI by a score of 24–3 (with Shula's team getting outscored 14–0 in the second half). His Dolphins also lost Super Bowl XVII by a score of 27–17, despite leading 17–10 at halftime, and lost Super Bowl XIX by a score of 38–16.

Could Don Shula have made halftime adjustments in the Super Bowl? History suggests not. In the six biggest games of his career—the six Super Bowls he coached—his teams scored 7, 0, 0, 7, 0, and 0 points in the second halves. The *only* fourth quarter points his teams ever scored in the six Super Bowls he coached came with a meaningless Unitas touchdown pass, which was scored with the Colts down 16–0 and less than four minutes remaining in the game. The only other time a Shula-coached Super Bowl team scored in the second half of the big game came on a two-yard touchdown run by Larry Csonka in the third quarter of Super Bowl VIII.

Tuohy: To me, if you strip away the legend and the nearly forty years worth of gloss painted over the Jets "miracle" win in Super Bowl III and look at the game objectively—what it meant to the league and what happened on the field—you cannot come away thinking the game was played on the level. Too much was at stake to merely "hope for the best." Too much money has been made by the NFL over the years as a direct result of that game.

EK: The public was already hooked on the NFL big-time by January of 1969. Super Bowl II was a blowout, yet CBS attracted more than fifty-one million viewers, garnering [a 36.8 share of the market, and a 68 share unclear]. Despite the Colts being overwhelming favorites the next year, NBC attracted a 70 share—meaning seven of ten television sets that were in use that day were tuned in to the football game. To me, the game could have been 98–0 and the league—merger and all—would have still prospered. I do not believe the game was fixed. It was an important game in the history of the league, and it came when the Jets and Namath represented the counter-culture. Shula didn't fix the game (although he made terrible coaching decisions; Rosenbloom didn't fix the game (although he may have bet on the game, and associated with a variety of unsavory characters); and the Colts players certainly didn't fix the game. Morrall was moral, as were the rest of the participants, as they battled through Super Bowl III.

CONCLUSION:

Isiah Thomas left off the 1992 Olympic Dream Team

Was there a conspiracy to keep Hall of Fame guard Isiah Thomas off of the 1992 U.S. Olympic basketball team, known throughout the world as "the Dream Team"? Enough evidence exists to support such a conspiracy. For this kind of glaring omission to occur, however, a man must have powerful enemies with enough influence to sway others. Let's examine the situation closely.

Isiah Thomas is one of those people, like his college coach Bob Knight, for whom there is no middle ground. He has plenty of admirers, and an equal number of critics. Isiah was seen as the culprit—the main instigator—in freezing out a young rookie named Michael Jordan in Jordan's first NBA All-Star Game (in 1985). Thomas, who grew up in Chicago, was drafted by the Bulls' rival, the Detroit Pistons, and by 1985 he was being jeered even in his hometown city, taking a backseat to Chicago's much-beloved hot-shot rookie.

Thomas always played like he had a chip on his shoulder, and he was a lightning rod for controversy. Although the mercurial and wacky Dennis Rodman, after the 1987 Eastern

Conference Finals between the Pistons and Boston Celtics, said, "Larry Bird would be considered just another player if he were black," it was Thomas that got ripped for the remark. That's because, when asked as the team leader about the quote, Isiah didn't go far enough in distancing himself or minimizing the statement.

His entire professional career has been filled with incredible highs and lows, sometimes experienced simultaneously. The pinnacle of Thomas' career as a player came in June of 1990, when his Detroit team defeated the Portland Trailblazers to win their second consecutive NBA Championship. In the Finals, Isiah was, as they say, "Jordanesque." In Game One, Isiah scored thirty-three points, including sixteen in the fourth quarter alone to lead his team to a come-from-behind victory. In Game Four, he scored thirty points in the second half (including twenty-two in the third quarter). In the final game, with the score tied at ninety, Thomas passed up a potential game-winning shot. Instead, he passed the ball to Vinnie Johnson on the wing. Johnson, dubbed "The Microwave" because he heated up in a hurry, froze defender Jerome Kersey and hit a series-clinching jumper in the final second. Isiah averaged 27.6 points per game in the series, and made eleven of sixteen three-point shots.

Less than forty-eight hours later, local FBI officials held a press conference for the purpose of clearing Isiah Thomas' name. There had been a report that linked him to an FBI investigation of an alleged multi-million dollar sports gambling ring. A report by Detroit television station WJBK said Thomas wasn't the target of the investigation, but that investigators were interested in checks from Isiah that were cashed by Emmet Denha, a close friend and former neighbor. Thomas was forced to explain that he often had Denha cash checks for him at one of Denha's stores, to save himself the hassle of signing autographs or serving as a distraction at local banks.

For whatever reason, Thomas always seemed to find controversy. He found it as a player, and he found it in his messy divorce from the Pistons following his playing days. He found it as an executive when he was accused of running the CBA (Continental Basketball Association) into the ground after twenty years as the Minor League of the NBA. He found it as the President of the Toronto Raptors, where he made several questionable personnel moves, and as coach of the Indiana Pacers, where he clashed repeatedly with the team's top brass. Most recently, Thomas encountered controversy in his role of President of Basketball Operations with the New York Knicks, in his clashes with former head coach Larry Brown, and the following year with Brown disciple George Karl, an opposing coach.

When Isiah was still a college student at Indiana University, he was selected for the 1980 U.S. Olympic team. Just months before the team was scheduled to go to Moscow, President Jimmy Carter pulled the United States out of the games, boycotting the games for political reasons. The American athletes therefore never had a chance to represent their country in Olympic competition.

In the 1984 Olympics, it was the Soviets' turn to boycott the games, and the United States (with Michael Jordan and Patrick Ewing) won the gold in basketball. By the time the U.S. men's national basketball team played the USSR in the semifinals of the 1988 Olympic tournament, the U.S. had compiled an Olympic record of 77–1. But the USSR, led by professional players like Sarunas Marculonis and Arvydas Sabonis, shockingly defeated the American amateurs by a score of 82–76.

The loss led FIBA (International Amateur Basketball Federation) to vote 56–13 on April 17, 1989, to allow NBA players to play in future Olympics. (The U.S. actually voted against NBA participation.) This vote not only paved the way for the U.S. Dream Team, but it opened the NBA doors to great Europeans like the aforementioned Sabonis. The United States would finally be able to send their best and most deserving players to Barcelona for the 1992 games. And when Detroit Pistons head coach Chuck Daly was selected to be the coach for the 1992 U.S. Olympic National Team, it seemed like Isiah Thomas would finally get the chance to represent his country.

After all, Thomas had done wonders on the court in his Pistons career, mostly under the watchful eye of Daly. And there had to be some bias toward allowing at least one or two of the 1980 U.S. team a shot at the Olympics. The 1980 squad had some very good players, but by 1992 the best candidates (apart from Isiah) were Mark Aguirre and Buck Williams. Aguirre was a bona-fide scorer who had won two championship rings, played in three All-Star Games and averaged better than twenty-one points per game in his eleven-year career. Williams had toiled his first eleven years for relatively anonymous NBA stomping grounds New Jersey and Portland, yet he had averaged sixteen points and eleven rebounds per game. Buck had made three All-Star teams, and had been a valuable starter on teams that went to the NBA Finals in 1990 and 1992. In addition, Buck had been named to the NBA's All-Defensive first team in both 1990 and 1991.

USA Basketball, the organizing committee that selected the team, had an abundance of riches, and although they knew the games would be lopsided in favor of the United States *regardless* of whom they chose, still they ignored Williams, Aguirre, and Thomas.

Larry Bird and Magic Johnson were easy choices, and they were made co-captains. They came into the NBA together, and the Olympics would serve as an encore to their marvelous careers. Johnson had been prematurely forced to retire from the NBA due to HIV in November of 1991, but he would return to play in the 1992 All-Star Game (and would comeback again in 1996 to play thirty-two more games with the Lakers). Bird had struggled with back pain through an injury-riddled 1992 season, and would never play another game in the NBA. Not knowing how much the team could rely on Bird and Johnson, USA Basketball filled out the rest of its roster like this:

Centers: *Patrick Ewing, David Robinson*

Well, there were three great centers in the NBA at the time, and one bubbling up on the horizon. Shaquille O'Neal was still a pup in college, and Hakeem Olajuwon didn't become a naturalized American citizen until after the 1993 season. That left two great players to pick. Ewing won gold for the U.S. in 1984, and Robinson won bronze for the U.S. in 1988. There is no question that these were the right selections.

Forwards: *Larry Bird, Scottie Pippen, Karl Malone, Chris Mullin, Charles Barkley, Christian Laettner*

Bird was a no-brainer. Karl Malone and Charles Barkley were in their prime, the two best active forwards. Mullin was a scoring machine (1992 was the fourth year in a row he had topped twenty-five points per game), and the team needed an outside shooter (the main weakness of the 1988 U.S. team). Mullin had Olympic experience as well, having played with Jordan and Ewing on the 1984 team. Pippen was one of the greatest defensive players of all time. He was a complimentary player, who had shown that he could flourish on the court with Michael Jordan. Laettner was the lone college selection.

Guards: *Magic Johnson, Michael Jordan, Clyde Drexler, John Stockton*

Johnson had been retired from the NBA for a year at that point. Everyone was drooling about having Jordan and Bird play alongside Magic Johnson. At that point, Jordan was the one of the most popular figures in the world, and easily the best NBA player.

Drexler was selected with one of the two last picks saved to fill out the squad. I really thought then, and I still think now, that Drexler deserved to be on the team. In 1992, he averaged twenty-five points, 6.5 rebounds, and 6.5 assists per game. He was, in my opinion, the second best player in the game at that time, behind Jordan. Between 1985 and 1992, only three men—Jordan, Karl Malone, and the defensively challenged Dominique Wilkins— scored more points than Drexler.

Stockton was just one year younger than Thomas, yet Thomas had done so much more than Stockton by the end of the 1992 season. Stockton did have 7,381 assists in his career at that point, but Thomas had 7,991. That was third-most of all time, trailing only Magic Johnson and Oscar Robertson. Stockton, to that point, had averaged thirteen points per game in his career. He had never been named to the First-Team All-NBA (Thomas was, three times), nor had he led his team into the Finals. Thomas, on the other hand, had not only taken his team to the Finals three years in a row, but had led the Pistons to consecutive championships. Isiah was a supreme playmaker, and a talented and clutch scorer. In the 1984 playoffs, he scored sixteen points in ninety-four seconds in the fourth quarter of the decisive Game Five of a series against the Knicks. Twice, he was named MVP of the NBA All-Star Game.

You can quibble with the choices, but most were rock-solid. The one real glaring piece that was missing was Thomas. How could that be, especially with his own coach, Chuck Daly, coaching the Olympians? In the spring of 2007, I spoke by phone with Daly about the omission.

Chuck Daly: Isiah *absolutely* should have been on the 1992 Dream Team. I didn't have a vote. It was done by committee [USA Basketball]. I don't know the reason why. They didn't want me to address it. I did make a call, but it went unheard.

EK: Wait a minute. Who did you call?

Daly: I brought up Isiah on a conference call, so it wasn't [just] one person. But I had a problem. I had [Pistons] Joe Dumars and Dennis Rodman and Thomas all available. All of them thought they should be on the team. Coaches didn't have a say in those days—I imagine they have more of a say today. Hey, they didn't put Shaq on the team, either. I took what I had, though, and made do . . . but yes, Isiah absolutely belonged.

★   ★   ★   ★   ★

Daly told me to check out *America's Dream Team: The Quest for Olympic Gold*, his journal of the experience, written in 1992. On page 36, Chuck wrote that many people didn't realize that the coach did not select the U.S. Olympic team, and actually had very little input. The team was selected by one of the USA Basketball Committees, known as the Men's Olympic Team Subset. It originally consisted of thirteen members, including C.M. Newton, Wayne Embry, Bob Bass, Quinn Buckner, P.J. Carlesimo, Billy Cunningham, Charles Grantham, Mike Krzyzewski, Jack McCloskey, George Raveling, Rod Thorn, Jan Volk, and Donnie Walsh. Daly wrote that Buckner and McCloskey withdrew from the committee during the period when the team was being chosen, and Willis Reed was added as a replacement.

Hold on. Quinn Buckner and Jack McCoskey *withdrew* from the selection committee? Buckner was an Indiana graduate, and fiercely loyal to Bob Knight (and Isiah). McCoskey was the then-General Manager of the Pistons.

Daly went on to include Newton's reasoning for not including Daly in the process. "If [Daly] were to make the selections, you put an active coach in a very difficult position," Newton reportedly said. "By keeping him in an advisory capacity, you try to take some of the pressure off him." Chuck didn't buy that totally, although he wrote, "having the committee pick the players did relieve me of some, if not all, criticism in the area of player selection."

Again, it's hard to argue with the selections. Coach Daly never had to call a single time-out in the tournament. The average margin of victory for the U.S. team was more than forty-three points. The closest game came against Croatia, when the USA won 103–70. Opponents were simply in awe of the Dream Team.

Still, if I had been making the decisions, Thomas would have been on the team instead of Stockton. Why wasn't Isiah Thomas on the team? People who believe in conspiracy theories claim that there must have been a secret negotiation between Michael Jordan and the higher-ups at USA Basketball. Jordan and Thomas were never warm to each other.

Thomas must have had mixed emotions towards Jordan. He wanted to be the hometown hero in Chicago, but that role was taken by Jordan almost as soon as he arrived there in 1984. Thomas wanted to be draped in red, white, and blue, representing his country and winning a gold medal, but that was a role that Jordan got to play early in 1984. Isiah had to be content with playing the role of the villain, the competitor that would rip your heart out. He became a fan of the Oakland Raiders, because of their commitment to winning and their rebellious nature.

And so, when Jordan made his initial NBA All-Star Game, Isiah Thomas apparently led his eastern teammates to "freeze-out" Jordan. This wasn't the polished Jordan, adept at being in center-stage for the world. It also wasn't the classiest move in Thomas' career. Close to two decades later, Thomas would play a part in Jordan's final All-Star Game, as well. Coaching the Eastern All-Stars, Thomas and Vince Carter convinced Jordan to start the game in Carter's spot, at the urging of nearly everyone.

Thomas and Jordan waged quite a rivalry in the years leading up to the 1992 Olympics as well. The Bulls and Pistons were and still are heated rivals. Scottie Pippen labeled Thomas "a cheap-shot artist," and implied that he wouldn't play on the Olympic team if Thomas were named to the squad. The Pistons met the Bulls in the playoffs four consecutive years (1988, 1989, 1990, and 1991), and Daly's Pistons eliminated Chicago three straight seasons before Chicago broke through and swept the Pistons in 1991. When the Bulls did eliminate the Pistons, dethroning the two-time defending champions, Isiah Thomas walked off the court before the final seconds had elapsed, in a display generally considered to be poor sportsmanship, refusing to acknowledge or congratulate the Bulls.

It's a little easier to understand why USA Basketball refused to hear Daly's plea for Thomas (and to a lesser degree, Dumars and Rodman). The U.S. needed Michael Jordan on the team, not to win a gold medal, but for the cache of having the greatest active player on the biggest world stage. Thomas, due in part to his competitive spirit, has never been a popular player. Jordan wasn't the only player who had a past with Isiah. Dream Teamer Karl Malone gave Thomas forty stitches over his left eye, after famously delivering a hard elbow in the lane in December of 1991.

MY OPINION

The U.S. could still have won the gold medal in 1992 with Thomas, Dumars, and Rodman replacing Jordan, Pippen, and Stockton. It's interesting that the coach of the Pistons, Chuck Daly, was the coach of the Olympic team but wasn't given any of his players. USA Basketball desperately wanted Michael Jordan to join forces with Magic and Bird for a once-in-a-lifetime Dream Team. I do believe accommodations for Jordan's preferences were made, but whether Thomas' exclusion was one of them is hard to say. It is one of those things that will never be able to be proven as fact.

At least we can be sure that it wasn't Daly who kept him off the team. Although there are a certain number of people who believe that Stockton was chosen over Isiah because of his skin color, I find that very, very hard to believe. The presence of Bird, Mullin, and Laettner is also good evidence against Stockton's inclusion solely because he was white.

Thomas sometimes had problems (in the words of preschoolers' report cards) playing well with others. It may not have been a conspiracy where a superstar forced the issue, but rather a meeting of minds concerning team chemistry. In either case, Thomas deserved a spot on the team, to my thinking, even more so than the great Michael Jordan.

CONCLUSION:

Michael Jordan's first retirement

Winston Churchill once said that "history is written by the victors." In basketball history, there was no bigger victor than Michael Jordan. The NBA released a bio of Jordan on the nba .com website that says, "By acclamation, Michael Jordan is the greatest basketball player of all time." The records and awards won by Jordan will be remembered for generations. Jordan retired for the first time in October of 1993 at the ripe age of 30, while at the apex of his brilliant NBA career. I think it's important to remember the time and circumstances surrounding Jordan's first "retirement," and what people were saying and writing about it at the time. There are many people who believe that Jordan was either serving a suspension, or was facing a situation where he felt he needed to "quit before he was fired." In either case, his retiring would have spared both Jordan and the NBA untold embarrassment. I don't necessarily believe or disbelieve Jordan's intentions at the time, but I do think it's important to look back.

Jordan completed his ninth season in the NBA in 1993, and although he missed all but eighteen games of the 1986 season with an injury, those first nine years were magnificent. He led the NBA in scoring seven consecutive seasons (1987–1993), was thrice named League MVP (1988, 1991, and 1992) and was named the Defensive Player of the Year in 1988. Most important, Jordan's Bulls won three straight championships (1991–1993), having won forty-five of fifty-eight playoff games (more than 77%) over the three post-seasons. Jordan was named MVP of the NBA Finals all three seasons. In the 1993 Finals, his last before his sudden retirement, Jordan scored fifty-five points in Game Four, and averaged a record forty-one points per game in the series. It was clear at the time of his retirement that he was going out at the top of his game.

Along with great players like Magic Johnson, Clyde Drexler, and Charles Barkley, Jordan's greatness on the court helped elevate the NBA to a level where the league began to attract non-sports fans. Jordan played a huge part in his team and his league gaining millions of new fans, and those fans meant millions of dollars in new revenue.

No basketball player in the prime of his career had ever voluntarily walked away like Michael Jordan did on October 6, 1993, days before training camp for the 1993–94 season started. Strange days, indeed.

Of the few athletes that had ever reached Jordan-like status in their sports, the few that had retired young were usually forced to due to health reasons, which was the case with the Dodgers' Sandy Koufax. The great running back Jim Brown retired after nine years with the Cleveland Browns, and that seems to be the closest parallel to Jordan. When Brown retired, he signed a multi-movie deal with Paramount Pictures. His first role was in *The Dirty Dozen*. (By the way, for those interested in astrology or numerology, Jordan and Brown share a birthday: February 17.)

There were a few all-time greats in individual sports that retired prematurely (Bobby Jones in golf and Bjorn Borg in tennis, for example) but even there, it was the rarity. As Isiah Thomas told me once, "Most great athletes leave on a stretcher." In other words, they leave when they can no longer compete physically.

Unlike Brown, who left the NFL for a blossoming movie career, or Jones, who retired from competitive golf in 1930 for a career in law, Jordan was evasive about his post-NBA career. He talked at his press conference about having achieved everything he could in basketball and "wanting to spend more time with his family."

The one aspect of Jordan's retirement that no one can judge is the grief he felt after his father was murdered. In July of 1993, James Jordan pulled over to sleep on the side of the road after midnight, headed just a few hundred miles to Charlotte, North Carolina. He was in the wrong place at the wrong time, the victim of two young men intent on robbing and shooting someone.

Additionally, Michael Jordan was physically and mentally overwhelmed when training camp approached in October of 1993. Jordan had put everything he had into the three previous championship seasons—meaning his seasons stretched until mid-June. And he had spent the entire summer of 1992 playing for the U.S. Olympic team at the Barcelona games.

When Jordan retired, NBA Deputy Commissioner Russ Granick told the press that Jordan had called the commissioner to tell him his intentions. Granick then said: "Whether it's permanent or not remains to be seen." That was an odd thing for Granick to say, unless he knew something that others did not.

The 1997 book *Money Players: Days and Nights Inside the New NBA* by Harvey Araton, Armen Keteyan, and Martin Dardis set up the situation.

> Did he, as he claimed, simply want a chance to move on with his life, get closer to his family, and take a swing at becoming a Major League baseball player? Was some clandestine deal cut between [Commissioner David] Stern and Jordan to allow the stench of Jordan's

gambling sprees to go away? Or did Jordan, knowing he would soon be suspended, if only for the sake of the league's saving face, decide to show Stern who was calling the shots and walk away on his own?

I'll remind you why there may have been questions about whether Stern would let Jordan back in the league: It concerned Jordan's ongoing gambling investigation. Remember, Jordan admitted writing a $57,000 check to a convicted cocaine dealer named Slim Bouler. Jordan at first said it was a loan to help Bouler build a driving range, but it eventually came to light that it was a repayment of a gambling debt. That would have been bad enough, but then a man named Richard Esquinas came forward with even more revealing info. Esquinas self-published a book claiming that he had won over $1 million in golf bets with Jordan. He claimed that the great basketball star didn't make good on all the money, either.

Jordan's response at the time was a statement that said, "Because I did not keep records, I cannot verify how much I won or lost. I can assure you the level of our wagers was substantially less than the preposterous amounts that have been reported." This news came to light during the 1993 Finals, which had to infuriate Jordan, when he and his fans wanted nothing more than to concentrate on his play on the court. *Money Players* also reminds us of Stern's words to *Sports Illustrated*, dismissing any possible deal between the league and Jordan. "The mere notion of that is scurrilous and disgusting," said Stern. (After looking up the definition of scurrilous, which means "grossly or obscenely abusive," one would wonder why a question about a deal would be out of line, especially considering the league's ongoing investigation.)

Three days after Jordan retired, however, the NBA announced the end of its investigation into Jordan's gambling, and found that he had violated no league rules. The league also admitted that its investigation did not even include an interview of Michael

Jordan. Although David Stern has been nothing but vigilant over a quarter-century to maintaining sacred trust in his sport, he did not tie up the loose ends of a player's gambling, at least publicly. I suppose an exit interview would have been, er, scurrilous? Remember, before Jordan's October 6 retirement, Stern had said publicly that the investigation would be concluded before the start of the season at the end of October. I'm not sure anything done or not done was improper, but the timing of the retirement and the ending of the investigation looked funny.

WHAT CONSPIRACY THEORISTS SAY ABOUT JORDAN'S "RETIREMENT"

In an online article posted in 2001 on disinfo.com (a website billed as "the gateway to the underground news, politics, and conspiracies"), Brian Tuohy wrote,

> Although some have speculated that his father's death had something to do with Jordan's gambling, I don't believe that to be the case. James Jordan wasn't a saint, truth be told. He was found guilty and sentenced to three years in prison (which were suspended) for being a cog in a larger embezzlement scheme in 1985, and at the time of his death, he was the subject of several lawsuits concerning the unpaid bills of his clothing company, JVL Enterprises, Inc. And even though there are some odd facts surrounding his murder (like the fact that a man like Michael Jordan's father decided to sleep in his car on the side of a rural highway rather than find a hotel or stay overnight at a friend's home), there is no real evidence to support a conspiracy.

At the announcement of his retirement, Jordan said, "Now that I'm here, it's time to be a little bit unselfish in terms of spending more time with my family, my wife, my kids, and just get back to a normal life, as close to it as I can." When asked what he intended to do now, Jordan replied, "In retirement, you do whatever comes to mind. Relax. Enjoy the time you've been deprived of for many years." In spite of those remarks, what "came to Michael's mind" in retirement was playing baseball. Not spending time with the wife and kids, unless of course they could travel on the bus with him and the rest of the Birmingham Barons from small town to smaller town across the bush leagues.

One of the reasons Jordan was even given an opportunity to play professional baseball was because Chicago Bulls' owner Jerry Reinsdorf also owned the Chicago White Sox. The Barons were an affiliate of the White Sox, so Jordan could easily cash checks from Reinsdorf for working in another part of the man's business empire. Reinsdorf stood to lose as much as anyone from Jordan's retirement, yet after Jordan's announcement, how did Reinsdorf respond? By paying Jordan $4 million and leaving a contractual window open for him to return to basketball—even though when Jordan was asked if he would ever return, he replied, "No—if so, I'd still be playing."

Jordan also made a very interesting comment during his retirement press conference. When asked, "Will you miss the sport?" he replied: "I'm pretty sure I'll miss the sport. To come back is a different thought—I can't answer that. I'm not making this a 'never' issue. I'm saying right now I don't have the mental drive to come out and push myself to play with a certain focus. Five years down the line, if the urge comes back, if the Bulls will have me, if David Stern lets me back in the league, I may come back." No reporter there bothered to ask him, Why wouldn't the commissioner let you back in? It's a very interesting choice of words, and one that lends itself to a certain interpretation of the situation.

MY OPINION

I tend to believe Jordan, especially after reading his former coach Phil Jackson's 1995 book *Sacred Hoops*, in which he wrote,

Michael always said that when basketball stopped being fun, he was going to walk away. . . . He'd been dropping hints all season that he might retire early, and that summer when I heard the news on the radio that his father had been murdered, my first thought was that he wouldn't be coming back for another season. . . . Michael had thought it through from every angle. I tried to appeal to his spiritual side. I told him that God had given him a talent that made people happy, and I didn't think it was right for him to walk away. He talked about impermanence. "For some reason," he said, "God is telling me to move on, and I must move on. People have to learn that nothing lasts forever."

According to Jackson, Jordan then asked him if there was a way he could only play in the playoffs. "Until we can come up with a solution for that one," he told Jackson, "I must retire."

I also think about what Bob Greene wrote in his 1995 book, *Rebound: The Odyssey of Michael Jordan*: "More than anything, it has been the story of a man who had all that a person could ever want—or so it seemed—and then, having lost something that was so important to him that his pain was unfathomable, had to decide what to do. In plain sight, Jordan faltered, and then, in his mourning, abandoned one of the parts of his life that he cherished the most while the world wondered what he might be doing."

Jordan went into baseball's Minor Leagues and didn't perform very well. He didn't pick the best time to begin a baseball career, either. After playing the 1994 season for Birmingham, Jordan left the White Sox organization feeling betrayed and used, thinking the organization wanted him to serve as a "replacement player" during the baseball owners' lockout. Baseball's loss was basketball's game, though, and in March of 1995 Jordan considered coming back to the NBA. In the ten days of rumors prior to his comeback announcement, there was something like a $2 billion increase in the stock prices of the five companies that he endorsed.

Jordan spoke with Commissioner Stern about his return. "I had to see if he wanted me back in the league," Jordan said. Again, Jordan used odd terminology that begged follow-up questions. Finally, after seventeen months and 157 regular and postseason Bulls game, Jordan returned. And there was nothing written or said publicly about the dropped investigation into Jordan's gambling during 1993.

All athletes die two deaths. One at the end of their playing days, and one at the end of their life. Jordan has already died three times, resurrecting himself twice on the basketball court. All three times, he left on his terms. He did it his way.

CONCLUSION:

Alan Eagleson colludes with NHL owners to keep hockey salaries down

As I mentioned in chapter two, Major League Baseball encountered a situation in the late 1980s where the team owners conspired to keep players' salaries down. In that same time period, the head of the National Hockey League Players Association was conspiring with League owners to serve the same purpose.

Alan "The Eagle" Eagleson was the most powerful man in hockey for so many years that it defies logic. He was one of the first player-agents. He was also the first Executive Director of the NHL Player's Association. He wore so many hats, it seemed the only one he didn't wear in the 1970s was that of the Prime Minister of Canada.

The question isn't how this man conspired with NHL owners to keep salaries down and limit player salaries and pension benefits. The question is how it took until 1989 for the players to revolt and until 1991 for the FBI and grand jury to begin their investigations which ultimately sent him to prison. And why did the team owners that conspired with Eagleson go unpunished?

"The Eagle" might have turned into a great criminal lawyer (he became a lawyer in 1959), but he got sidetracked while playing amateur lacrosse with his childhood friend Bob Pulford, a future star with the Toronto Maple Leafs. Pulford became a four-time Stanley Cup champion with the Maple Leafs in the 1960s, and it was Pulford who introduced Eagleson to his Toronto teammates. Eagleson would socialize with the players, provide legal services for them, recommended investments, and advise them on financial and legal matters.

He became especially close with Toronto defenseman Carl Brewer, which helped earn him some leverage with Toronto ownership. Maple Leafs owner Punch Imlach resisted negotiating with Eagleson, or any lawyer, for that matter. Brewer, a four-time All-Star, retired at the start of the 1965–66 season and enrolled at the University of Toronto. Eagleson helped Brewer regain his amateur status so he could continue to play for Canada's National Team. (Brewer, after a year playing in Europe, would eventually return to the NHL).

At the players' request, Eagleson formed the National Hockey League Players Association (NHLPA) in 1967. "The Eagle" became a hero to the players after he took on Eddie Shore in 1966. Shore, a former great player, was the owner of the Springfield Indians from the American Hockey League. Shore treated his players like slaves, refusing to let them get X-rays or proper medical clearance. Several of the Indians called on Eagleson, who had established a reputation with Pulford and Brewer, and by negotiating the young Bobby Orr's first NHL contract.

When Eagleson headed up the first NHLPA, anything he accomplished would have been considered a great improvement. The players had attempted to unionize ten years earlier and had failed miserably, but Eagleson had the support of the best players in the league, including Orr and Pulford.

According to William Houston and David Shoalts' 1993 book *Eagleson: The Fall of a Hockey Czar,*

> The attitude of the owners toward Eagleson and the proposed union seemed almost ambivalent. They did not want a union and would have jumped at the chance to crush it. But with Eagleson, they felt they could do business. He wasn't a labor lawyer, had no experience in labor negotiations, and showed no signs of militancy. Better him, the owners felt, than Marvin Miller, the head of the baseball union and a man with sixteen years' experience with the United Steelworkers of America. Or Jimmy Hoffa and the Teamsters, who in 1966 had announced plans to unionize all of professional sports.

Bobby Orr was a teen legend in Minor League hockey in the mid-1960s. He was coveted by NHL teams, and became the property of the Boston Bruins before he turned eighteen. Eagleson became Orr's agent and negotiated a monumental deal for the era, basically a two-year contract worth $80,000. That may not seem like much by today's standards, but it was more than the established superstars were making at the time. Orr became the lure that reeled in everyone else, as he went on to became one of the greatest players in hockey history. From 1968 to 1975, Orr captured eight consecutive Norris Trophies (awarded to the league's top defenseman) and twice led the NHL in scoring, to this day the only defenseman in league history to accomplish this feat. Players flocked to Eagleson for representation, and by the early 1970s his firm represented more than 150 NHL players. I spoke with Helene Elliott, a columnist with the *Los Angeles Times* and the first female reporter elected into the Pro Hockey Hall of Fame, about Eagleson.

Helene Elliott: He would organize the 1972 Summit Series or the 1976 Canada Cup, and that's great. But then he would set himself up with an incredible salary, and [set up] his family with jobs that paid incredible salaries as well. And in the meanwhile, great hockey stars would get cheated and ripped off on basic pension funds. He and his law firm represented close to half the league. People who did question him didn't get insurance benefits and pension benefits and got screwed later on. He was very powerful in his day.

Alan Eagleson was powerful because he was tight with NHL owners, especially Bill Wirtz of the Chicago Blackhawks. For a few years in the early 1970s, the player's salaries increased, thanks to leverage from the WHA, no thanks to Eagleson.

Superstar Bobby Orr had a great season in 1975, at the age of twenty-six. The Boston Bruins made him an offer that included five years (at close to $300,000 per year) and either a $925,000 payment, or 18.5% ownership in the team. Eagleson turned down the offers, without informing his client.

Eagleson denied that he hadn't kept Orr informed of his negotiations with the Bruins, and said that Boston's offer was conditional on Orr's passing a medical examination. Eagleson would later explain that Blackhawks owner Wirtz made a quality offer of $500,000 per year for Orr. Wirtz was accused of tampering with Orr when he was still under a Boston contract, and by 1979 Orr was essentially broke, and at odds with Eagleson.

Helene Elliott: How did Bobby Orr not wind up with a piece of the Bruins? I don't want to say tragedy, it's too strong a word . . . but it's one of the saddest things in sports that Orr didn't end up with the Bruins—as a general manager, or club executive even. And why didn't he? Because his agent—whom he implicitly trusted—was in bed with the Wirtz, and delivered him to the Blackhawks.

In retrospect, it seems odd that Boston would make an offer to Eagleson that included an 18.5% stake in the team and that Orr would feel that the Bruins weren't interested in keeping him. Eagleson had plenty of motive to deliver his player to the Blackhawks (where his longtime friend Pulford was by then the head coach). Wirtz felt that Boston had taken advantage of the Chicago franchise years earlier, when Phil Esposito was traded to the Bruins.

In 1957, the average annual salary in Major League Baseball was $20,000, while in hockey, it was only $8,000, 40% of the baseball figure. By 1979, with the WHA–NHL war still going on, the average hockey salary had increased $101,000, roughly on par with baseball's $113,558. By 1979, Hockey salaries were 89% of baseball's, but by 1989, three years after Eaglesons' collective bargaining sessions, the average baseball salary had shot up to $497,254, while hockey salaries, with the WHA having long been disbanded, had regressed to 38% of baseball's at $188,000.

Ed Garvey, a former executive director of the NFL Players Association, was retained by the growing number of disgruntled NHL players to investigate the NHLPA. In 1989, Garvey summarized his findings, saying, "The conflicts of interest are shocking, but even more shocking is a pattern of sweetheart agreements with the NHL over all these years." Garvey called the NHL's collective bargaining a charade.

Garvey's findings in 1989—and Sports Illustrated's *1989 article on Eagleson—pushed whistleblowers to stop Eagleson.*

Helene Elliott: Who blew the whistle eventually? Carl Brewer, of course, who knew Eagleson as a friend and agent all those years, and also a Boston-area writer named Russ Conway, who did some incredible investigative work [were primarily responsible]. It was more of a natural progression with men like Conway and Orr becoming more assertive and telling people that this is just not right. Carl Brewer did an incredible job for the players, although most of today's players don't even recognize who he was and what he did.

Eagleson billed hundreds of thousands of dollars in sometimes questionable expenses to the players' union, and union funds were put into high-risk real estate investments involving Eagleson, his friends, and his associates. He claimed that money from international tournaments went into the pension fund for players. But it didn't. The money just helped to reduce what the NHL and teams were supposed to pay into the pension fund. Eagleson made loads of money selling advertising on rink boards at those international tournaments. He also allegedly worked to keep disability payouts low, and in return, demanded kickbacks from the insurance companies.

In 1992, a Canadian judge ruled that more than 1,300 former NHL players were owed more than $20 million in pension money. Due to mounting interest during the appeals process, the judgment swelled to $41 million after the Canadian Supreme Court upheld the ruling in 1995.

Former NHL players Dave Forbes, Rick Middleton, Brad Park, Ulf Nilsson, and Doug Smail filed a class-action lawsuit against the NHL and most of its individual teams in 1995 on behalf of about 1,000 NHL players who were employed during Eagleson's tenure. They were hoping to sue for hundreds of millions of dollars, and they should have received it—or close to it. Instead, the U.S. District Court in Philadelphia dismissed the players' lawsuit in August of 1998, saying that the retirees should have known by at least 1991 about the allegations against Eagleson (which they certainly should have), and that the four-year statute of limitations in civil racketeering cases had run out by their 1995 filing date.

Here's the reason those owners and team executives did not go directly to jail: Bill Wirtz and former NHL Commissioner John

Ziegler cut a deal with the government to turn on Eagleson (and eventually, they testified against him). Ziegler and Wirtz were co-defendants in the civil racketeering and conspiracy lawsuit filed in 1995 by a group of former players. That suit could have buried the entire National Hockey League.

The defense argued that the players should have known about Eagleson's abuses long before the suit was filed. They argued that the statue of limitations had expired. Eagleson tried to argue that the U.S. court had no jurisdiction over him. He tried to argue that player reps all backed him, pretty much unanimously.

Finally, in 1998, Eagleson pled guilty (to fraud and theft) in both the United States and Canada, and was sentenced to an eighteen-month prison term in Canada. He was paroled after six months.

The scope of the abuses that went on is unbelievable. The president of the player's union in the mid-1970s, Flyers great Bobby Clarke, was never elected—he was appointed by Eagleson. Clarke had a personal services contract with his owner, guaranteeing him an income long after his playing days were over. Is it any wonder that the owners loved Eagleson? Hockey gave Eagleson control of the players' disability insurance and the international hockey tournaments. In return, the NHL had labor peace and salaries were kept artificially low.

Eagleson wasn't the only head of a player's union that also represented individual players. (For example, in the late 1980s, Charles Grantham was not only the head of the NBA players union, he also represented players like Michael Ray Richardson.) But Eagleson *was* the only one that conspired to betray the players' interests in collective bargaining. Eagleson was the one who agreed to a merger (the 1979 merger of the NHL and WHA) which caused salaries to plummet, without attempting to gain concessions. Eagleson was the one that gave in on inadequate minimum salaries, free agency, the removal of player representation from the board of the players' pension funds, and the owners' practice of offsetting pension contributions by the amount the players contributed with international hockey.

Eagleson repressed salaries for a tremendously long time, but he didn't do it alone. He needed co-conspirators in the form of the owners. The National Hockey League players are still paying for the crimes that Eagleson and those co-conspirators committed.

CONCLUSION:

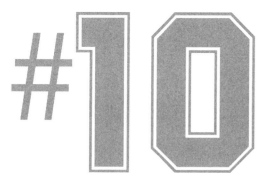

Gamblers attempt to fix the 1946 NFL Championship Game

- - - - - - - -

Even the biggest NFL fans seem surprised to learn that one of the NFL Championship Games was the subject of a conspiracy. This tale of point-shaving and game-fixing is one of my favorite conspiracies in the book—precisely because it's largely forgotten about (or swept under the rug).

I can't believe that a movie or stage show hasn't yet been made of the gamblers' attempt to fix the 1946 NFL Championship Game between the New York Giants and the Chicago Bears. This true story has more colorful characters than *Guys and Dolls*, and situations right out of *Goodfellas*. This story has great potential scenes. (How about a scene where Giants head coach Steve Owen, on the eve of the Championship Game, tries to enter the interrogation room where the police were attempting to beat a confession out of the suspected front-man for the gamblers and his starting quarterback and fullback? How about a beautiful B-list actress—dubbed a "tomato" by the tabloids of the time—telling the press of her dates with the married football stars? How about the pre-game prayer in the Giants' clubhouse, where the team chaplain reminded the players that the game had sunk into the shadows of doubt? "It's up to you to restore the fans' faith in pro football," he reportedly said.)

The 1946 NFL Championship Game marks one of the great sports conspiracies of all time, and despite the fact that authorities caught wind of the matter just days prior to the big game, it is my opinion that the game might still have been fixed. After all, one of the players who was approached, quarterback Frankie Filchock, played in the game and threw six interceptions. At the very least, the game was played under conditions where the sold-out stadium didn't know if the home-team players had "sold out" their honest effort for money.

Before addressing the particulars of the players and gamblers who conspired to fix this game, I have to set the scene. World War II had just ended, and the NFL was evolving. The league faced competition from a new rival, the All-America Football Conference. The NFL, forced to reduce roster size because of the war to twenty-eight players per team, had increased the rosters to thirty-three for the 1946 season. The threat of the AAFC forced the NFL to make some real changes. The 1945 NFL champion Cleveland Rams moved to Los Angeles to secure the west coast for the league. In doing so, they were able to use the Los Angeles Coliseum only by integrating and signing two former UCLA football stars (Kenny Washington and Woody Strode).

The New York Giants finished just 3–6–1 in 1945, but in the off-season, the Giants signed Filchock, a backup to Sammy Baugh at Washington, for a reported $35,000. With the new competing league, pro football players had a little leverage for the first time.

Also, before that 1946 season began, the NFL named Bert Bell as the new commissioner. According to Jeff Davis' 2004 book, *Papa Bear*:

Some owners thought Bell was a clown, a football version of baseball's Casey Stengel before he donned Yankee pinstripes. George Halas knew Bell as the man who dreamed up the draft and as smart, honorable, and an able negotiator. With [Steelers owner Art] Rooney's endorsement and [Redskins owner George] Marshall's help, Halas and his supporters stood fast for Bell and persuaded everyone to step in line. It was a move the National Football League never regretted.

Davis' book also points out that right after the war there was another significant invention that changed pro football. "Nobody can say with any authority who devised the point spread system," Davis wrote. "But it goes back at least to World War II. Any big-time bettor and a lot of small-timers agree with the anonymous gambler who told Nevada operator Peter Ruchman, 'The invention of the point spread is the single greatest creation since the zipper.'"

Now that we understand the times in which this story unfolded, it's time to introduce the main characters. First, there was Alvin J. Paris, a small, dapper twenty-eight-year-old man known around New York at the time as a playboy who escorted beautiful women around (think Leonardo DiCaprio, if we're casting the movie). He worked in his father's novelty store, but he made his real money fronting three bookmakers. The bookmakers had their offices in New Jersey, and used Paris for giving and taking tips and introductions in New York. It was in November of 1946 that Giants backup fullback Merle Hapes (Seth Rogin could play him) met a man named Sidney Paris. Paris invited Hapes to a cocktail party on November 30 at his son Alvin's apartment in midtown. It would be reported in January of 1947, following the sworn testimony in court, that there were more than fifteen people at this cocktail party, including Ida McGuire, the movie starlet.

Hapes, the Giants' backup fullback, didn't know that the elder Paris was a convicted felon who had served four years in prison for mail fraud. On November 30, the night before a big Giants–Rams game at the Polo Grounds, Hapes found himself at Alvin Paris' apartment. He also found, for lack of a better word, bait. He found beautiful women. And he did what many men would do in a similar situation. Being a team player, Hapes asked Paris if it would be alright to call his good friend, Giants quarterback Frank Filchock, and tell him to come over. Paris probably didn't take too long to decide that it would be just fine. The players made dates with two of the women for the following Wednesday. It was a classic seduction. At one point in the evening, Paris asked Hapes how he thought his team would do the next day against the Rams. Hapes said he didn't think the Giants should be seven-point favorites. Paris called his gambling connection Harvey Stemmer, and Stemmer suggested (according to Paris' later testimony) that he needed to pass the information along to Jerome Zarowitz. Paris would testify that Zarowitz was employed at an Elizabeth, New Jersey, office operated by his stepfather Eddie Ginsberg, and there was subsequently a $200 bet placed on the Rams. Yes, the figure seems a little low—a lot lower than anyone would think—but rest assured, there is no extra zero missing. The $200 bet was what was reported. Perhaps it was just a test by the gamblers.

Convicted of bribing Brooklyn College basketball players to throw games in 1945, Harvey Stemmer was in Rikers Island at the time (though continuing his bookmaking operation).

After the December 1st game, Hapes and his wife took two other Giants teammates (tackle Vic Carroll and back Howie Livingston) and their wives to his new friend's apartment. It was there that Paris dangled the prospect of getting jobs in the novelty business. Apparently, there was room in this company for both players; each would oversee sales in different parts of the country for about $15,000 per year. Paris took the couples to the Copacabana night club. As the United Press would report months later, "Girls, restaurants, and Cabarets were among the enticements used . . ." It was on Tuesday that Paris sought information from Filchock and Hapes about the Giants' upcoming game against the second-place Redskins. The players told the gambler that the team was determined to beat Washington and play the Bears for the title. There were no postseason games then, except for the Championship Game. The winner in the Western Division played the winner of the Eastern Division in the NFL Championship Game. The standings for the Eastern Division entering into the final weekend's games on December 8 were:

1. New York Giants, 6–3–1
2. Washington, 5–4–1
3. Philadelphia, 5–5

Therefore, a Giants victory over Washington would put them in the Championship Game on December 15 against the Bears. And the Giants had already earned a victory over the Chicago Bears in late October, shutting out the Bears 14–0 in New York.

The players were falling hook, line, and sinker. They allowed themselves and their families to be wined and dined at the Copa. They fell for Paris' lure of an off-season job. And they fell for the women provided. According to Leonard Shector's 1969 *The Jocks*, one of Paris' best-looking ladies was the aforementioned Ida McGuire. "Also," Shector wrote, "a perfumed dream named in trial records only as Emmy Lou, and then somebody called Betty Bigelow or Betty Bartholomew, or both. They were *all* together a lot." Somehow, it didn't take Alvin Paris long to become good friends with the two star gridders, as the newspapers called them.

On Wednesday, December 4, Stemmer asked Paris if Hapes and Filchock could be talked into throwing the Redskins game. Paris didn't think so, so the gamblers bet $2,500 on the Giants, which included a $500 bet for each of the two players.

On December 8, the Giants routed the Redskins 31–0 before 60,000 fans in New York. After the game, Hapes, his wife, and brother went to dinner with Paris. Later, Hapes and Paris went out partying, and it was then that Paris made his move to fix the Championship Game.

That Sunday night, Paris was to testify later, he gave each of the players $500 apiece for having won the bet on the Giants against Washington, setting up the title clash with the Bears. In the trial record, when asked if he had had any conversation with the defendant [Paris] about football, Hapes testified: "Yes, he asked me if the Bears would win by ten points. I said, 'What do you mean?' Alvin said, 'I want you to throw the game.' I said, 'What do you mean?'"

Hapes went on to testify that, when he finally found out what Alvin meant, he told him, "No soap." Also on the witness stand, Hapes said, "He told me there would be money in it for him if the Bears won by ten points. I told him to speak to Frank Filchock himself. I told him I could only fumble the ball, and that was a no go. I told him Frankie Filchock would be the man if anything like that could be done. I told him he should speak to Filchock himself, and he went to the phone." Fitchock also said "No soap," and swore, "Hot damn, Alvin, I just ain't going to do it. The boys have too much confidence in me, and they got much more at stake than any dough I can make."

When the two were asked why they didn't report the bribe, the players said that they still hoped to get the off-season job. Filchock turned down the offer when it was presented to him on Tuesday by Paris. It was then that Paris introduced him to a car dealer that might have been able to land him the car that he was interested in buying. Later in the week, Paris had to advise his associates to hedge their bets, as the quarterback still wouldn't go along with letting the Bears win by at least ten points. When the syndicate hedged their bets, and started making sizable wagers the other direction, the resultant change in the betting odds attracted the attention of detectives.

Coach Steve Owen took his Giants up to Bear Mountain, New York (about two hours away), on Thursday, for three days prior to the Championship Game, which would be played at the Polo Grounds in New York. Paris drove Hapes' wife and daughter, end Jim Poole's wife and daughter, and Mrs. Poole's sister up to Bear Mountain for the afternoon to watch practice. While there, Paris was introduced to some more of the Giants players. Paris spoke with Hapes by phone on Saturday, telling him that he was going to get some money down on the Giants, and to play well. Paris reminded Hapes of their plans to get together for dinner after the Bears game—Paris, the two players and their wives (Filchock's wife was up from their Washington home).

The police lucked into finding out about the bribery attempts just in time. As it turned out, Eddie Ginsburg's phone was tapped by the District Attorney in an investigation into other bribery matters. The D.A. found out about Paris' connection to the Giants almost by accident.

On Saturday night, New York Mayor William O'Dwyer summoned Hapes and Filchock to Gracie Mansion and confronted them with evidence, gathered by police, of the fix attempt. Hapes admitted to being offered a bribe. Filchock admitted nothing of the sort. The quarterback was questioned well past midnight. Hapes wasn't sent home until 6:30 in the morning, and then told he might be needed further. The Mayor had called Giants owner

Tim Mara as well. Mara, with his sons Wellington and Jack and coach Steve Owen, showed up to see their starting backfield being grilled by cops hours before the biggest game of their lives. Commissioner Bell consulted with the authorities, and made his ruling: Hapes would not play in the title game, "Although it doesn't mean in any way that Hapes is guilty of anything more than a failure to report the bribery charges." Filchock was, according to Bell, "absolutely in the clear, and was only approached by innuendo."

The conspiracy in this case is not the fixing of the Championship Game, it's the conspiracy by the two players and their families to keep quiet about the bribery, and the nature of their sudden friendship with the shady Paris.

The story was big news around the country on Sunday morning. Was this game a legit contest, and should the commissioner give either player the benefit of the doubt?

The Bears won the NFL Championship 24–14.

Because the Bears' margin of victory was only ten points, and the point spread went off at ten, the game was a push (neither side winning their bet) for gamblers who bet on the game. In the months to follow, Commissioner Bell suspended both Hapes and Filchock indefinitely for failing to report the bribe. Paris received a reduced one-year sentence for turning state's evidence.

EVIDENCE AGAINST A CONSPIRACY

According to the Chronology of Professional Football section in the league's annual *Record and Fact Book*, "Backs Frank Filchock and Merle Hapes of the Giants were questioned about an attempt by a New York man to fix the Championship Game with the Bears. Bell suspended Hapes but allowed Filchock to play; he played well, but Chicago won 24–14 on December 15."

The commissioner found out at the trial of Alvin Paris that Filchock had lied about receiving an offer to fix the Championship

Game. At least he hadn't accepted it. Hapes and Filchock eventually wound up playing professionally in Canada. Filchock returned to the United States to play for the Baltimore Colts in 1950, and actually became the first head coach in the history of the Denver Broncos franchise.

EVIDENCE TO SUPPORT A CONSPIRACY

This game was fixed, pure and simple. Just because the District Attorney had tapped into phone calls made by Paris to Ginsburg doesn't mean they tapped into all his phone calls. He easily could have made phone calls from delicatessens and bars and friends' homes. The police stumbled onto Paris, who was a small-time guy. Could Paris—or others—have gotten to other members of the Giants or Bears? Could threats have been made—subtle or otherwise—regarding the health of Filchock or a member of his family if the game didn't go a certain way? The Giants' quarterback had assured the gamblers that "the fix is no-go," and that the gamblers were able to hedge their bets and make even bigger ones on the Giants to win (or lose by less than double-digits). If that were the case, Filchock had to deny any involvement In a fix attempt to all the authorities, and do everything he could to play in the game and keep the Bears from covering the spread.

Papa Bear describes the game thus: "With blood pouring from his Sprinkle-administered broken nose, a vindication-seeking Filchock played the game of his life. He threw two touchdown passes to send the game into the fourth quarter tied 14–14 . . ." Bears quarterback Sid Luckman called the title game "the most vicious football game I'd ever played in my entire life."

I have to put some perspective into Filchock's performance, described as "the game of his life," in *Papa Bear* and described as "playing well" in the NFL *Record and Fact Book*. If one views the quarterback's performance with 1946 eyes, one sees a very different effort than with 2007 vision and sensibilities.

Carl Lundquist wrote on December 15, 1946, for UPI, "Frank Filchock did everything a football player can do to win a game, but it wasn't enough." Filchock completed 9–26 passes for 128 yards, two touchdowns, and six interceptions (one returned for a touchdown). He would never be forgiven if he posted those numbers in a modern day playoff game (look at the criticism that Bears quarterback Rex Grossman received in Super Bowl XLI for throwing just *two* interceptions). But it was a different game back then, and even fans in their late sixties need to be refreshed about some of the changes. First off, quarterbacks threw interceptions at that time, and it wasn't looked upon with the disdain that it is today. All the great quarterbacks threw as many picks as they did touchdowns. In 1946, Filchock threw twenty-five interceptions in the eleven-game season. In 1947, legendary Bears quarterback Sid Luckman threw thirty-one. Hall of Famer Sammy Baugh threw 187 touchdowns and 203 interceptions in his career (including 8 TD/17 INT in that 1946 season for the Redskins).

Here are some incredible facts about this game: The score was 14–14 going into the fourth quarter, despite the Giants being depleted. Hapes, normally the backup fullback, was ruled out while cops investigated the attempted fix. The number one fullback, Bill Paschal, was out with a broken jaw. Halfback Frank Reagan was rushed to the hospital at halftime with a fractured nose. Another halfback, George Franck, also got sent to the hospital with a banged-up shoulder. And Frank Filchock played the final three quarters with a broken nose. The bottom line on Filchock's performance was that he kept a severely depleted team in the game until the fourth quarter.

In researching this story, the one thing that still puzzles me is the point spread being set at ten points. I found a UPI story advancing the game that was published on Saturday, December 14, 1946, and that article mentioned that the Bears were ten-point favorites. Testimony in March of 1947 would prove that Paris knew the Bears would have to win by more than ten points as soon as the game on December 8 was over! Does anyone else find it peculiar that the Giants—playing at home and playing a team it had beaten soundly early in the season—would be ten-point underdogs?

All I can say is that I have to use my 1946 eyes again. The Bears had a mystique about them. After all, they were the "Monsters of the Midway," and this victory marked their fifth NFL Championship. In discussing the Bears being favored by double-digits on the road in the 1946 Championship Game with historian and author Jeff Davis, we agree that the spread was due to the mystique of the Bears. Clearly, the betting public overwhelmingly sided with Chicago.

MY OPINION

How much did the league know at the time they made the decision to bar Hapes from the game and let Filchock play? Did they know about the $500 that the players took from Paris? This had to be a tough call for the new commissioner. Do you go on with the Championship Game as scheduled, despite the known attempt to fix the game? Do you allow the quarterback, who was denying everything, to play in the game? The game went on as scheduled, and even if the game hadn't been taken off the boards by the bookies, the final score was a push against the point spread. How convenient.

I believe the game was tarnished. The players didn't even have lawyers with them when the decision was made. The quarterback made a decision to perjure himself and deny being offered a bribe. Why? What was going through Filchock's mind? At some point, he might have thought that his teammate, the backup fullback, had confessed to being offered money to fix the game. Wouldn't the authorities assume that he was offered the same deal or better? Wouldn't he assume that Paris might sing like a bird for police at some point? What was the quarterback doing not confessing the night before the game? Did he have a reason, or co-conspirators, that made it imperative for him to play in the Championship Game?

We'll never know.

CONCLUSION:

Was there a secret agreement between Pete Rose and Bart Giamatti?

As the all-time leader in hits, games, and at bats, Pete Rose is without a doubt one of the greatest Major League Baseball players in history. He once hit in a National League record forty-four straight games. He had five hits in a game no less than ten times, and finished his career with 4,256 hits, breaking Ty Cobb's record of 4,192.

Rose was also at one point the highest paid player in the game, and often the most popular. A fierce competitor, his nickname was "Charlie Hustle," in part because he would *run* to first base after receiving a *walk*. No one, it seemed, respected or loved the game as much as he did. He once famously barreled over a catcher, Ray Fosse, to score the winning run in the 1970 *All-Star* Game, effectively ending Fosse's career as an elite catcher.

The late, great sportswriter Jim Murray wrote, "Rose seemed the eternal fourteen-year-old, cap on backward, socks flopping about his ankles, knickers with a hole in them from sliding. . . . He was born to play baseball. He never wanted to do anything else. He never could do anything else."

Rose had great baseball intelligence, and was able to remember dates and records and stats, as well as detailed information on thousands of his at-bats. But he was not book-smart. Instead of reading books, he read box scores and horseracing forms. He loved to gamble, and bet on everything, including the sport he knew most about, baseball.

If Rose was the blue-collar dream of baseball lovers everywhere, then Commissioner Bart Giamatti was the white-collar counterpoint. Giamatti was a scholar and an academic, in addition to being a steward of baseball, a game he cared passionately about. Unlike Rose, Giamatti was one of the most intelligent, book-smart men of his generation. The one-time president of Yale University, he was one of the world's foremost authorities on Renaissance poetry. What Rose and Giamatti shared was the sense that baseball was their religion. Giamatti equated baseball with high mass. In Rose's 2004 autobiography, *My Life Without Bars*, he wrote that his daughter Fawn used to refer to baseball as her father's religion, and he confessed that he "worshipped" baseball.

Giamatti suffered a massive heart attack in 1989, at the age of fifty-eight, just days after ending his summer-long battle with Rose, which resulted in the banishment of the sport's career leader in hits, due to gambling. Still out of the game nearly twenty years later, some have suggested that Giamatti took a secret to his grave. Was there an unwritten agreement with Rose that made clear his re-entry into baseball? Is there any credence to this theory?

A secret agreement between these two men would explain much of Rose's behavior over the years, certainly his refusal for more than fifteen years to admit betting on baseball games.

Giamatti's deputy, Fay Vincent, succeeded his friend as commissioner, and was intimately involved in the gambling investigation in the spring and summer of 1989. It was Vincent who brought in Washington lawyer John Dowd, a man who had experience as head of a Justice Department strike force conducting Mafia investigations. Dowd was relentless in his pursuit of Rose's gambling activities; some detractors say he was overly zealous, and trying to make a name for himself.

Dowd's report would contain enough evidence to permanently ban Rose, and it was Vincent who was the go-between between Dowd and Giamatti. That's why Vincent, as we shall see, was so vehemently against Rose being reinstated. That's also why some people believe there was a secret agreement between Giamatti and Rose that bypassed Vincent.

There were three books that gave me the clues to piece together what happened: Pete Rose and Roger Kahn's *Pete Rose: My Story* (1989), Fay Vincent's *The Last Commissioner* (1992), and Rose's 2004 confession, *Pete Rose: My Prison without Bars*.

Toward the end of Peter Ueberroth's commissionership, Paul Janszen, a convicted felon awaiting sentencing, approached *Sports Illustrated* in February of 1989 with a damning story about Rose, then the manager of the Cincinnati Reds. The magazine went to Major League Baseball's top brass, and Ueberroth, Giamatti, and Vincent met with Rose to discuss the allegations.

It quickly became apparent, after initial small talk, that the meeting was going to be serious. Vincent asked Rose the question that everyone assembled wanted to hear the answer to. The Reds manager made a decision to adopt a strategy that he rarely veered from: deny, deny, deny. "No, sir, I did not bet on baseball," said Rose. He did this without knowing how much Ueberroth knew about what really had transpired. The baseball executives accepted Rose's answer, but laid it on the line. If they found out after an investigation that Rose had been untruthful, they told him the consequences would be extremely serious. Since Janszen was a convicted felon who was desperate for money, extortion of the famous Rose was not totally out of the question.

The *New York Times* caught wind of the story and reported it a day or two later, infuriating Rose. But what was he really upset about? Ueberroth was quoted by the *Times'* Murray Chass as saying, "We asked Rose to do it. We didn't order him. There's nothing ominous and there won't be any follow through."

Of course, Ueberroth could afford to say that, to appease Rose and his fans. He was leaving his office on April 1st of that year. The April Fools joke he gave to Giamatti was to investigate the most popular and beloved figure in baseball. Giamatti was clearly torn: disappointed that a baseball hero was so flawed, and yet excited about the prospect of uncovering the truth.

Vincent brought in John Dowd. In Vincent's words, "Dowd was a pro, a former Marine with a towering physical presence. He had the charm of the Irish and the hard-edged tenacity of a big-time prosecutor. He knew what he was doing and thus had a calming effect on Bart (Giamatti), on all of us."

The baseball offices had more than Dowd to help calm the investigation. A lot of people (including Rose) thought the influential *New York Times* was serving as the mouthpiece for Giamatti's office. Remember, this was 1989. There was no Internet and there were far fewer media outlets. Not only was the *New York Times* extremely influential, it was especially influential to Giamatti. According to Vincent, his trusted deputy, the commissioner would complain to the Sports Editor of the *New York Times* if he thought that Rose was being portrayed too sympathetically. It appeared that the new commissioner cared very much about his own popularity, and how he was being portrayed.

Meanwhile, a bookmaker named Ron Peters agreed to plead guilty to one count of drug trafficking and one count of filing false tax information. It was at this point that the meticulous Dowd made a costly mistake. Peters' lawyer asked Dowd to draft a letter from the commissioner to the sentencing federal judge on

Peters' behalf, saying that Major League Baseball had found Peters to be "candid, forthright, and truthful" in his testimony regarding Rose. In retrospect, it seems a little odd that Dowd drafted the letter, and send it to Bart Giamatti to sign. It seemed—especially to the Rose camp—that Dowd cut a deal. The deal apparently specified that if Peters cooperated with Dowd, Dowd would have Giamatti write a letter to the judge who would be sentencing Peters for felony charges of drug dealing and tax evasion. Did Dowd really think that Peters had nothing to gain from spreading dirt about Rose? If Giamatti was duped—or naive—it went to the grave with him.

Legendary sportswriter Jim Murray wrote in the *Los Angeles Times* about that.

> You had the undignified spectacle of Giamatti bursting his moorings in a way when he penned a letter to a judge who was sentencing a Pete Rose associate for cocaine trafficking. Giamatti was the last man in the world you'd expect to find in bed with a character of this low appeal, but there he was appealing to the judge for leniency on the grounds the dope dealer (and admitted addict) "had given significant and truthful cooperation" to Baseball in its investigation of Pete Rose.

Rose and his attorneys had found a defense, and it was handed to them! They argued that the commissioner had already concluded, as evidenced by his letter to the judge, that Rose had gambled on baseball. How else would they know that Peters had been truthful and all those other wonderful things they said about him?

This defense was so effective that a temporary restraining order against Baseball briefly shut down the investigation. Giamatti was having a very stressful summer, in what turned out to be the final weeks of his life. His reputation was on the line, as well as Rose's.

Eventually, baseball officials were able to move the injunction case before a federal judge in Columbus. Once that happened, Rose was down to two options: truth (and cutting a deal) or more lies. If he cut a deal, he could at least spare himself a public finding by the commissioner that he had bet on baseball. Rose was backed into a corner. He was told that Baseball, by virtue of their anti-trust exemption, had absolute power based on whatever was in Baseball's best interests. He also knew that he had bet on baseball, a very big sin known by every Major Leaguer who entered a clubhouse.

It was also in Baseball's best interests, however, to cut a deal with Rose. According to Rose, "The commissioner approached my lawyers and offered a settlement—twelve years suspension. I said, 'No thanks.' Within hours, he came back with another offer—six years. I still said 'No.' I thought I had leverage. Baseball did not want to go to court with the Dowd report. You can't win a case which is based on manufactured and circumstantial evidence. On the third try, Baseball hit the jackpot. The commissioner offered a suspension with the right to apply for reinstatement after one year."

Despite evidence that included hundreds of interviews, telephone records, and canceled checks, Dowd's report was criticized by many. Bill James, the noted baseball historian, supported Rose in *The Baseball Book 1990* and claimed that Dowd's report was flawed. Pete had many people who believed—or wanted to believe—that he had not bet on baseball. And he let them believe that he had not bet on baseball. That was his story, and he was sticking to it.

Would Baseball give him an opportunity to save face? Rose's attorney, Reuvan Katz, told Baseball that Pete was ready to accept a harsh sanction. Vincent, by now long past his star-gazing, was intent on running Rose out of the game. He would only be satisfied with a lifetime ban. It was important for Rose that any sanction—including any ban—not include his admission that he bet on baseball. From his days with the Security and Exchange Commission, Vincent had experience with "no admission/no denial" agreements. Basically, the negotiation for a deal sounded like the old joke about prostitutes where a woman is questioned about whether she would sleep with a particular man for an outrageous amount of money. The punch line is, "We've already established what kind of woman you are, now we're just negotiating the price."

It seems to me that they had already established what kind of person Rose was, and all they were doing was "negotiating the price." Rose wanted to apply for reinstatement after two years, maybe three. Baseball countered with ten years. Then Vincent Burke, Jr.—a Washington lawyer working for Major League Baseball—found that the rules say that anybody thrown out of baseball may apply for reinstatement after one year.

Giamatti was forced to admit that Rose could apply after only one year. He also agreed to a stipulation that made no formal finding that Rose had bet on baseball. Giamatti may have even given Katz a personal assurance that he would be open to Rose's bid for reinstatement. In Rose's mind, he was going to take a year off, get his life together, and then be back in baseball.

Vincent told Giamatti to be clear to Katz and Rose on Rose's chances for reinstatement after one year. Giamatti may or may not have been clear. He did reportedly say that "Pete must reconfigure his life" (whatever that means). Giamatti was clear that there could be no understanding, no commitment. Rose had, in effect, a constitutional right under baseball's rules to apply for readmission.

The deal was signed, with Rose being permanently barred from baseball but able to apply for reinstatement in a year. Rose admitted to betting, but not on baseball. At the time, everyone wondered what Rose had gained from the agreement. Johnny

Bench, Rose's one-time teammate, was vocal about it. "If Pete didn't bet on baseball, why doesn't he just say so?" But Katz and Rose were able to get Baseball to sanction Rose without an admission of guilt to the most serious of baseball crimes. Katz did a great job, if you look at it. He had nothing to work with. He got the best outcome he could get, and in some people's minds, a secret agreement with Giamatti to reinstate Rose, possibly in as soon as twelve months.

Giamatti, who was not a lawyer, may have opened his mouth a little too wide in expressing his opinion to the press the very next day. He thought he only couldn't say that he had made a "finding" that Rose had bet on baseball. In response to one of the first questions reporters asked him, Giamatti answered, "In the absence of a hearing, and therefore in the absence of evidence to the contrary, I am confronted by the factual record of Mr. Dowd. On the basis of that, yes, I have concluded he bet on baseball."

Rose was livid, and he probably had a right to be. Would Giamatti, if there were an agreement, back down from that? Vincent wrote, "Rose's lawyer, Reuvan Katz, may not have been wholly candid with him. I don't think Rose understood the latitude Bart [Giamatti] had to speak about the agreement and how difficult it would be for Rose to be reinstated."

My Opinion

Was there a conspiracy to reinstate Rose in a year (or two) if he sought treatment, or reconfigured his life? I suspect that there was, due to the following: Rose accepted his punishment rather quickly for a man who had spent months proclaiming his innocence. It was almost plea-bargaining, with Rose fearful of what further disclosures might do to him. He had to know that in the fourteen previous lifetime bans there hadn't been a single case of reinstatement. But Rose acted like a man who knew he would be back in the game before long. And why wouldn't he be? Couldn't you imagine a scenario in which Giamatti (assured privately by Rose that he would make major life changes) would make a grand gesture of allowing the legendary baseball superstar back in the game's good graces? It would have had to have been done without the knowledge of Vincent or Dowd. Giamatti, ever mindful of his reputation, could have had it both ways. He could play the moral father figure and the benevolent mother-hen, the commissioner who had an unconditional love for the game and all who played it. In this scenario, only one thing could have prevented Rose from getting reinstated in the 1990s: Giamatti's death.

Everything that happened after the agreement pushed Rose further and further from the game. Giamatti passed away. Shortly after Rose's ban, he went to prison for income tax evasion. He pleaded guilty to failing to report $348,720 in earnings from baseball memorabilia sales. Vincent was not going to reinstate Rose, and neither was Bud Selig, his successor. The question remains, why didn't Rose just come clean and confess to having bet on baseball? He finally did, in true defiant spirit. He did it to sell his book. "I knew that I had broken the law," he wrote. "But I really didn't believe I had broken the 'spirit' of the law, which was designed to prevent corruption. I never bet more or less based on injuries and inside information. I never allowed my wagers to influence my baseball decisions."

On an ESPN radio show in March of 2007, Rose admitted to betting "every day" on the Reds, as proof of his "competitive fire," not as a manipulator of games. If he thought that would ease his way back into baseball, he was probably wrong. That information not only contradicts the Dowd report (available to all on the Internet) but also contradicts Rose himself in his 2004 book. On page 158 of *My Prison without Bars*, Rose wrote that reports of betting "an average of $2,000 per game on as many as four to eight games a day, approximately four days per week," during May 1987 were fairly accurate. To me, that means that even if he bet on his team to win approximately four days per week, he did not bet on his team the other game days. That means that as manager, Rose did influence pitching decisions and lineups in games whose outcomes he had a vested interest in.

He spent over a million dollars in legal fees and investigations, fought the worst scandal in baseball history (until the modern-day steroids scandal), and came away with the same settlement that he would have received (a permanent ban) if he had just told the truth from the beginning! The one thing he negotiated and won was the agreement that "made no finding that he had bet on baseball." Maybe the reason was that he needed that to protect his eventual (and secret) reinstatement into baseball.

Rose himself wrote in 2004 that, "Perhaps things would have been different if Mr. Giamatti hadn't died. I might have gotten a fair hearing on reinstatement after a year's suspension as we had all agreed."

Giamatti was not a bad person. He was just thrust into an impossible situation. He was given the position of caretaker for the game he loved, and to do his job properly he had to ban one of its (and his) most beloved players. Perhaps he was tortured for trusting and listening so closely to bulldogs Vincent and Dowd? Perhaps he let them play bad cop, while he played good cop—privately—to Rose?

Reuvan Katz did an amazing job for Rose with the agreement, and didn't feel that he had any need for a secret unwritten agreement. He and Rose had everything they wanted in writing. And then Giamatti blew it up within twenty-four hours. Reuven desperately needed something in writing to exonerate Pete, and he thought he had it with the original agreement. To some people, it's not that Giamatti died before he could live up to the secret agreement, it's that he couldn't adhere to his signed agreement for more than a day.

I believe that there was an understanding that Rose would be back in the game within a year or two. Maybe Rose wasn't contrite enough for Giamatti when the agreement was signed, and that pushed the late commissioner into damning Rose with his statement that he had bet on baseball. Maybe Giamatti wanted it both ways: He would be the judge and jury to "prove" Rose had bet (what a delicious detective story!), and also be the benevolent forgiver in due time.

CONCLUSION:

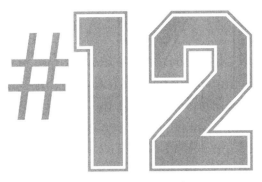

Why were Ty Cobb and Tris Speaker allowed to remain in the league after being found guilty of gambling?

More than sixty years before Pete Rose was banished from his sport, there was a gambling scandal that featured not one, but two of the very best players in Major League Baseball history. The scandal became exposed when a disgruntled former teammate and friend went public with letters that implicated Ty Cobb and Tris Speaker for fixing and gambling on a game played seven years earlier.

There were several parts to this conspiracy. First, the American League president, Ban Johnson, was presented with evidence and tried to make the situation go away before the Major League Baseball Commissioner Judge Landis knew of it. Then there was blackmail and various cover-ups. This was one juicy story, concerning two of the greatest outfielders of all time.

There really isn't any modern-day equivalent. Rose, despite being the all-time hit king, wasn't as good of a ballplayer as either Cobb or Speaker. More than eighty years after his final game, Cobb is still considered one of the three or four best players ever. Speaker is still considered one of the top twenty. Imagine if in their final playing years it was found out that modern NFL star quarterbacks Tom Brady and Peyton Manning had (seven years earlier) conspired to fix a regular season game; and since the outcome wouldn't be in doubt; one of them had a third party place a sizable wager for all concerned. If that happened, and there was incontrovertible evidence linking and implicating both, you can see why efforts were made to cover everything up before the commissioner found out about it.

One has to be aware of the times in which this conspiracy took place to fully grasp it. In 1919 baseball had returned, after having been shut down on Labor Day the year before (Secretary of War Newton Baker had issued a "work or fight" order for all non-essential industries, and baseball owners didn't need much more of a cue to end their season early). The first World War, the war to end all wars, had just ended, but many doughboys never made it home.

In the final days of the 1919 season, the White Sox had pulled away from the pack and clinched first place. The Indians, with first-year player-manager Speaker, were solidly entrenched at second. The Yankees were battling the Tigers for third. In those days, teams were paid based on whether they finished in first, second, or third place. The Tigers and Yankees were battling for the third place money when the Indians and Tigers met for a series in the final week of the season. The Yankees had a record of 75–59 at the time of the series, mere percentage points better than the Tigers.

So it was that on September 24 in Detroit, Tiger players Cobb and Dutch Leonard got together for a "friendly chat" under the stands with Indians player-manager Speaker and outfielder Joe Wood. Leonard, Wood, and Speaker were all one-time Boston teammates. The thirty-two-year-old Cobb was more than friendly with fellow Southerner Speaker. Cobb had led the American League that year with a .382 batting average, and Speaker was one of the few opponents he deeply respected.

According to Timothy M. Gay's *Tris Speaker: The Rough and Tumble Life of a Baseball Legend* (2007), Leonard and Cobb told Speaker and Wood how much they would appreciate finishing with the third-place money. By Leonard's account, Speaker told Cobb he had nothing to worry about. With all four players knowing the outcome of the next day's game, it was then decided to put some money down on it. Cobb reportedly got a clubhouse attendant named Fred West to collect the bets and get them placed with a local bookie. Supposedly, each of the four co-conspirators bet between $1,000 and $2,000. Leonard would later claim that Wood and Cobb each wrote separate letters to him in the coming months, saying West had been unable to bet more than $600—which, because the Tigers were favored, only netted $420 for the four to split (the letters would implicate Speaker as a co-conspirator). Leonard eventually released those letters, which were printed by the *New York Times*.

That's Leonard's story. Cobb testified seven years later to Commissioner Landis that he had recommended West as a trusted person with whom to place a bet—implying that he did nothing more than serve as an intermediary to the making of a bet. Cobb's letter to Leonard mentioned a "business proposition," but never the word "bet."

Detroit won the game, and the four players won their $600. The Tigers, even with their 9–5 victory on September 25, finished the season 80–60. The Yankees won their final five games of the season to finish 80–59, a half a game better than Detroit. The White Sox won the pennant, and eight of their players would go on to throw the World Series against the Cincinnati Reds.

Speaker, in his second year as player-manager, won the 1920 World Series as a member of the Cleveland Indians. The next year, Cobb took on the responsibilities of being a player-manager with the Tigers.

Leonard continued to pitch for the Tigers until he was cut by Cobb in the middle of the 1925 season. In his 1961 autobiography, *My Life in Baseball: The True Record*, written with Al Stump, Cobb said "I'd dropped him from the roster for a good and sufficient reason. . . . Speaker, as Cleveland manager, had refused waivers on him. For this, Leonard openly had vowed revenge on both of us."

This is where I get suspicious. Cobb gave Leonard the ball for eighteen starts in 1925, and Dutch went 11–4 with an ERA right around the League average. When Cobb released Leonard, the Tigers were 48–46, meaning that the team was 37–42 in games that Leonard didn't earn a decision in, and 11–4 in games he did. What were the "good and sufficient" reasons that Cobb had? Maybe Leonard was trying to extort money from Cobb, being that he was in possession of Cobb's 1919 letters?

It was at the beginning of the 1926 season that Leonard, who never pitched another game in the majors after Cobb cut him, gave his evidence of the 1919 fix (of the Indians–Tigers game) to American League President Ban Johnson.

Johnson wanted to handle matters privately, without the press or even Commissioner Landis finding out about things. Some reports claim that Johnson and the league owners tried to buy the letters from Leonard in exchange for his silence. Apparently Johnson and Landis had been feuding for years, ever since Landis came in and demanded total authority over baseball in his attempt to clean up the game.

Ban Johnson needed to conspire with Tigers owner Frank Navin as well as with Cobb and Speaker to get them all out of this mess started by Leonard's accusations. Johnson met with Cobb and Speaker separately and privately (Wood was long gone from the majors by this point). In October of 1926, Navin announced that Cobb would not be retained as the Tigers' manager for 1927. "Georgia Peach Declares He is Through With Baseball, Moriarity Named New Pilot," was the banner headline in most newspapers across the country. The stories put out by the Associated Press reported that Cobb had tried to buy into the Tigers, to no avail, and that he might take over managing the Atlanta team in the Southern League. The story also pointed to dissention in the Tigers clubhouse.

Three weeks later, it was announced that Speaker would not be retained as the Indians manager, either. That item, also unexpected, raised considerable eyebrows. The plot to have both Cobb and Speaker retire as players and be fired as managers was hatched by A.L. President Johnson. Landis apparently went crazy when he found out that Johnson had permitted the two stars to quietly resign. He didn't get wind of any evidence of scandal until months later.

Johnson said, "When I found that two of our managers were not serving us properly, I had to let them go. Now isn't that proper? As long as I am president of the league, neither one of them will manage or play on our teams."

The story soon broke, and real reason Cobb and Speaker stepped down came out. Landis asked Leonard to come to his office to face Speaker and Cobb and make his accusation directly. Leonard refused to go to Chicago, where there were people, he reasoned, who were adept at knocking off guys like him for a price. Baseball didn't have a lawyer like John Dowd, but there was an investigation.

By late December, the story had unfolded in the press, and it was clear which side had won in the media and court of public opinion. Billy Evans, the former umpire and one of the leading sportswriters of his time, wrote that Leonard had been branded the "Squealer." Evans said, "Even in our kid days, the 'tattle-tale' was never a very popular person." Evans wrote that Leonard's charges "were purely a matter of personal revenge." The column could have been written by Cobb, or one of Cobb's attorneys. Evans wrote as if Leonard had squealed on him personally. "To use the slang of baseball, Leonard never was regarded as a real game guy. . . . Leonard was a southpaw with good speed and a fast-breaking curve, a truly great pitcher had he possessed the proper heart and temperament. . . . He liked to pick his spots. He would pitch often against teams against which he was effective, but either had a sick stomach or a sore arm when named to work against a club that liked his stuff." One bold sub-headline read, "Leonard's Temperament Not Unlike *Chorus Girl*." As in the case of many conspiracies, it is often imperative to knock the whistle-blower. "It is a crime that men of the stature of Ty and Tris should be blackened by a man of this caliber with charges that every baseballer knows to be utterly false," Evans wrote.

When re-reading the microfilm from Evans' 1928 column, I learned something that I hadn't known about the case. Apparently, if Leonard had accumulated ten years of Major League service time, he would have been able to get his unconditional release on the ground that he was a ten-year man in the majors, which would have enabled him to sign a fat contract with a National League club that wanted his services. Remember how Cobb dropped Leonard for "good and sufficient reason" in July of 1925? That reason was that Leonard was about to accrue ten years of service. Cobb released him, but Leonard wasn't a free agent able to hook on with a National League club. No wonder Leonard was peeved.

The play-by-play of the fixed game was reprinted in all the newspapers. The Tigers scored two runs in the first inning, and two more in the second. They cruised to an easy victory. The reaction of the baseball fans around the country was predictable. The NEA service (another wire service) questioned fans in baseball cities. There is no doubt that the court of public opinion was in the favor of the two ex-managers. Most fans severely criticized Baseball. There were many assertions that Cobb and Speaker were innocent. Many fans felt that the best interests of Baseball would have been served by burying the charges.

Many fans also opined that it was wrong to dredge up a scandal after seven years had passed, and that there should have been a statute of limitations on the transgression. "The exposé should have been made long before, or not at all," the Los Angeles reporter observed after canvassing fans. Obviously, Dutch Leonard held on to his letters—his evidence—waiting for the right time and place.

Cobb and Speaker joined forces and hired attorney W.H. Boyd. Making their defense in the investigation, the future Hall of Famers came out swinging. They received testimony from clubhouse attendant Fred West, who said that the money he received was *not* for a bet on the Tigers–Indians game, but rather a horseracing bet. (Even in the 1920s, it was a safe route for baseball players to admit betting on the horses!) Since Leonard had testified that it was West who was given the money to place the bets, it was a good day in court for the former outfielders. "The bet on the game was Leonard's idea, but when Wood gave me the money, I convinced Wood that the money should be bet on a 'hot tip' at the racetrack," West testified.

Could Cobb and Speaker—both rich and powerful men—have gotten to witnesses Wood and West, as well as the leading sportswriters of the day? Sure they could have. Of course, they also had a compelling case.

Speaker had three hits in a game his team was supposed to lose. Cobb had only one in a game his team was supposed to win (and did). As Cobb put it, "The paltry profit in betting on a game was the last thing I needed. Likewise Speaker, who was a man of substantial means. For any trio of men [Wood didn't appear in the game] to attempt to rig a ballgame is ridiculous on the face of it."

Cobb proclaimed his innocence and was believable. "I am branded a gambler on a ballgame in which my club took part. I have never in the twenty-two years I have been in baseball made a single bet on an American League game."

Which raises my antennae, into thinking he may have made bets on National League games.

EVIDENCE TO SUPPORT A CONSPIRACY

If Cobb and Speaker were not guilty of fixing and betting on baseball games, why did they agree to quietly step down in October of 1926?

Cobb believed that Ban Johnson wanted to make a grandstand play in which the two veteran stars were ruthlessly sacrificed to prove that baseball was honest. It makes sense that Johnson wanted the matter dropped with the two stars retiring (with enough space apart to make them seem unconnected). It also makes sense that Landis wanted the exposure of a public sacrifice even greater than the banned "Shoeless" Joe Jackson. And Tigers' owner Navin wanted out of Cobb's huge contract.

Cobb had big-time political connections, even playing poker in the White House with President Harding. Al Stump's 1996 biography of Cobb reported that Cobb had arranged a meeting with Charles Evans Hughes, the former U.S. Supreme Court justice. Several wealthy men in Georgia had offered to meet Hughes' fees for handling Cobb's libel and slander suits.

On January 27, 1927, Commissioner Landis made his ruling. "This is the Cobb–Speaker case. These players have not been, nor are they now, found guilty of fixing a ball game. By no decent system of justice could such finding be made." Landis declared.

In Cobb's 1961 book, *My Life in Baseball*, Cobb revealed that Landis' verdict was dictated to him by attorneys representing Speaker and himself. Neither Cobb nor Speaker ever managed another Major League Baseball game, although they were able to play for other teams. Cobb signed with the Philadelphia Athletics. Speaker signed with the Washington Senators. The two stars were acquitted, and nothing was said of their gambling ever again.

Ban Johnson was slapped the hardest. Because he had prejudged the great Cobb, he took a forced leave of absence, and stepped down soon after. Somehow, Landis knew which gods he could take on, and which he couldn't. Some stars—like Shoeless Joe Jackson—were at Landis' mercy. Others, like Cobb, clearly were not.

Cobb agreed not to sue Baseball on a defamation of character suit, and was elected into the charter class of Baseball's Hall of Fame in 1936, earning 222 of the 226 votes cast (higher even than Babe Ruth's vote). Speaker was enshrined into the Hall of Fame a year later.

When Speaker died in 1957, not a word about the scandal was mentioned in any of the obituaries or sidebars. There was nothing about the fixed game. The first paragraph of the Associated Press story read: "Baseball men everywhere mourned Tris Speaker today as a great center fielder—perhaps the best of all time—a fine and understanding manager, a good influence on younger players and a wonderful person."

Folks, if you committed the cardinal sin in your sport, and walked away with this legacy, you would be able to rest in peace. This was the case for Cobb, who died in 1961. Ban Johnson was among many who praised Cobb after his passing, calling him the greatest player of all time. Again, not a word was uttered about the scandal.

Speaker and Cobb came out unscathed, with their souls and reputations in tact.

Landis didn't come out looking as great. The esteemed sportswriter Shirley Povich wrote in 1989 (after Giamatti had banished Rose):

> It is to be recalled that Landis' reputation suffered in 1927 when he surprisingly took no action against Ty Cobb and Tris Speaker despite solid evidence that they not only bet on baseball games—Rose's sin—but actually

were involved in fixing a game, the ultimate baseball crime. . . . When Landis chickened out on that one it was startling because was he not the very model of the no-nonsense commissioner before whom all baseball trembled? Had he not swiftly banished for life the eight Black Sox who fixed the 1919 World Series? Was he not the stern old federal judge who once fined the Standard Oil Company $10 million in 1917?. . . . Yet Landis, after a hearing, let Cobb and Speaker off as "not guilty because of insufficient evidence." Therein his critics said Landis got satisfaction in what was his long and bitter feud with Ban Johnson, who had already declared both players guilty and banned them from the game.

My Opinion

When Cobb was being questioned by Landis, he reportedly leaked news of a 1923 series between the Tigers and Browns that was fixed by St. Louis Browns players. Cobb said that certain Browns players approached members of the Tigers, saying they would see to it that the Tigers won. Cobb claimed that he took the matter to the Tigers' owner, Navin. When questioned by the commissioner about the story Cobb had leaked to reporter Bert Walker of INS (International News Service), Cobb was coy, saying, "He does not wish to testify in any more scandals, barring the one involving himself." Cobb also hinted to reporters that he had inside information about certain club officials filing false ticket sales figures to tax collectors and scalping World Series tickets.

There were so many cans of worms that Cobb could have opened that he could have ripped baseball apart single-handedly. Every game, every series could have been scrutinized and investigated *ad nauseum*. In my view, Landis knew that Cobb was a wealthy man with powerful friends in politics. He was also very vindictive, and wouldn't go away easily, like the uneducated and illiterate Joe Jackson had. In consideration of those factors, he let the aging Cobb and Speaker remain in the game.

This was, without a doubt, one of the greatest sports conspiracies of all time. The players conspired to fix the game, and then bet on the outcome. The league president conspired with the team owner to quietly make the problem go away. And the commissioner ultimately bowed to the attorneys, rewriting history.

CONCLUSION:

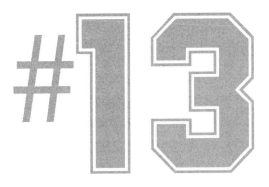

Are some NASCAR outcomes too good to be true?

One of the best things about sports is that it's unscripted. One never knows when a powerful, emotional moment will come. When the events are scripted and planned out in meetings, as they are in professional wrestling, the entire event is cheapened (in my opinion). But with so much at stake, sometimes the players, teams, and leagues have incentive to manufacture theatrical outcomes to tug at the heartstrings of the fans.

It makes sense that there would be conspiracies to alter the results of auto races. Motorsports has seen its popularity grow by leaps and bounds in the last two decades. Strangely, there have been more than one Hollywood-type ending in a key race, with many ways to exploit and nudge the outcomes. That makes for a powerful recipe for conspiracy.

People who cover NASCAR (the National Association for Stock Car Auto Racing) and who know a whole lot more about it than I do tell me that there is still a lot of mistrust between NASCAR and its core fan base. There are phantom caution flags—often when no debris appears on the track. Some skeptics believe that cautions are thrown because the racing is boring, or because officials want someone other than the front-runner to win the race. Some think that the governing bodies might have caution flags thrown so that certain drivers (like Dale Earnhardt, Jr. and Jeff Gordon) can be more competitive. NASCAR doesn't help the matter, since they don't share their information with the media. Drivers are thus trained not to speak up or criticize NASCAR. Sometimes, the saying goes, NASCAR has to show the drivers who the boss is.

Clearly, there are ways that NASCAR can fix races, if they wanted to. Here is what fans of conspiracy theories might say about certain races that raised some eyebrows.

1998 Daytona 500

In his 2002 book, *Daytona: From the Birth of Speed to the Death of the Man in Black,* Ed Hinton wrote how, to Americans and Canadians these days, Daytona is synonymous with NASCAR. Hinton wrote that "NASCAR's showcase race, the Daytona 500, has supplanted even the Indianapolis 500 as North America's premiere motorsports event." The Daytona 500, sometimes referred to as "The Great American Race" has the largest purse in all of auto racing, attracts the largest television audience, and is generally considered the most prestigious race of the year.

It makes sense that everyone wanted to see Dale Earnhardt win Daytona in 1998. The man known as "The Intimidator" and "The Man in Black" had won everything else, beginning with his 1979 Rookie of the Year season. Yet despite winning seventy-six Winston Cup races (and seven championships), Earnhardt had always come up short at the Daytona 500. By February of 1998, Earnhardt had entered nineteen previous Daytonas and had come away empty-handed each time. The forty-six-year-old had few chances left at the most prestigious of races. During pre-race ceremonies on February 15, 1998, at Daytona International

Speedway, NASCAR (owing to a tradition borrowed from the NBA a year earlier, and to be copied by Major League Baseball the year after) honored its own. The thirty-four living members of NASCAR's Fifty Greatest Drivers were honored before the race. It would have been a perfect script for Earnhardt to win his first Daytona 500 on the fiftieth anniversary of the first stock car race, and in front of all the surviving members of the Fifty Greatest Drivers. It would have been good for the sport.

What happened was storybook. According to Hinton, when Earnhardt crossed the finish line and made his way down the pit road to victory lane, "Virtually every member of every team had lined up to slap hands with him as he drove by. It was the most monumental salute in the history of American motor racing—not even when A.J. Foyt won the Indy 500 for a then-unprecedented fourth time, in 1977, had there been such an emotional outpouring for a winner as he brought his car in."

Jeff Gordon had dominated the first half of the race and appeared to be in good shape. Gordon hit a chunk of rubber from a tire off Dale Jarrett's car, however, and that threw off his engine the rest of the way. On lap 123, Earnhardt finally passed Gordon. "With twenty-seven laps to go, teammates Jeremy Mayfield and Rusty Wallace were hooked up and preparing to draft past Earnhardt when John Andretti and Robert Pressley crashed together, bringing out a caution," Hinton wrote. "All the leaders pitted under the yellow, and Earnhardt got back onto the track first." Hinton heard Gordon's plaintive radio transmission during a round of pit stops: "Damn! If that Three [Earnhardt] ain't speedin' off the pit road, I don't know what is!"

Hinton continued:

> For safety, NASCAR now requires speed limits on the pit road, usually about fifty-five mph, and officials used radar guns to enforce it. But pit road speed checks had

become very similar to ball-and-strike calls in baseball. Could NASCAR—on this twentieth try by Earnhardt, on this fiftieth anniversary of the first NASCAR race—be giving Earnhardt a little bit larger strike zone to pitch? Perhaps. But it was a judgment call, and not blatant massaging of the situation.

My Opinion

Superstars—real, honest-to-God superstars—get calls in every sport. Very few NBA Finals games were decided when a mega-star was called for traveling in the final seconds. Part of the reason is that elite stars don't commit infractions at the worst possible moment. But more likely, the legends know how to get away with things that give them a little bit more of an advantage. Calling speeding on "The Intimidator" off the pit road—in that situation—would not have been the right call. We don't live in a perfect world, but sometimes our live sporting events just happen to turn out, well, perfect.

1994 Brickyard 400

Here's another race that was a little too close to how a perfect script would end: Jeff Gordon's 1994 victory at the Brickyard 400. There was more than a little animosity that stock cars were there in Indianapolis for the inaugural Brickyard 400. Gordon was a young, up-and-coming superstar, who happened to have grown up in Pittsboro, Indiana, a tiny city about fifteen miles outside Indianapolis.

Let's just say that the newly-turned twenty-three-year-old Gordon, the youngest driver in the field, was an appropriate choice to win the race. How storybook could you get? I mean, Gordon was a guy who grew up seeking autographs from drivers like four-time Indy 500 winner Rick Mears. Who better to give stock car racing a needed push in the Hoosier city?

The race wasn't exceptionally close. It was written the next day that the final four laps were a victory parade for Gordon, whose only other win to that point had come in May in the Coca-Cola 600 at Charlotte, North Carolina.

Before the start of the race, the crowd was eerily quiet, unlike it usually was at the 500. But it didn't take long for the race-happy fans in Indianapolis to embrace the first Winston Cup race held there, or its local hero.

Conspiracy theorists will say that the sport needed a victory by local hero Gordon. Others will counter with the argument that Gordon put forth after the race: "It's tough to race on those tracks where all those guys have been racing so many years." In other words, that particular track was new enough that all the great drivers were just learning the ropes and its nuances.

Gordon's victory was widely celebrated in Pittsboro, with banners and a hero's welcome. It was a perfect way for the inaugural Brickyard to end.

My Opinion

Where there's smoke, there's fire. And where there's a local kid making a name for himself in a place that desperately needs some help pumping up an event, there's a conspiracy theory. On the other hand, this was not just another "kid" being hyped. Not everyone realized in 1994 how great Gordon would become. In just a few years, he would dominate his sport. In 1998, he tied the record with thirteen victories. Earnhardt would call him the "Wonder Boy." Was this race fixed, or just another case of an unscripted race imitating Hollywood movies and their perfect endings? I think it's more likely that it was just a terrific coincidence.

2001 Pepsi 400

There is nothing more dramatic than a good father and son story, and NASCAR has a history filled with them. But nothing equaled what happened in July 2001 at the Pepsi 400, when Dale Earnhardt, Jr. won the first race to be held at the Daytona International Speedway since his father—and racing legend—was killed in the last lap of the 2001 Daytona 500.

Conspiracy theorists can't stretch their imagination enough to figure out how "in a late charge from seventh to first, Earnhardt's car seemed to defy the laws of physics on a track where carburetor restrictor plates limit horsepower and almost always keep drivers close." That's according to the Associated Press' Eddie Pells, writing on July 11, 2001. Rusty Wallace said, following the race, "I can't think of a better script to play than to come back to the track that took his father away from him. To have him be able to honor him with the victory is pretty cool. I wish I would have been the one shoving him across the line. I almost was." (Michael Waltrip actually was.)

Chris Jenkins wrote in *USA Today*:

> It's one of the touchiest subjects in NASCAR, and it almost never comes up while cameras and tape recorders are rolling. Privately, some drivers and teams suspect that NASCAR officials show favoritism to Earnhardt, Jr. in his biggest races. Earnhardt, Jr. only recently stopped seething about a comment from driver Jimmy Spencer, who questioned the legitimacy of his emotional Daytona win in 2001. Spencer said immediately following the race, "I knew going in [that] the No. 8 car was going to win the race. Something was fictitious. . . . I mean, you know, it's not ironic the No. 8 car would win at all."

Spencer now says that Dale Jr. has won so many restrictor plate races, he no longer thinks the July 2001 race was fixed.

A restrictor plate is a device used to limit the car engine's power. The restrictor plates used in NASCAR reduces engine power from approximately 750 hp to approximately 430 hp. It's apparently much easier to fix a restrictor plate race than other races, where speed isn't controlled. Teams will work an entire year to gain one extra horsepower, but if NASCAR gives you a plate with 1/32 of an inch bigger hole in the restrictor plates, you can gain as much as ten more horsepower than your competitors, which is a huge advantage.

They only run restrictor plate races at the Daytona and Talledega race tracks. That's because cars were getting airborne when racing over 200 mph there. Officials saw the need to slow them down, after Bobby Allison flipped, hit the catch-tents, and his car came within only seven feet or so of winding up in the stands. So, it is more for the safety of the fans than the drivers that they began using plates. Why just those two tracks? Because the danger isn't so great at the other tracks. One of the fastest tracks is in Atlanta, where turns can be taken around 205 mph, but that's still not as fast as the turns that were being taken in Daytona and Talledega. With the plates, speeds are closer to 190 mph there.

"No fewer than a half-dozen newspaper columnists wrote about the 'wink-wink, nod-nod' aspects of the result," in the words of *Tampa Tribune* columnist Martin Fennelly. "You don't go by yourself on the outside and make that kind of time up," Johnny Benson said of Earnhardt's late-race push to the front. "But it's okay. It was good that Junior won," wrote Eddie Pells.

My Opinion

It seems an awful lot like a movie. At Daytona, cars usually need drafting help. To dart in and out of the pack alone, and to go from seventh place all the way to first, seems almost unreal. In fact, I wouldn't believe it if I saw it in a movie. It happened, though, in real life. I certainly understand those who think it was fixed. It was almost too perfect. And NASCAR had the technical ability—especially on that kind of restrictor-plate race—to tweak the cars accordingly.

Usually, I would think that most cheating would be exposed in this sport because so many people are involved. When crew members eventually have a falling out and leave a crew, they are the ones that rat out the cheaters. In this case, though, that hasn't happened. In fact, Earnhardt, Jr. has won other restrictor-plate races since, including the 2004 Daytona 500.

I see this as looking more shady immediately after the race, but like with Jeff Gordon's 1994 Brickyard victory, time has a way of showing us that the storybook finish was logical. After all, Earnhardt (and the other racers at Dale Earnhardt, Inc.) do have some intangible edge in restrictor-plate racing. I believe the edge was on the level.

2004 DAYTONA 500

If the 2001 Pepsi 400 victory by Earnhardt, Jr. wasn't emotional enough, how about his victory at the 2004 Daytona 500? It provided one of the most memorable outcomes in the sport's history. Earnhardt, Jr. won the prestigious race six years to the day his father won it—and three years after the crash at the race that killed his father. In the 2004 Daytona 500, there were more whispers of a conspiracy concerning the controversial son. This time, it seems that he was not only helped from above (NASCAR officials), higher above (his father), but from other drivers as well. Did Tony Stewart allow Junior to race by him in the final laps?

Stewart was quoted after the race as saying, "I'm just flat tickled to death. Normally, I wouldn't be this excited about second [place]. He outdrove us and beat us, plain and simple." Stewart took the lead at Lap 175, with twenty-five laps remaining. Earnhardt took the lead from him on Lap 181. The race lacked any real drama after that. Bloggers were incensed. They wrote that NASCAR wanted Earnhardt to win. They wrote that it appeared only one person was racing that day. That it was not a race so much as a foregone conclusion.

MY OPINION

Superstars get favorable calls in all sports, and in modern sports, there is a disturbing (to me) tendency for athletes to glorify or revel in their opponents' good fortune. How dare opponents congratulate Mark McGwire when he hit record-setting home runs? How dare opponents hit Michael Jordan up for autographs before games, and acquiesce to him during play? It's happening more and more lately. The Chicago Bears were not thrilled about losing Super Bowl XXXXI, but at the same time the Bears and their coach were happy for opposing quarterback Peyton Manning and head coach Tony Dungy, who had each won their first Super Bowl. That's crazy to me. Now, I realize that in this case Earnhardt, Jr. and Tony Stewart had a history of working together, and the entire sport is made up of individuals needing help from opponents to win. It's not a conspiracy theory, but a fact of life. Athletes not only root for themselves, but they have their favorite opponents that they root for, too. It's just that when those opponents pass them, sometimes they look a little too happy. Especially someone like Stewart, who is known for being an intense competitor. My opinion is that there was not a fix, or foregone conclusion.

1984 FIRECRACKER 400

The crowd in Daytona Beach for the 1984 Firecracker 400 included, for the first time ever, a sitting president of the United States. Ronald Reagan was in attendance, in large part hoping to see history (and appeal to the millions of NASCAR fans who would reelect him five months later). Reagan was the president, but to race car fans, Richard Petty was The King. And forty-seven-year-old Petty was attempting to win his 200 race.

It was a perfect scenario. With the president there and the advantage of a big engine, Petty out-dueled Cale Yarborough as the two took the yellow caution flag with two laps to go—meaning no driver could improve his position during the last five miles of the 400-mile event.

Incredibly, Yarborough lost the chance to finish second when he rolled into the pits one lap too early, thinking the race had ended. Petty and Yarborough were so close heading into the decisive third and fourth turns that the winner said their cars actually touched two or three times.

Come on, now. A mental error by Yarborough, in which he thought the race was over, with one lap left to go? It seems odd, to say the least. After all, Yarborough and Petty had by far the strongest cars, linked up in a draft, and they built up a lengthy lead over the rest of the field. With thirty-seven laps remaining, Petty made his final pit stop, taking on right-side tires in 14.8 seconds. Yarborough pitted one lap later, and received left-side tires and gasoline in sixteen seconds. Yarborough caught Petty with twenty laps to go.

The two ran bumper to bumper in a thrilling conclusion. What a backdrop to set a historic milestone! There are many who think the race was just too perfect a set-up.

My Opinion

Cale Yarborough had a strategy to win the race, but it proved to be unsuccessful because of the late caution. "I got beat at my own drafting game," Yarborough said after the race. Intending to sling-shot his way into victory, he didn't anticipate the late caution flag. To me, this is like accepting the fact that Ali "forgot" that he had to go to a neutral corner after knocking out Sonny Liston.

Great athletes are supposed to know their whereabouts—and their opponent's—at all times, especially in the late stages of the biggest of matches. For almost any other race, I would have accepted Yarborough's explanation, but I'm a little skeptical of this one.

CONCLUSION:

Cheaters conspire to steal signs, throw illegal pitches, steal pennants

Everyone cheats sometimes. That's just a simple fact. Average men and women, when they don't exploit the cheating on a large scale, simply don't get caught. If they are exposed, the punishment is often inconsequential. That is why—whether by exaggerating their deductions when filing taxes, omitting items on their resume, or getting out of speeding tickets by flirting with or currying favor with officers—people cheat all the time.

Of course, most people don't consider their indiscretions to be very serious. Recent studies have shown that the percent of high school students who admit to cheating at least once is close to 75%. There is evidence that the desire to cheat—and the willingness to do so—has become the norm.

Baseball players and managers are the same way. For over a century, players have cheated (it's called "gamesmanship," for those who like to rationalize) a number of different ways.

On offense, batters have often been tipped off by teammates as to the type of pitch about to be thrown. On defense, pitchers have often doctored baseballs with foreign substances and throwing illegal pitches.

In the past, students cheated by copying answers off a friend's paper, or by smuggling notes into class. In more recent times, they have surely used technology for less-than-virtuous means. Baseball, too, has had to stay ahead of technological cheaters, who have tilted the playing field with illegal drugs not previously available. To me, cheating is cheating, and this chapter will deal with the more traditional forms of cheating as they pertain to baseball: stealing signs and throwing illegal pitches. Another form of skullduggery is the corking of bats—using a substance other than wood, like cork—to make the bat lighter.

In a book about sports conspiracies, all the cheaters in baseball that were caught with corked bats get a free pass. The late Norm Cash batted .361 in 1961 with a bat that he drilled a hole in and filled up with sawdust and cork. Slugger Albert Belle was caught and suspended for seven games in 1994 because he used a corked bat. Graig Nettles and Amos Otis both reportedly used superballs (rubber balls) in their bats. Billy Hatcher was suspended for using a corked bat in 1987. These are just a handful of the players that were caught. It's a perfect crime, if the player doesn't break his bat. But there's no conspiracy to be found there, really, as these cheaters, generally speaking, act alone.

But players at bat can't steal signs alone; they need help from co-conspirators. In an effort to get a better idea of the location and velocity of the pitch, offensive players can steal signs from the defense. And, unlike the doctoring of pitches, there is no official rule in the books against sign stealing. The most famous sign stealing incident in baseball history concerns the New York Giants, who overcame a thirteen-game deficit to the Brooklyn Dodgers to win the National League pennant in the final weeks of the season in 1951.

The three-game playoff to determine the National League champion ended with Bobby Thomson's "Shot Heard 'Round the World," the most famous home run in baseball history. In January of 2001, an article by Joshua Prager appeared in *the Wall Street Journal* that quoted three Giants players admitting that the Giants stole signs by means of a buzzer which sounded in the Giants' bullpen. The three Giants players that initially spilled the beans were Monty Irvin, Sal Yvars, and Al Gettel. It's important to remember that there was no written rule against sign stealing.

The Giants played their home games at the Polo Grounds in Harlem, where the home clubhouse was located deep in center field, complete with an unobstructed view of the opposing catcher. Beginning in July of 1951, the Giants' placed someone (either coach Herman Franks or infielder Hank Schenz) in the clubhouse to steal signs using a high powered telescope or binoculars hidden in a mesh grid along the distant wall. They would buzz the bullpen once or twice, depending on whether a fastball or curve was coming. Backup catcher Yvars was the tip-off guy, signaling the batter by the simplest of means: tossing a ball up in the air.

After reading Joshua Prager's *Echoing the Green: The Untold Story of Bobby Thomson, Ralph Branca, and the Shot Heard 'Round the World* (2006), it seems clear that the Giants indeed cheated, and conspired for fifty years to keep it a secret. There are hints of Watergate involved in this conspiracy—the Giants hired an electrician to wire a connection between the clubhouse window and the Giants bullpen, within easy sight of the batters— and of course, an elaborate cover-up.

The Giants stole signals in the final two months of their furious comeback, but did Thomson receive a signal before his dramatic, pennant-winning home run? It appears that he did. When asked in 2001 if he received the sign, he responded that it was basically impossible to stand in the batter's box and not get it. When asked if he took the sign on the 0–1 pitch, Thomson said, "I'd have to say more no than yes." He was being honest, although he let an honorable man and pitcher, Ralph Branca, believe for all those years that the home run was hit fair and square.

I really don't think the Giants needed to steal signs to win the 1951 pennant. In late May, they called up a rookie named Willie Mays, who was standing on deck when Thomson hit his home run. Thomson had hit a home run off Branca in the first game of the playoff series as well, in a game played in Brooklyn. That home run was obviously on the level. Thomson hit nine of his thirty-two home runs that season off Dodgers pitching. Was he signaled on any of the others that were hit at the Polo Grounds?

The game on October 3, 1951, was dramatic. I believe it was the first nationally televised non–World Series game. It was a thrilling finish to a thrilling season at a time when baseball faced no real competition from professional football, basketball, or hockey. But the Dodgers didn't lose the pennant because Thomson was tipped off.

First off, the Dodgers made a poor choice upon winning a season-ending coin toss. It was their decision to play either the first game in Brooklyn, or the last two. They chose to have home field for only the first game. Dodgers manager Charlie Dressen let his hottest pitcher, Clem Labine, pitch all nine innings of a 10–0 Game Two victory. If I could have taken a time machine back to that afternoon and advised Dressen to get Labine out of there, that he might be needed to get one or two batters the next day, I would have. Even if managers didn't have computer charts showing how batters did against individual pitchers back then, Dressen shouldn't have put Branca in that difficult spot in Game Three, after witnessing Thomson's earlier blast off Branca in the Series.

The Giants were hardly the only baseball team to steal signs, but they became the most noteworthy because of the time and place of the dramatic home run. No less than ten years later, it appeared that there was just as much evidence to conclude that the Cincinnati Reds won the 1961 National League pennant in the same fashion as the 1951 Giants had.

★ ★ ★ ★ ★

How the 1961 Cincinnati Reds Stole the National League Pennant

Both the 1951 Giants and the 1961 Reds finished ahead of the Dodgers, then lost the World Series to the Yankees. Both stole signs in their home ballpark, from a station in deep center field. The similarities are remarkable.

Jay Hook pitched for the Reds until he was moved to the Mets in the 1962 expansion draft. In spring training with the Mets, Hook accused Brooks Lawrence (a former teammate with the Reds who had last played in 1960 and had served as a scout in 1961), of stealing signs for the Reds in their pennant-winning season. Hook said the Reds had Lawrence posted in the center field scoreboard at Crosley Field at some home games, and that Lawrence relayed information by telephone to a coach in the Cincinnati dugout, who would then relay signals to the Reds batters.

Lawrence, who passed away in 2000, denied the accusations at the time, saying that he used to slip into the scoreboard before games for a smoke, but couldn't see anything. I call this the "smoke signal" defense (where there's smoke, there's also sign stealing).

The Reds manager at the time, Fred Hutchinson, who passed away in 1964, issued a "no comment." After that 1961 season, National League President Warren Giles warned that he would forfeit any game won with the aid of mechanical devices.

Reds relief pitcher Jim Brosnan admitted the scheme to author Richard Lally in *Bombers: An Oral History of the New*

York Yankees (2002). Brosnan admitted that then-manager Hutchinson assigned then-coach Otis Douglas to be on the phone in the dugout. When he would holler or chatter at a batter, it was a sign of an incoming fastball. The former Reds pitcher said his teammates knew every pitch that was coming, but it hardly mattered against the 1961 Yanks—one of the greatest teams of all time.

Was There a Motive for the Reds to Steal Signs?

Yes. In my opinion, the Reds likely wouldn't have made it to the World Series without cheating.

The Reds simply were not a very good team. In 1960, the Reds won only sixty-seven games. The next year, they increased their wins to ninety-three, earning a trip to the World Series. The Reds had two great batters in those days, and both Frank Robinson and Vada Pinson remained healthy in both seasons (Robinson/Pinson combined for 1,116 at-bats in 1960, and 1,152 in 1961), so essentially, a team comprised of mostly the same players improved by twenty-six wins in just one season.

Cincinnati won the pennant with their regular lineup: Jerry Zimmerman as catcher and Gordy Coleman, Don Blasingame, Gene Freese, and Eddie Kasko on the infield. They beat out a Dodgers team that included stars like Drysdale, Koufax, Maury Wills, Gil Hodges, and others. They beat out the Mays–McCovey–Cepeda-led San Francisco Giants. And they beat out Hank Aaron's Braves, the team that had won National League pennants in 1957 and 1958, and finished second in 1959 and 1960.

That the Reds won was a fluke. They played the 107-loss Philadelphia Phillies twenty-two times that summer, and won nineteen of the twenty-two contests. Against everyone else, the Reds were ordinary.

The Reds scored 710 runs and allowed 653 that year. According to retrosheet.com, the Pythagorean winning percentage (a formula devised by Bill James to estimate a team's winning percentage given their runs scored and runs allowed) would be .538 (or 83–71 over the course of a season). Instead, the Reds won ninety-three games, or ten more than they would have been expected to. This raises my eyebrows quite a bit.

The Reds finished with a home record of 47–30. If you take away the eleven home games played against Philadelphia, the Reds were 37–29 at home, despite being outscored by thirty-one runs. But no one *really* got up in arms because the Reds weren't *that* much better than everyone else. They actually hit more home runs on the road than at home. They won almost as many games on the road (forty-six) as they did at home. And, like the 1951 Giants, the Reds didn't win the World Series against the Yankees. In three Series games played in Cincinnati, the Reds lost 3–2, 7–0, and 13–5.

My Opinion

If the 1961 Cincinnati Reds had defeated the Yankees (the team that went 109–53 and set a Major League record for home runs, led by Mantle and Maris' combined 115) in the World Series, everyone would have made a much bigger deal out of the sign-stealing. As it was, Baseball put out a memo against sign stealing that winter. But of course, the Yankees had Bob Turley stealing signs and Whitey Ford scuffing baseballs, so they could hardly have complained. I do believe that the Reds stole the pennant that year, and there was an agreement among the conspirators not to talk about it in the years afterward. How come Hank Aaron and other stars of his era grumble about modern day home run hitters having unfair advantages, but didn't utter a peep now or then about home run hitters like Frank Robinson (who would later become a league official that oversaw discipline) being tipped off about what pitch would be thrown?

There was a conspiracy in 1961 with the Reds, just as there was a conspiracy in 1951 with the Giants.

In baseball, the offensive team isn't the only one that bends the rules to give themselves a better chance. There are teams throughout history (most notably the Chicago White Sox in the 1950s) that froze their baseballs. This doesn't seem to be practical, as any umpiring crew worth its job would throw out any suspiciously cold ball. The most common way for pitchers to conspire is to throw illegal spitballs—with help from their teammates. Hall of Fame pitcher Whitey Ford used to have his catcher Elston Howard scuff the baseball by scraping it against his belt buckle. Catchers—even if they didn't actively participate in the subterfuge—had to throw the illegally-altered baseballs back to the pitcher, often hiding the evidence from the home-plate umpire.

Pitchers applied Vaseline, K-Y jelly, oily hair tonics, and other slick substances to the balls. Hall of Fame hurler Gaylord Perry did this to great advantage, using gobs of the stuff. Pitchers hid the grease or the Vaseline in several places. They could have hidden it in various cap locations or put some under their thumbnail. They could have hidden the substance in their sideburns, or behind either or both of their earlobes. The hiding places were endless. Some pitchers in the 1980s were caught using emery boards to shave a little off the ball. (If they were caught, well, they could say they just needed the emery board to file their nails!) Two-time American League All-Star Rick Honeycutt even taped a thumbtack to his finger to cut the ball. And the conspiracy in all of this was that the catcher had to know. According to Perry, "I always had a few special signs to let [the catcher] know I was loaded up."

Because of Perry, a 1974 rule gave umpires the latitude to make a judgment call on whether or not a baseball was loaded up with a foreign substance. Really, though, they can make all the rules they want, but there will always be cheaters, and there will always be pitchers who get away with it. Maybe even on the biggest stage in the world.

In the 2006 World Series, Detroit Tigers pitcher Kenny Rogers started the second game. The television cameras noticed that he had a brown spot on his pitching hand in the first inning. Rogers was warned by the home plate umpire to clean up his hand. Was he using something to aid his pitching?

It was a cold night, and a clump of dirt wouldn't necessarily have helped him grip the ball better. But pine-tar, mixed in the clump of dirt, would have. Dirt is part of the playing field, and therefore not technically a foreign substance. Two things make me suspicious. First, Rogers was seen with a similar clump of dirt (in virtually identical spots) in his earlier divisional series start. And Rogers had been one of the worst postseason pitchers in history, allowing twenty earned runs in his twenty postseason innings prior to 2006. Remember, conspiracy theories suggest that dramatic events happen not by accident, but because of other secretive reasons.

But opposing manager Tony LaRussa didn't make a big deal out of Rogers dirty hands, preferring to wash his own of the mess. "A guy pitches like that," LaRussa said, "we as a team don't want to take anything away from him." Yeah, Tony, we wouldn't want to take away anything a cheater does in baseball. This quote was taken from the same man that managed both Jose Canseco and Mark McGwire in their bulked-up, "Bash Brothers" days.

According to rule 8.02(a)(2), (4) and (5), the pitcher shall not:

(2) expectorate on the ball, either hand, or his glove;

(4) apply a foreign substance of any kind to the ball; [or]

(5) deface the ball in any manner.

According to the penalties set forth in the Official Baseball Rules, "For violation of any part of Rules 8.02(a)(2) through (6): (a),the pitcher shall be ejected immediately from the game and shall be suspended automatically for ten games." However, in reading the penalties further, the umpires can decide that the pitcher did not intend by his act to alter the characteristics of a pitched ball. And then it would be up to the umpire's discretion to just warn the pitcher in lieu of applying a harsh penalty.

This is akin to a parent telling a youngster that if he's caught with something bad, he's going to be grounded immediately—unless, of course, there's a big family outing or event, in which case the child will be warned to just cut it out. Rogers was told to wash his hands, and Major League Baseball avoided the embarrassment of having to impose a suspension.

Let me just say one more thing about Kenny Rogers. He didn't pitch again in the 2006 World Series (although he was slated to start if the Series had continued on to another game). On March 30, 2007, it was reported that Rogers would miss the first three months of the season following surgery to repair a blood clot in his pitching shoulder. He made his first appearance of the season on June 22, in the Tigers' 71st game of the season. I have no evidence of a suspension, but the timing of the surgery and the announcement surprises me.

Conclusion:

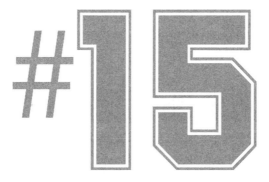

The steroids era in baseball

Labor strife in baseball led to the cancellation of the 1994 postseason, and the beginning of the 1995 season was shortened and scarred as well. In 1996, when Major League Baseball played a full season for the first time since 1993, it was crucial for baseball to win back its fans at a time when too many had adopted a "pox on both their houses" attitude and vowed to stay away.

Here's what happened in that 1996 season that should have sounded alarms and bells and sprung investigations, indignations, and congressional hearings: Major Leaguers began hitting more and longer home runs than ever before. A player named Brady Anderson hit fifty home runs for the Baltimore Orioles. Anderson had played eight previous seasons in the Major Leagues, and had only once hit as many as twenty-one homers. How could this nondescript leadoff batter fashion the only 14 season in Major League history of 50+ home runs, especially coming off a season in which he only slugged sixteen?

There were other home-run hitters who were hitting balls out of the park with a frequency that would have made Mays or Aaron blush. One was Todd Hundley of the New York Mets. Hundley hit forty-one home runs in 1996 (a record, at that time, for catchers), after hitting just fifty in his first six seasons *combined*. Another was Bernard Gilkey, who crawled out from under a rock and hit thirty home runs, in addition to setting the Mets club record for RBI in a season with 117 (up from just sixty-nine the previous year). Then there was Kevin Elster, a previously light-hitting shortstop, who hit twenty-four home runs in one powerful season for Texas after never hitting more than ten in any single Major League campaign.

In 1996, a record 4,962 home runs were hit. The Orioles themselves hit 257, setting a new Major League record. The Rockies hit 247, tying the National League mark set by both the 1947 Giants and the 1956 Reds. Seventeen players hit forty or more home runs in 1996, and forty-three players hit at least thirty. Mark McGwire hit fifty-two, despite missing thirty-two games with injuries.

The fans and the media and the baseball executives struggled to process these numbers. I worked the All-Star Game for NBC that year and drew up many of these numbers and comparisons for Bob Costas, one of the few media members who warned that something was happening, although he didn't know what it was.

I wasn't in the locker rooms, so I didn't see the creatine, the dietary supplement that was being used in vast quantities. I just saw the numbers. Of course, I had covered the 1987 season as the statistician for NBC, working on the Game of the Week, and home runs had exploded in that season as well. But the next season, home runs went down by almost a third. All the stories in 1987 were that the ball was juiced. In 1996 it could have been the ball, but just maybe it was the *players* that were juiced.

One of the changes in baseball that Howard Bryant alluded to in *Juicing the Game: Drugs, Power, and the Fight for the Soul of Major League Baseball* (2005) that may have contributed to the increase in home runs was that batters—even leadoff batters—attacked the plate and were no longer ashamed of striking out.

It was something that I had long noticed, and that has continued to this day. In 1992, thirty-four different Major League players struck out more than 100 times. In 1996, sixty-two players reached the century mark in strikeouts. That figure went up again the next year, as seventy-two players struck out 100 or more in 1997.

Major Leaguers striking out 100+ times in a season

1960: 7
1980: 11
1985: 29
1992: 34
1993: 41
1996: 62
1997: 72
1998: 73
1999: 71
2001: 74
2002: 71

It was a red herring for many people, myself included. Players were playing a different game, closer to "Home Run Derby" than conventional baseball. Everyone went up to the plate trying to hit home runs. Look at the numbers:

For baseball fans in need of a good trivia question, the seven players who struck out more than 100 times in 1960 were Pancho Herrera, Mickey Mantle, Jim Lemon, Eddie Matthews, Frank Howard, Dick Stuart, and Harmon Killebrew. Even the best baseball fans will have trouble remembering Pancho Herrera, who sounds more like a tennis player than baseball player.

Herrera was a first baseman for the Phillies. I can use any benchmark, not just 100 strikeouts in a season. In 1960, only fourteen players struck out as many as ninety times. In 1998, however, there were 104 players that struck out 90+ times. Even accounting for many more Major Leaguers in 1998, you can see my point. There were sixteen Major League teams in 1960, and only fourteen players (not even one per team) struck out ninety or more times. That rate would multiply 3½ times in the late 1990s.

It's not because the pitching has gotten better. If anything, pitching has gotten worse. Pitchers walk more batters, hit more batters, allow more hits, more runs, and more home runs. But they strike out far more batters. Maybe home runs were just hit at a greater rate before because players tried like hell to swing for the fences, which put them on nightly highlight shows and gave them ammunition when seeking new contracts.

Players worked out with weights—used supplements to do extensive weight training, like football players or weightlifters—and baseball became a hit or miss game.

The old-time baseball players didn't look like defensive ends or weightlifters. In fact, they didn't even lift weights. The best home run hitters of all time didn't even weigh 200 pounds. Hank Aaron hit 755 home runs, mostly with his powerful wrists, and never struck out 100 times in a season. Ted Williams hit 521 home runs, and never struck out more than sixty-four times in any year. Mel Ott hit 511 homers, but never struck out seventy times in a season. Willie Mays had exactly one year that he struck out more than 100 times.

So, one reason the players hit more (and longer) home runs was that they built up their bodies with weightlifting and supplements and went up swinging for the fences. They were able to generate greater bat speed. Another reason was little fear or repercussions from strikeouts. The computer-generated statistics—and men like Bill James who were capable of analyzing the numbers—further advocated the end of bunting, sacrificing, and giving up outs to play for a single run.

I was not only a member of the media in 1996, but also a fan. I took my sons to baseball games, and wanted them to become fans, too. They wanted to see home runs. I wanted to see home runs. I remember telling people that the baseball season was twenty-six weeks long. For most of baseball history, a batter would be considered a home run threat if he hit *one home run per week*. Beginning in the mid-1990s, however, the best home run hitters were hitting two or three per week. It was like chocolate: a little was good, a lot was better. We fans ate up the home runs like chocolate, and were supersizing baseball.

Last five full seasons prior to work stoppage (1989–1993)

Players hitting 40+ homers in a season: 12
Players hitting 50+ homers in a season: 1 (Cecil Fielder 50 in 1990)

First five full seasons after work stoppage (1996–2000)

Players hitting 40+ homers in a season: 70
Players hitting 50+ homers in a season: 10

In 1998, four players hit 50+ homers, including Mark McGwire (seventy) and Sammy Sosa (sixty-six). McGwire hit sixty-five the next year, and Sosa hit sixty-three. Oh, and by the way, one player that had continued to play "old-time" baseball was the supremely talented Barry Bonds. Bonds always had low strikeout totals (only once, in his rookie season of 1986, had he struck out more than 100 times). Bonds, according to Mark Fainaru-Wada and Lance Williams' book *Game of Shadows*, saw what was happening around him in 1996, 1997, and especially 1998, when McGwire and Sosa both broke the single-season home run mark. Even when McGwire was found with androstenedione (a stimulant that mimicked a steroid) in his locker, there were no real repercussions. Players were admitting to using creatine, which at the time was not a banned substance. McGwire admitted to "andro." Was that a red herring? What else did he take, that wasn't on display in his locker? Bonds didn't like what he saw, which was less-talented players setting records and gaining admiration. It's funny how everyone turned a blind eye when lower-level players became instantly muscular to make a roster. Although we saw the effects of those players, they got a pass from Baseball, from the media, and from the fans. Superstars who attacked records—like Bonds, beginning in 1998—became a victim of a witch hunt. Bonds became the symbol for steroid cheaters, somehow.

Was there a conspiracy to "see no evil" in baseball in the years prior to 2002, when baseball finally put rules against steroids in writing? My opinion is that there was, but there are reasons that many (including me) looked the other way.

The same rationalizations were given as when, in previous eras, players were tipped off by pitches, such as "they still had to hit the ball." Yes, they still had to hit the ball. Plus, a certain number of pitchers were also juiced. Who knows how many?

In addition, there were other reasons for the increase in home runs. The Marlins and Rockies entered Major League Baseball as expansion teams in 1993, creating openings for twenty pitchers who wouldn't likely have otherwise made a Major League roster. In 1998, baseball expanded again with the addition of the Devil Rays and the Diamondbacks. That's another twenty pitchers to dilute the numbers. In addition, outside of the Marlins, the other three expansion teams played in ballparks that favored hitters (in the Rockies' mile-high altitude case, *greatly* favoring hitters).

Plus, so many other organizations built new ballparks that also favored the hitters. The Texas Rangers played in Arlington Stadium (which favored pitchers) until 1994, when The Ballpark at Arlington was built. The new park favored hitters. The Orioles played in Memorial Stadium (a good pitcher's park) until Camden Yards was built in 1992. Presto, the park caters to batters.

I'm fairly certain that there are other, legal technological advances that have helped batters, including vision-correction eye surgery and the use of videotape. So, I'm still not willing to place too much blame on anabolic steroids for the statistical imbalance in home runs and the baseball record books.

I do not like it that players who played after 1995 like Manny Ramirez, Todd Helton, Mark McGwire, Vladimir Guerrero, Jim Thome, and Larry Walker all have higher slugging percentages than legends like Stan Musial, Mickey Mantle, and Willie Mays.

But yes, everyone looked the other way during the growing steroid scandal. There were pitchers lasting into their forties, seeming not losing any velocity on their fastballs. There were pitchers—plenty of pitchers, as it turned out—that were juiced. And yet, managers said nothing. Major League Baseball did nothing. As Bryant recounted in *Juicing the Game,* "Though no one in baseball had any real education about andro, the Cardinals organization nevertheless released a statement that absolved McGwire of any wrongdoing, a message that was buttressed by Bud Selig."

Did baseball profit too much from the home runs, particularly the 1998 chase by McGwire and Sosa, to investigate the problems that baseball was facing? Did baseball create this mess by failing to act initially, beginning in the late 1980s, when Jose Canseco hardly made a secret of his success?

It was the biggest baseball story in a decade, yet it was mostly swept under the rug for years. It was Jose Canseco, incidentally, who was the chief whistle-blower. His 2005 book, *Juiced: Wild Times, Rampant 'Roids, Smash Hits and how Baseball Got Big,* was dismissed by many in the establishment, but probably will be seen as a valuable historical document decades from now. Canseco said the biggest names in baseball knew of the problem, and that some of the biggest players in the game were steroid users.

This time, it wasn't just a professional league that conspired to hide information. It was all of us. It was the reporters and broadcasters, blindly defending the users, and attacking or ignoring people like Canseco, Ken Caminiti and others. It was the Fantasy players that thrilled to watch the home runs, and all the fans. It was the organizations, which turned a blind eye, and opened their clubhouses to entourages that enabled players to allow individual trainers into locker rooms and team planes.

I can't blame this one on the commissioner. I really can't. There were good, valid reasons for the increases in offense, apart from the steroids. And since the commissioner was hit square in the face with a problem, he has not run from it. He has attacked it, albeit with a delicate balance. Selig has been genuinely troubled by baseball's steroid problem, the one negative in a decade full of growth in the industry. He has won concessions from the players association, and has instituted far tougher policies than most thought possible. And although the cheaters will always manage to stay a step ahead, progress is being made. Baseball's effort to punish those caught using steroids has brought balance back to the game. In 2007, home run levels were below two per game, the lowest levels since 1993.

Conclusion:

Who's keeping Dennis Rodman and Peter Vecsey out of the Basketball Hall of Fame?

Many of the conspiracy theories presented in this book have been talked about—or at least whispered about—for years. Permit me to add my own to the mix which, like most good conspiracy theories, cannot be proven. I believe that there is a conspiracy keeping some worthy men out of the Basketball Hall of Fame.

The election process for the Naismith Basketball Hall of Fame dictates that a player must be fully retired for five years before becoming eligible for enshrinement. But non-players (i.e., coaches and contributors) can be elected at any time. Four screening committees (one for North American players, one for women, one for veterans, and one for international players) review and recommend individuals to be reviewed for enshrinement by the Honors Committee. To advance to the Honors Committee, an individual must have a certain number of yes votes from the Screening Committee (North American players need at least seven of nine). The Screening Committee may put forth as many as ten North American players per year to the Honors Committee.

There are twenty-four people on each of the four Honors Committees. The names of these people are not made public, but we are told they are comprised of Hall of Famers, members of the media, basketball executives, and other contributors to the game. Twelve of the twenty-four people sit on all four committees, and a person needs a minimum of eighteen votes from an Honors Committee to be enshrined.

It's not as difficult as it sounds, as the Hall has enshrined nearly 300 individuals after the induction of the class of 2008. It's also not at all difficult to keep someone out of the Hall, though, especially if personal grudges are taken into account.

So why wasn't Dennis Rodman enshrined as soon as possible, five years after playing his final NBA game in March of 2000? Why wasn't he a even a finalist, for goodness sake? He's one of the greatest defensive players in the history of the game. Does anyone really think he damaged the integrity of the sport?

Judging Rodman strictly as a player, I see this as a no-brainer. Rodman is a Hall of Fame–caliber player, with credentials more worthy than all but a few players. But remember, Rodman is the player who threatened to strip naked on his final exit from the NBA. He kicked photographers, showed up for book signings in a dress, and was suspended multiple times by his teams and by the league. Following his career, he never failed to make the news every few months for various assaults or motorcycle crashes or boating-under-the-influence charges. You can bet there is motive for basketball people to want to keep the Worm out of the Hall of Fame.

Dennis Rodman never played high school basketball, and stood only five feet, eleven inches after his senior year. After graduating high school, he grew seven inches in one year. He played basketball for one semester at Cooke County Junior College, then transferred to Southeastern Oklahoma State University.

Who would have thought that someone with that kind of background would make an impact on the NBA, much less become one of the greatest players to ever play in the league? I'll make the case that Rodman, despite very low scoring totals, is a first-ballot Hall of Famer on paper. I believe he is the greatest defensive forward of all time, and the greatest rebounder of the last thirty-five years. His impact on his teammates and his team's winning percentage speak to his abilities to directly influence the outcomes of games.

Rodman pulled down 11,954 rebounds in his 911 NBA games. In his rookie year, the second-round draft choice played only fifteen minutes per game for the Pistons, averaging just 4.3 rebounds. After that, in his remaining 834 games, he averaged 13.94 rebounds per game. In his final game, on March 7, 2000, Rodman had fifteen rebounds for the Mavericks, playing alongside Dirk Nowitzki and Steve Nash.

In Rodman's era, there are only a handful of players besides him who ever averaged as many as fourteen rebounds in *a single season*, much less over the course of an entire career.

Rodman averaged less than thirty-two minutes per game in his career, meaning he pulled down close to twenty rebounds per forty-eight minutes of NBA action (the length of a complete game). Forget that he didn't play as much as most great players, and wasn't even a full-time player for half his career. He was, by far, the greatest rebounder of his generation. For a twenty-year span beginning in 1987,

Leading Rebounders

1987: Charles Barkley: 14.6 rebounds per game

1990: Hakeem Olajuwon: 14.0 rebounds per game

1992: Kevin Willis: 15.5 per game

2000: Dikembe Mutombo: 14.1 per game

2003: Ben Wallace: 15.4 per game

only two players (Karl Malone and Dikembe Mutombo) pulled down more total rebounds than Dennis. And in an era where no one else could manage to average as many as twelve rebounds per game, Dennis pulled down 13.94.

The players below Rodman on that list all played more minutes per game than he did, and yet all had fewer rebounds per contest. Compare Rodman with all the great rebounders in today's NBA, like Ben Wallace. They all come up short compared to Dennis.

For most of his first four seasons, Dennis came off the bench for Chuck Daly's Pistons. In his first full season as a starter, he finished second to David Robinson in rebounds (1991). For the next seven seasons, Rodman led the NBA in rebounds.

Most Rebounds per game, 1987–2007*

1. 13.9 Dennis Rodman
2. 11.9 Tim Duncan
3. 11.7 Charles Barkley
4. 11.6 Shaquille O'Neal
5. 11.4 Kevin Garnett

Minimum 4,500 rebounds or 400 games

He averaged more than eighteen rebounds per game in a three-year period beginning in 1993. No other NBA player had averaged as many as eighteen rebounds in a game since 1974, when Hall of Famer Elvin Hayes averaged 18.1.

And the Worm did more than just specialize in rebounds. He was also a defensive specialist, adept at guarding players at different positions. He was used at first by Pistons head coach Chuck Daly to play against the opposing team's big guard, small forward, or power forward. In later years, there wasn't a player at any size—including Shaquille O'Neal—that Rodman couldn't guard. In 1990, Rodman was named the NBA Defensive Player of the Year. He won the award the following year as well. Rodman was also voted a First Team All-Defensive forward seven times.

Rodman led the NBA in field goal percentage in 1989, hitting close to 60% of his shots. And in his first four seasons, he hit on more than 57% of his field goal attempts. Not only that, Rodman wasn't the one-dimensional (defense-oriented) player that he became toward the end of his career. He actually had more total points than rebounds after his fourth season in the league.

Beginning with his fifth season, Rodman averaged 6.4 points and 15.9 rebounds per game for the rest of his career. Chuck Daly, who coached Rodman for his first seven years, said that Dennis was a Hall of Fame player in his early Detroit years, and that the Chicago Bulls wouldn't have won their final championship without Dennis' offensive rebounding.

Putting aside both his rebounding excellence and his overall defensive brilliance, Rodman was also a winning player overall. In 1988, the Pistons went 20–4 with Rodman in the starting lineup. In 1989, Rodman was a key contributor to a team that won sixty-three games (the most in the league) and took home the NBA Championship. In 1990, the Pistons were champions again, chiefly because they went 34–9 in the games Rodman started.

In 1993, Detroit finished only 40–42. But they went 36–26 with Dennis in the lineup, and won only four of the twenty-four games they played without him. In the next five seasons, Rodman played on clubs that won fifty-five, sixty-two, seventy-two (a league record), sixty-nine, and sixty-two games. He played on the team with the best record in the NBA four times, in 1995 with the Spurs, and in 1996, 1997, and 1998 with the Bulls.

It wasn't a coincidence. Winning teams followed Dennis Rodman around. Dennis was a great offensive rebounder, averaging close to five offensive rebounds per game. In Dennis' first season with the Spurs in 1994, San Antonio finished first in the league in offensive rebound percentage (pulling down more than 35% of their missed shots), after finishing dead last in that category the year prior.

Rodman got into the head of opposing players, particularly Utah's great power forward Karl Malone. Rodman helped the Bulls defeat Malone's Jazz in both the 1997 and 1998 NBA Finals.

Dennis Rodman did all the dirty work, guarding everyone from Michael Jordan to Karl Malone to Shaquille O'Neal. He created extra possessions and shot attempts for his teammates, while needing few (if any) of his own. He successfully played along-side greats of the game like Isiah Thomas, Joe Dumars, Michael Jordan, Scottie Pippen, David Robinson, Shaquille O'Neal, Kobe Bryant, Dirk Nowitzki, and Steve Nash, helping each of them to elevate their respective games.

EVIDENCE AGAINST A CONSPIRACY

One argument some people make is that Rodman played in only 911 games, about 2/3 the amount most Hall of Famers play. But the real argument is that he played only one side of the court. I counter that by saying that many players were mere offensive weapons and some of those players, like Dominique Wilkins, are in the Hall. Dennis' offensive rebounding more than made up for his lack of scoring.

Detractors will say that Rodman was a specialist and not really a Hall of Fame caliber player, even though a field goal kicker (Jan Stenerud) is in the Pro Football Hall of Fame, and Harmon Killebrew (a great power hitter but a defensive liability at several positions) is in Baseball's Hall. Even for those who say that Dennis was a one-trick pony, you have to agree it was a pretty good trick.

MY OPINION

People remain unsettled and scared of Dennis. I spoke with several team executives who took a pass on answering when I asked if they thought Rodman was worthy of the Hall of Fame. I remain puzzled by the lack of support Rodman must be getting in those closed door meetings. He played the game with a fero-cious intensity, and could frustrate the greatest of players, like Karl Malone. It is my belief that there is a conspiracy, perhaps to spare the league the spectacle that Rodman's enshrinement would bring. Maybe Rodman burned too many bridges, with the wrong executives, media members, and past Hall of Famers who now determine his Hall of Fame fate.

*   *   *   *   *

While I'm thinking about it, there has to be a reason that someone else isn't in basketball's Hall of Fame, too. For more than forty years, reporter Pete Vecsey has covered the NBA with the tenacity that Walt Frazier displayed in guarding Jerry West, or Dennis Johnson in blanketing Andrew Toney. Vecsey, mainly through the New York tabloids (first the *Daily News*, later the *Post*), has brought inside basketball information to the masses through his "Hoop du Jour" column.

Does anyone else see that while Vecsey prepares legal briefs for worthy former players like the late Dennis Johnson to make the Hall of Fame, there has been no one to point out the absurdity of absurdities—Vecsey's own absence from the Hall?

Pete Vecsey belongs in the Hall of Fame as a contributor, just like longtime Laker broadcaster Chick Hearn. Vecsey was born roughly the same year as newest Hall of Famer, Coach Van Chancellor of the LSU Lady Tigers. Which individual has done more to advance the game of basketball? Which person served as the voice, the conscience, and the watchdog of the National Basketball Association for over four decades?

Since 1990, there have been prestigious Curt Gowdy Media Awards presented each year to a print reporter who has made a significant contribution to the game of basketball. I can count exactly four men of the seventeen recipients who belong in the same discussion as Vecsey. Sam Goldaper (*New York Times*), Leonard Lewin (*New York Post*), and Leonard Koppett (*New York Times*) were enshrined in consecutive years beginning in 1992.

Bob Ryan (*Boston Globe*) received the call in 1997. The point is this: Vecsey deserves this Curt Gowdy Media Award, and then some. He deserves to be enshrined.

He's covered everything in basketball from Rucker league tournaments to the ABA to international Olympic competitions to the NBA. He's usually given a complimentary team of editors or producers that allows him to get his information across, but occasionally there were gaps when he did not have that luxury. Remember when Pete took his "Hoop du Jour" column to *USA Today*? Neither does anyone from *USA Today*. Pete without column inches is like having LeBron James on your team and limiting his minutes and shots. What's the point? But in this age of the Internet, Vecsey's columns are now available to everyone. He operates in a much more competitive environment than the one in which he started out. Pete now competes not just against print reporters, but online reporters, national twenty-four-hour NBA television and radio networks, and a steady stream of all-knowing bloggers.

Vecsey has served as a mouthpiece for many, an ardent supporter for some, a vocal critic of others. Say what you will about the acerbic Pete, he doesn't just take on small fries. He'll attack the best players (like Charles Barkley), and is not afraid to bite the hand that feeds him. He's attacked his employers, especially when working for the league's television network or one of its broadcast partners.

Detractors love to claim that Vecsey doesn't get much correct, that he throws a lot against the wall and sometimes something sticks. Yet I defy anyone to show me where he got it wrong regarding a trade or firing. He has broken hundreds of stories through the years. He broke the story that Julius Erving was about to be sold to the 76ers in October of 1976. More than three decades later, he broke the story when Sixers great Allen Iverson demanded a trade and the team decided it was time to move him to Denver.

Although he prides himself on his record of breaking stories, he's at least as well known for his one-liners. Even critics find themselves laughing at his many jabs. In the spirit of full disclosure, I must admit to being a "column castigator," contributing one-liners on occasion. Seeing my lines in his column gives me a sensation probably not unlike a young Woody Allen, who wrote jokes for the great Sid Caeser in the early 1950s.

Vecsey's a tough guy with a set of steel balls, and he's also loyal as hell. He's loyal to his friends and he's loyal to his readers. Not once has he taken one-third of a superstar's book advance to write a "tell-all." Never has he left to join the establishment. In the mid-1990s, he was tempted by some offers to become a general manager, but he never stopped serving hoop fans. Vecsey, a Brooklyn Dodgers fan growing up, didn't even waste his time, or his employers' or his fans', covering other sports.

If he was called by the Hall, it wouldn't be a ceremonial honor given to him because of his years of service. There aren't many guys who can write like Pete. Some days he'll write a stream-of-consciousness column remembering everyone from the 1960s and 1970s and make it come off like poetry to basketball fans. Other times, he might write about spending a few days in Phoenix with a dying Cotton Fitzsimmons. He has a "six degrees of separation" connection with just about everyone vital in the history of the NBA. Lewin and Goldaper and Koppett have all passed away. Pete is the elder statesman of the league. He knew all the playground legends and corporate movers and shakers who made basketball what it is. And not only did he know them, but through his columns, he allowed all of us to know them as well.

MY OPINION

At first thought, Vecsey is the victim of a New York bias. But there have been three aforementioned New York print media members to win with the Curt Gowdy award. My second thought is that Vecsey has attacked (in print) some of the most influential members of the Basketball Hall of Fame. It's hard to say whether there is a conspiracy or just an abject loathing of the man. People fear both Rodman and Vecsey, for different reasons. But that shouldn't keep them from being enshrined with peers they far outclassed each and every day of their professional lives.

The Hall of Fame has to change its election process. In a league where several of the top officials have been suspended for having grudges against particular players, the voters have to be made public. This would make them accountable. Until that happens, voters can lurk in the shadows and conspire to keep worthy candidates out of the Hall of Fame.

CONCLUSION:

Funny business at the Kentucky Derby

One of the biggest sporting events in the world is the annual "Run for the Roses" at Churchill Downs Racetrack, otherwise known as the Kentucky Derby. Whenever there is a sporting event of that magnitude, especially in a sport where people are encouraged to gamble, there is always a chance of someone conspiring to fix the outcome of the event.

Here's a little background on the Kentucky Derby's prominence in the early 1920s. According to the *Thoroughbred Times Racing Almanac*, the years 1913–1915 would establish the Derby's credentials from both a romantic and qualitative standpoint. In 1915, New York owner Harry Payne Whitney shipped his unbeaten filly, Regret, to Louisville, where she became the first filly to win the Derby. While some Eastern stables still shied away from shipping their horses west for the Derby—most notably Samuel Riddle's decision not to run Man O' War in 1920—the Derby's reputation was set after 1915. In 1919, Sir Barton won the Derby, although it wasn't yet referred to as "The Triple Crown."

It's safe to say that by 1921, only baseball and boxing held the same grip on the American sporting public as the Kentucky Derby. In 1921, the betting favorite for the Kentucky Derby was a Harry Payne Whitney filly named Prudery. Prudery actually went off at odds of 1.1–1. But Colonel Edward Riley Bradley had other ideas, and other horses with which to defeat Prudery. He owned a fine three-year-old horse named Black Servant—a horrible name for a horse, considering it was in the South just fifty years after the Civil War—that was one of the favorites to win the Derby. Bradley planned to enter a second horse, Behave Yourself, and with proper instructions to the jockeys, Black Servant would win. A week earlier in the Blue Grass Stakes, Black Servant beat Behave Yourself and three other horses that would race in the Derby.

Bradley wagered $250,000 on Black Servant to win. The first place purse that year was only $38,000, and a quarter-million dollars was a huge amount of money in those days. The grooms and stable hands were in on the plan, and wagered their own money as well. Bradley didn't make the bet all at once, which would cause suspicion, instead, he spread his $250,000 out all over the winter books.

Bradley hired Charlie Thompson to ride Behave Yourself. Before the race started, Thompson was given strict instructions by the owner and trainer H.J. "Dick" Thompson (no relation). The riding orders to the jockey were relatively simple. He was ordered to come out fast, grab the lead, and set an early pace for Black Servant. He was told that he could win *only if it looked like Black Servant couldn't*. Otherwise, if Black Servant were out in front, or coming up from behind, he was told to let Black Servant get out on top.

At the mile mark, Black Servant took the lead and was out in front of the pack hitting the stretch. At that point, in sixth place, Charlie Thompson proceeded to gain ground, and with only 150 yards to go, he had Behave Yourself in second place. The owners and co-conspirators had to be dancing, with the biggest race and even bigger bets about to be won in a matter of seconds. After all, it was assumed that Thompson would stay back with Behave Yourself and let Black Servant win.

Here's a little clue about fixing races: It's easier when everyone in on the fix is a human being. It was widely reported at the time that Thompson tried to reign his horse in, but the horse didn't cooperate. If Strangler Lewis, the most well-known wrestler of the time, had been the jockey, he would not have been able to reign in Behave Yourself, who sprinted to a first-place finish.

EVIDENCE TO SUPPORT A CONSPIRACY

Some say Charlie Thompson had a bet in on Behave Yourself, with everyone else betting down the favorite filly, Prudery, or the owner's favorite, Black Servant. Others say the jockey might not have been cut in for any (or enough) of the winning payoff if stablemate Black Servant had won. Still others think that maybe someone else got to him.

It could have been that Thompson simply forgot the instructions. (Unlikely, as the big bet was probably laid out for him, as well as what might happen to him if he didn't follow orders.) In Pamela K. Brodowsky and Tom Philbin's *Two Minutes to Glory: The Official History of the Kentucky Derby*, there is yet another explanation.

> Then it happened; a spectator skimmed his hat near Black Servant's head (in the final seconds of the race), and for just a heartbeat the colt pricked up his ears and lost stride. Thompson grabbed the moment and drove by Black Servant. . . . Black Servant's jockey, Lucien Lyke, knew that Thompson wanted to win the race, but he wasn't supposed to. He screamed above the thundering hoofbeats, "Take back, you son of a bitch!"

In the end, by a head, Behave Yourself won the race over Black Servant in 2:04 1/5. The horse couldn't behave, I guess, any better than Thompson (who, for all we know, had a bet down on his own horse). Even though Bradley had the Derby winner, he could hardly be consoled. The $250,000 bet to win the race was lost, and he had virtually nothing down on the winning horse. The winning jockey was promptly fired, and was bluntly informed that, for disobeying orders, Colonel Bradley would see to it that no other horse owner in Kentucky would ever hire him again. Of the twelve jockeys entered in the 1921 Derby, only two never mounted another horse in any subsequent Derbys. One was George King, who finished tenth. The other was Charles Thompson, who won his only Kentucky Derby start.

When Charlie Thompson returned to his dressing room after his triumph, the grooms and stable hands that had wagered and lost their money beat him up mercilessly. Bradowsky and Phillips wrote that Bradley (who reputedly carried a derringer in his coat) looked for Thompson, but fortunately didn't find him.

★   ★   ★   ★   ★

1957: Sit Down, You're Rocking the Derby!

Another controversial Kentucky Derby took place in 1957. Legendary jockey Bill Shoemaker was riding Gallant Man, and just after the last turn, Shoemaker moved his horse up from third place and passed 8–1 long shot Iron Liege to take the lead in the stretch. At the sixteenth pole, Shoemaker apparently thought he was at the finish and suddenly stood up in the stirrups. Realizing his error, he immediately sat down again, but the mistake slowed Gallant Man down enough to lose the race, along with the nearly $108,000 purse.

Jockey Bill Hartack won his first of five Kentucky Derbies aboard Iron Liege, and Shoemaker would end his career with only four. It was, without a doubt, the most controversial of Shoemaker's twenty-six Derby starts.

Just before the 1957 Derby, the owner of Gallant Man, Ralph Lowe, had a nightmare. He dreamed that his colt had the race won in the stretch when suddenly his jockey misjudged the finish line, rose up out of his saddle prematurely, and lost the race. Did Lowe suggest to his superstar jockey that his dream should become a reality?

Stewards at Churchill Downs suspended Shoemaker for fifteen days for misjudging the finish line. The suspension also prevented Shoemaker from riding the horse in the Preakness. When he learned of the suspension, Shoemaker said "They think they're doing the right thing, so I guess there's little I can say about it. I just made a stupid mistake in judgment—and that's it." He went on to say that he realized his mistake as soon as he stood up, and silently cursed himself. "Then I laid the whip to Gallant Man again, but it was too late. . . . The change in my position caused him to hesitate momentarily—just enough that we dropped from a nose to a head behind. He didn't break stride, though."

He also commented, "I've never done anything like that before." However, it was reported by the UPI that "western turf writers recalled that a year ago in the $100,000 Californian race at Hollywood Park, Shoemaker eased up on Swaps in the stretch and allowed Porterhouse to zoom by to win the race. There he didn't misjudge the finish line, but merely thought he had a safe margin in the stretch and stopped driving." Shoemaker's miscalculation of the finish line cost him 10% of the purse (over $10,000). Conspiracy theorists would note that that was not a huge amount of money in 1957.

CONCLUSION:

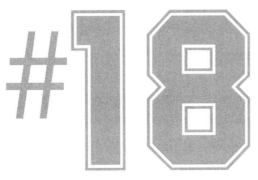

Why weren't any Japanese players signed to major league contracts from 1965–1995?

In July of 2007, the Boston Red Sox announced a deal with the Chiba Lotte Marines of Nippon Professional Baseball, in the areas of scouting and baseball development. I wrote to Jim Small, a Vice President for Major League Baseball, to ask him about this latest deal. He emailed that "the Red Sox/Chiba deal is identical to the other agreements that currently exist (Yomiuri Giants/Yankees, Nippon Ham Fighters/Diamondbacks, etc.) They can share baseball information and development ideas." Let's just say there is a real spirit of cooperation that exists now.

In the 2007 All-Star Game, Ichiro Suzuki represented the Mariners for a seventh time and stole the spotlight, winning the MVP award. It doesn't seem possible that not too long ago there was a conspiracy that kept Japanese players from playing in the Major Leagues.

The success Ichiro—as well as others like Hideo Nomo and Hideki Matsui—has had in the Major Leagues has opened the door for many other Japanese ballplayers to come to the United States to play in the world's top baseball league. Signed as a free agent by the Los Angeles Dodgers in 1995, Nomo became the Jackie Robinson of Japanese players, breaking a barrier that had existed for decades. Did he shatter the myth that the Japanese players weren't as good as their peers from the States? You bet he did, starting the All-Star Game in his rookie MLB season (1995), and pitching no-hitters in both the American and National Leagues before his career was through.

Nomo's success was miniscule compared to that of the Mariners' Ichiro Suzuki. Ichiro spent eight years in Japan playing for the Orix BlueWave, his team in the Nippon Professional Baseball League. He won seven Japanese batting titles before his owner let him follow his dream and come to the states. Ichiro has been playing at a Hall of Fame level for the Seattle Mariners ever since. In 2001, his first year in the states, Ichiro led Seattle to 116 wins while batting .350, stealing fifty-six bases, and becoming a worldwide superstar. That year he became only the second player in Major League history to win the Rookie of the Year Award and the Most Valuable Player (MVP) award in the same season, following Fred Lynn's magical 1975 season with Boston.

Matsui has not become the elite superstar that he was in Japan, but instead a valued and trusted star with the New York Yankees. Matsui, a former number one draft pick by the Yomiuri Giants in 1993, spent ten years with the Giants, hitting fifty home runs in 2002, his last year in Japan. Matsui hit only 112 home runs in his first six Major League seasons, but has a batting average of .295 with the Yankees, not far off from his earlier days in Japan. He's also got a .302 batting average in the postseason.

On opening day of the 2007 season, there were eighteen players on Major League rosters born in Asia, including twelve players born in Japan, one being Boston's right-handed pitcher Daisuke Matsuzaka. He'll make more than $52 million in a six-year deal, and that's not including what the Red Sox had to spent ($51.1

million in a sealed bid) in the posting system for the exclusive right to negotiate with him.

There have been other hits (and some misses) with the Japanese players that have made the long flight to the United States to play in the Major Leagues. With enough evidence in after more than thirty Japanese-born players have made league rosters since 1995, we still have to ask the question and look for conspirators. Why were there no Japanese players in the Major Leagues in the 1970s, 1980s, and half of the 1990s?

For that, we have to give some background and answer the question in several parts. First, why where there no Japanese players in the majors prior to 1960? Second, why were there no Japanese players outside of Masanori Murakami in the mid-1960s? And third, why did it take more than thirty years after Murakami for the next Japanese player to come to the States and play in the Majors? Incidentally, I compared Nomo (and not Masanori Murakami) to Jackie Robinson because their immediate success paved the way for others in their race to make the Major Leagues. Nomo (and Jackie Robinson) weren't the first ever but the first in decades, as there were African Americans playing in the Majors almost sixty years before Robinson.

Let's look at the first question about what took so long. According to Robert Whiting's 2004 *The Samurai Way of Baseball: The Impact of Ichiro and the New Wave From Japan*,

> By the time the first professional league in Japan had been established in 1936, amateur baseball had a solid grip on the Japanese public. A team of Major Leaguers from the States first toured Japan in 1908. Other tours followed, including one in 1934 that Babe Ruth played in. The team of Americans won all of its sixteen games against a team of former college players, semi-professionals, and high-school players.

It would take years for Japanese players to compete with the Major Leaguers. As late as 1955, when the Yankees made a tour of Japan following their World Series loss to Brooklyn, the team from the United States won every game. Even if a Japanese player had wanted to overcome the language barrier and the increased caliber of competition, there would have been problems with the Japanese players locked into their own reserve clauses.

In 1961, the Tokyo Giants began training in Vero Beach, Florida, the spring training home of the Dodgers. The Tokyo team had a young third baseman, Shigeo Nagashima, that piqued the interest of Dodgers owner Walter O'Malley. Matsutaro Shoriki, the owner of the Giants, had grand illusions of his team soon battling a Major League team in a true *World* Series, and turned down O'Malley's advances. Nagashima and Sadaharu Oh, the Japanese home run king, formed the most lethal one-two punch in Japanese baseball history. There was no way that the Giants would have let either of them go.

Hundreds of American players had played in Japan, both before and after World War II. In the early 1960s, Japan became a lucrative market for aging Major Leaguers no longer in demand for their Major League teams. However, traffic the other way was nonexistent, thanks to a combination of NPB contractual restrictions and cultural barriers. The stars had to align for a Japanese player to finally be allowed to wear a Major League uniform. The year it happened was 1964, and the player's name was Masanori Murakami.

Murakami was a very young left-handed pitcher who pitched in the Minor League system of the Nankai Hawks of the Japanese Pacific League. In 1964, the twenty-year-old Minor Leaguer was sent to America, along with two other young players, to spend the season in the lower Minor Leagues of the San Francisco Giants. It was like an exchange program. He was part of a player exchange agreement, approved by both the American and Japanese baseball commissioners. The Giants organization anticipated that one day they might be able to send players from their minor league farm system to train in Japan, and inserted a standard option clause in the agreement which allowed San Francisco to purchase the contract of any of the Japanese players who made the parent team for only $10,000. The Hawks signed off on this clause, figuring that the odds that any of their players would ever advance out of the Minor Leagues was virtually unthinkable. The three players that the Japanese Hawks were sending over couldn't even make the Hawks.

But Murakami pitched extraordinarily well in the Minors and was needed by the Giants in a September call-up. On September 1, 1964, he became the first Japanese player to play in the Major Leagues. And this guy wasn't just a curious footnote. He was a real pitcher. Murakami pitched fifteen innings that September, and gave up only two earned runs. The Giants moved quickly to send him a 1965 contract, and Murakami was happy to sign it.

Murakami changed his mind, however, and signed a contract to remain in Japan for the 1965 season. The Giants' owner, Horace Stoneham, complained to the commissioner of baseball, Ford Frick. Stoneham, and every other Major League Baseball owner, believed in the reserve clause. Every player that had a contract for one season was "property" of that team for the next season. How dare a player have a choice in what team to play (even if one team was in Japan and another in San Francisco)?

Frick wrote a letter to Japanese Commissioner Yushi Uchimura demanding the Hawks send Murakami back to San Francisco for the 1965 season. The next step in the controversy was the reply of Uchimora. Ford said that in the best interests of U.S.–Japanese baseball relations, the Hawks should live up to their agreement and send Murakami back to the Giants.

Nankai saw it differently. They explained that they had rented Murakami to San Francisco for the year. That's how on February

17, 1965, Frick suspended baseball relations between the Japan and the United States. He told the Pirates to suspend their off-season goodwill tour. On March 17, Uchimura came up with a counterproposal—a compromise with Frick whereby Murakami would return to San Francisco for 1965, but would come home to stay for good in 1966. Frick declined the offer, averring that Murakami's return to Japan in 1966 would still constitute a violation of the reserve clause.

On April 28, the Giants caved in. It was reported that Giants vice-president Chub Feeney had an iron-clad agreement with Nankai showing that the Hawks had released Murakami to San Francisco. But Feeney capitulated slightly, allowing Murakami to choose for himself where he wanted to play in 1966. This was followed by an international crisis of sorts, which was settled by the baseball commissioners of both nations. Frick ruled that Murakami still had to play with San Francisco in 1965, but could return to Japan in 1966 if he wished. The Hawks returned the $10,000 to the Giants, and Murakami flew to San Francisco to play the remainder of the 1965 season.

There would be unconfirmed reports that the U.S. State Department had intervened at the behest of the Japanese government and asked MLB to back off, supposedly because it needed the support of the Japanese government on the Vietnam War.

Murakami pitched very well (4–1, six saves), and the Giants offered him a contract for 1966. He was their top left-handed reliever. In the end, he decided to stay home, signing a deal with the Hawks for less money. He was not, however, treated like a conquering hero in 1966, back in his native country. Whenever he failed to do well, fans taunted him with cries of "Go back to America!" The Hawks converted him into a starting pitcher and discouraged him from intimidating hitters with his brush-back pitch, which had been so effective in the States. The sports pages of Japan wrote that the players wondered how he was ever good enough to pitch for the San Francisco Giants.

Obviously, by the mid-1960s, Murakami wasn't the only Japanese professional player capable of gracing Major League rosters. Why, then, were there no Japanese players in the Major Leagues after 1965? Surely everyone knew that the talent gap was closing.

After the 1965 season, the Los Angeles Dodgers made a trip to Japan and won only nine of their seventeen games. It was estimated at the time that there were maybe twenty-five players in the NPB that could play in the U.S. Majors, mostly pitchers.

One of the players who would have surely been a star in the U.S. was pitcher Masaichi Kaneda, perhaps the best pitcher in the history of the NPB. The stars could have easily aligned for Kaneda to come to the States, as both the San Francisco Giants and New York Yankees were very interested in him. After the 1966 season, Kaneda was coming off a twenty-seven-win campaign, and was released from his contract with the lowly Yakult Swallows. The second-division team couldn't afford him anymore, and the pitcher finally had an opportunity to go someplace where he could win. But Masaichi was hesitant to come to the U.S. because of the language barrier. He also wanted to set career pitching marks in Japan. (He would finish his career in 1969, after piling up 400 wins.) Even more important, Masaichi was being paid 15,000,000 yen at the time, which worked out to about $125,000 plus living expenses. No Major League team was going to pay a Japanese player as much as Willie Mays. It would have been unthinkable.

Was there a conspiracy to keep Japanese players out of America? As a result of the trans-Pacific tiff over Murakami, the U.S. and Japanese commissioners had signed something called the United States–Japanese Player Contract Agreement, informally known as the "Working Agreement," in which both sides pledged to respect each other's baseball conventions.

American baseball players won the right to play out their contracts and sign with any team of their choosing by 1975. The reserve clause, however, still existed in Japan. The Japanese players union was much less effective and vocal than their American counterparts. It wasn't until 1985 that they managed to obtain the "right" to strike. Free agency finally found Japanese ballplayers in 1993, and then only because the owner of the Tokyo Giants wanted to sign all the superstars to his team. Other owners finally caved on free agency, but it was very different than what the U.S. was used to. Players could only become free agents in Japan after ten full years of service on the parent team, and that didn't include time spent in the Minor Leagues. It wasn't until after the 1997 season that free agency eligibility was lowered to nine years.

Years went by, and then decades. All the time, however, the Japanese players were quickly closing the talent gap. In 1990, a Japanese All-Star squad swept the first four games of a seven-game series against a visiting team of American stars that included Cal Ripken, Jr. and Randy Johnson. Hideo Nomo pitched in this series, as well as he had in the 1988 Summer Olympics in Seoul, when he led Japan to a silver medal.

Nomo was the best pitcher in Japan in the early 1990s. An agent named Don Nomura helped get Nomo to the States while he was still young and healthly. Nomura took Nomo's Japanese contract to powerful U.S. agent Arn Tellem, who found a loophole with the "voluntarily retirement" clause: a voluntarily retired player was obligated to return to his former team only as long as he stayed in Japan. Nomo, calculatingly, asked for much more money in his contract negotiations than he could have expected to receive. Knowing he wouldn't get a close counter-offer, he then voluntarily retired (he said it was to pursue other areas outside of baseball). Nomo was the first to find this loophole, and sprang free of his contract, headed for the Major Leagues.

Who were the conspirators that caused three decades to pass between Japanese Major Leaguers? One party was the Japanese media, who made it hard on Murakami and who would later call Nomo an ingrate. (Interestingly, Murakami was a member of the Japanese media, and a strong critic of Nomo.) Other conspirators included the commissioners of the Major Leagues and the Japanese Leagues. And then, there were the Japanese players themselves. Sadaharu Oh said, "In my era, if I had tried to go the States to play, the public [in Japan] would have turned overwhelmingly against me."

According to Whiting's book, "Some published reports speculate that there was a de facto ban in place. The U.S. needed Japan's cooperation in matters relating to defense. Assuming the government played no part, why was there no scouting by the owners? Why was there an idea that the Japanese players weren't good enough to play in the Majors?"

In December of 1998, a new agreement was forged between the commissioners of MLB and Nippon Professional Baseball called the Posting System. Players in Japan could become free agents after nine years with their club, and Japanese clubs could "post" a player a year or two before free agency, to get something for the player (rather than lose him to the Major Leagues as a free agent). This aided the Japanese owners, because U.S. teams that wanted to sign Japanese players had to pay for them twice, once to the team that owned the player's rights and once to the player himself. There had to be a system in place that kept the game competitive in Japan and in other Asian countries.

My Opinion

There has to be some sort of conspiracy that keeps good Japanese high school players from signing with Major League teams rather than Japanese teams. "I've been trying for ten or twelve years," agent Don Nomura told *USA Today* on March 29, 2007. "But it's such a strong cultural thing. I've gone to college and high school coaches, I've gone to the parents, I've gone to the kids. So far, no go."

There must be more than cultural barriers. There must be intense pressures on Japanese families to keep the Japanese Leagues competitive. There is obviously no de facto ban or pressure from the United States to keep Japanese youngsters from signing. As you can see from the following lists, it isn't just Japanese pitchers, and it isn't just superstars that are making the move to the United States and Major League Baseball. That's why the de facto ban on Japanese players for thirty years—that wasn't widely talked about—remains one of the more intriguing conspiracy theories in sports.

Japanese-Born Ballplayers on Major League Baseball Rosters on Opening Day, 2009:

Kosuke Fukudome	Akinori Iwamura
Kenji Johjima	Kenshin Kawakami
Masahide Kobayashi	Hiroki Kuroda
Hideki Matsui	Kazuo Matsui
Ichiro Suzuki	Daisuke Matsuzaka
Hideki Okajima	Takashi Saito
Koji Uehara	Keiichi Yabu
Yasuhiko Yabuta	

CONCLUSION:

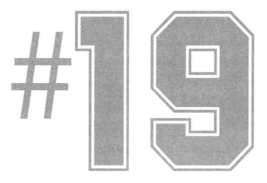

Attempts to keep minorities from breaking cherished baseball records

Here's the thing about sports records that inspire and capture the imagination of the public: Most people don't want to see those marks broken. If they must be broken, people want them to be broken after a suitable amount of time by a suitable hero. It is perfectly acceptable in 2007 or later for a true superstar like Peyton Manning or Brett Favre to break longstanding records held by Dan Marino, for example. The late Dick Schaap once wrote that, regarding the chase on Babe Ruth's home run record, most fans rooted like this: 1) for Ruth, 2) for Mickey Mantle, and 3) for Roger Maris. Maris was not a beloved player, and not seen as a worthy successor to the great Ruth, who had set his mark of sixty home runs in 1927.

Maris was under tremendous pressure in 1961, and found out the hard way that it's not easy to break a legend's record. Not only did he have to overcome the memory and mystique of Babe Ruth, but had to put up with being hounded by the press and jeered by fans who didn't want him to erase Ruth's name from the record books. Even the commissioner, Ford Frick, downplayed Maris' accomplishments, citing how, though Maris eventually toppled Ruth's mark, he did it in a slightly longer season.

The challenge that Hank Aaron faced in breaking Ruth's career record for home runs was harder than the one that Maris faced. Aaron faced the same annoyances that Maris had faced, but also had to deal with racism. It is well known that Aaron faced death threats by fans who didn't want him to break the record simply because of the color of his skin.

Aaron, thankfully, overcame the obstacles and broke Ruth's record of 714 home runs. However, there are several times in history where there were conspiracies to keep other players from breaking records held by cherished players. The most famous was the instance when a Jewish Major Leaguer, Hank Greenberg, challenged Ruth's single-season home run record in 1938. There are many conspiracy theorists who believe that there were those in Major League Baseball—including Commissioner Landis—that did not want to see Ruth's record broken by a Jew, and conspired to see to it that it wouldn't be.

In the days when the Detroit Tigers were the main challengers to the Yankee dynasty, native New Yorker Greenberg's star shone brightest. Because Hank lost five years of his career to military service, he finished his career with just over 5,000 at-bats. That's about one-half of the at-bats that most legendary batters reach. How good a player was he? In the sixty-year stretch beginning in 1933, only one player—the great Ted Williams—had a higher slugging percentage than Greenberg.

Greenberg was only sixteen years old when Babe Ruth hit his record sixty homers in 1927. Greenberg was of course aware of the Yankees, and in short order they became aware of him. But the Yankees also had a first baseman named Lou Gehrig. The Yanks offered Greenberg a contract, but Greenberg didn't think it was smart to sign with a team that already had a star first baseman. Other teams coveted Hank and he decided to sign with Detroit, which agreed to wait until he had completed college and to pay for his tuition.

The slugger lasted just one year at New York University, unable to resist the craving to test himself in the Majors. The Tigers brought him up from the Minors in 1933. In his rookie season, he played in just 116 games, and drove in eighty-seven runs. In 1934, Greenberg batted .339, with twenty-six homers, 139 RBI, and a League-leading sixty-three doubles. He led the Tigers to the American League pennant that year, although the Tigers lost the World Series to the Cardinals.

Greenberg's career began during the Depression, and he had to face a torrent of anti-Semitic behavior from those in and out of baseball. In Lawrence Ritter's 1966 classic of sports literature *The Glory of Their Times*, Greenberg said that when he was in the Minor Leagues, he was probably the first Jew many people in some southern towns had ever seen. "They seemed surprised I didn't have horns and a long beard," he was quoted as saying. In the 1934 World Series, it was reported that St. Louis shortstop Leo Durocher shouted to Cardinals pitcher Dizzy Dean, "Don't waste your fastball. Throw the son of a bitch a ham sandwich!"

Several weeks earlier, Greenberg (who had been raised in an observant Jewish household) made big news in the September pennant race by playing—and belting a pair of home runs—on the Jewish high holiday of Rosh Hashanah. But Greenberg made even bigger news the next week, when he sat out against the Yankees to observe Yom Kippur as his father ordered.

In 1935, Greenberg had a truly great season. He drove home 170 runs, fifty-one more than his closest competitor, Lou Gehrig. (If you're *really* into conspiracy theories, you could point to the fact that Greenberg—the MVP of that 1935 season—didn't even make the All-Star team, despite having 110 RBI at the All-Star break! However, let me point out the two established first baseman that made the team ahead of Greenberg. Gehrig finished second in the League to Hank Greenberg in RBI in 1935, and third in homers. Gehrig batted .329 and walked a League-leading 132 times. And Jimmie Foxx batted .346, was third in the American League in RBI behind Greenberg and Gehrig, and had a .636 slugging percentage.

Greenberg's Tigers again made the World Series in 1935, this time facing the Chicago Cubs. The Cubs were no angels, having famously tormented the aging Ruth in the 1932 World Series. Ruth's biographer, Robert Creamer, told me in 2003, while researching another book, "In 1932, the Cubs were calling Ruth the n-word from the bench. The Yankees weren't much better. They would heckle Cubs pitcher Guy Bush, who had a dark complexion and curly hair, and say that he looked black himself. The anti-black prejudice was just so strong in America then, it's hard to imagine the inferior place in society black people occupied." Some people speculate that Ruth's "called" shot in the 1932 World Series was his way to get back at the Chicago players for taunting him constantly.

African Americans weren't the only ones with an inferior place in society in the mid-1930s. According to Eldon Ham's *Larceny and Old Leather: The Mischievous Legacy of Major League Baseball*, Greenberg was "an immediate lightning rod for storms of ethnic insults poring out not only from subversive hate groups or even from the fans [of] that day, but directly from the Cubs' bench." Greenberg's memoirs, and many other sources, say the Cubs players screamed "Christ Killer!" and "Jew Bastard!" at Greenberg. The home plate umpire, George Moriarity, threatened to kick at least five Cubs out of a Series game, led by their manager Charlie Grimm, if he heard any more profanity.

Ham's 2005 book details how "Commissioner Landis was appalled too—but apparently in a different way: Landis fined the umpire." Landis also fined some of the Cubs, but according to Ham, "whether doing so reflected real outrage or was just a sham to hide his true feelings is irrelevant. The fining of an umpire who not only maintained order and avoided an ugly escalation, but admirably defended the integrity of the game, speaks volumes for itself regardless of any feigned mitigation or obfuscation by the bigoted Landis."

Greenberg broke his wrist late in that 1935 World Series, which the Tigers would go on to win. In 1936, Greenberg broke his wrist for a second time in an on-field collision. In 1937, a fully-recovered Greenberg drove in 183 runs—the third most of all time, and a number that no one has topped in seven decades. Yet that year, he didn't win the MVP. Despite the Yankees winning the pennant, Greenberg's Detroit teammate, Charlie Gehringer, won the MVP. Gehringer led the League in batting with a .371 average, helping to set the table for the slugging first baseman.

It wasn't a good season for the Tigers in 1938, as they slid to fourth place. However, Greenberg challenged the most admired record in sports then and now: He went after Babe Ruth. It was like tugging on Superman's cape.

Like most sluggers, Greenberg had hot streaks. He had eleven multiple home-run games in 1938. On September 27, he hit a pair, giving him fifty-eight home runs with five games remaining in the season, the last three to be played in Cleveland.

In one of the five games, Greenberg was walked four times. In another, Cleveland's Bob Feller set a strikeout record (since broken), striking out eighteen Tigers (including Greenberg twice). The final game of the season was called on account of darkness in the sixth inning. The Feller performance notwithstanding, one thing is clear regarding those five games: Greenberg did not see many hittable pitches.

EVIDENCE TO SUPPORT A CONSPIRACY

The Indians played their home games in two stadiums: League Park, a small, relatively hitter-friendly park, as well as Municipal

Stadium, where center field was 470 feet from home plate. All of a sudden, there was a change in the venue for the final two games in Cleveland, and the final two games were rescheduled to be played in the bigger ballpark. In other words, if Hank were to break the record, he would really have to earn it—really earn it in cavernous Muncipal Stadium. Not only that, but there were pitchers who would not pitch to him. They would not allow the Jewish Greenberg to break Ruth's record.

One has to understand what was going on in the world in 1938. For one thing, *Time* magazine named Adolph Hitler its Man of the Year because he was the most influential man in the world, which was hard to dispute. In 1938, he led Nazi troops to their occupation of Austria. In November, Nazi troops and sympathizers looted and burned thousands of Jewish businesses in numerous German cities in what would be called *Kristallnacht* (Night of Broken Glass). Less than a year later, Germany would invade Poland, sending Europe into war. There *was* a growing anti-Semitism in the United States, some of it fueled by the preparation of U.S. armed forces to resist Hitler.

In Ritter's *The Glory of Their Times* (1966), Greenberg told him, "Some people still have it fixed in their minds that the reason I didn't break Ruth's record was because I'm Jewish, [that] the ballplayers did everything they could to stop me. That's pure baloney. . . . The reason I didn't hit sixty or sixty-one homers is because I ran out of gas; it had nothing at all to do with being Jewish."

While it is true that some teams down the stretch had pitchers who wouldn't give Greenberg anything good to hit, the Cleveland Indians pitchers that walked him did so because it was the strategic thing to do, as the Indians and Tigers were fighting for third place money. It is commonplace now to walk a Barry Bonds–type hitter, but it was less common then. Most hitters were challenged. Still, it made sense then and now to walk Greenberg repeatedly.

Historians who don't believe in the conspiracy against Greenberg also have an answer to why the American League decided to play the additional games at the giant Municipal Stadium: The move simply allowed many more fans to see the great slugger go for the record.

My Opinion

The argument that the Indians were battling the Tigers for third-place and therefore didn't want to let Greenberg beat them with a home run is ludicrous. I checked the standings on September 26, 1938. The Yankees were entrenched in first place, and the Red Sox were firmly in second. Cleveland had a record of 83–63 and Detroit had a record of 78–69, which means the Indians had a 5½ game lead on the Tigers, with a week left to play. Detroit won five of its last six games, and finished three games behind the Indians. It's a nice rationale, the third-place money argument, but it doesn't jive.

As for the game being moved from League Park, the Indians played the entire season at Municipal Stadium in 1933, after which the Indians returned to League Park—playing only occasionally at the Stadium. It wasn't until 1947 that the Indians began to play all of their games at Municipal Stadium. It is possible that they moved their games to a bigger venue to maximize attendance, but I'm not sold on that. Teams averaged one doubleheader per week in those days, rather than squeezing out every last dollar by playing as many dates as possible. Organizations had to be cognizant of the Depression-era economics. If the Indians were concerned about gate receipts, they would have played every game at League Park, rather than moving a season-ending double-header to Municipal Stadium.

In the final two games of the season, a doubleheader in Cleveland's huge stadium, Greenberg had a 420-foot hit in the first game that didn't even reach the fences. In the second game, with the shadows coming across the infield, the game was called after seven innings. It was called by home plate umpire Moriarity, who apologized to Greenberg, saying that he had gone as long as he could go. (In the off-season, the Indians apparently put in lights. The first night game at Cleveland Stadium was held on June 27, 1939.)

Oh, and by the way, Greenberg had two ground-rule doubles in 1938, resulting from the batted ball hitting a screen in Tigers Stadium that wasn't there in 1927. Both would have been home runs in Ruth's day.

Greenberg was the first Jewish Major League player to win an MVP award, and the only one to win the MVP twice (1935 and 1940). He also was the first Jew to be elected to Baseball's Hall of Fame, and the first Jewish owner/general manager of a Major League ballclub (of the Indians, ironically).

More importantly, Greenberg's baseball prime was interrupted by World War II, when, at thirty years old, he was the first baseball star to enlist in the Armed Forces. He spent 4½ years serving his country, coming out of the service just in time to hit a pennant-clinching home run for the Tigers in 1945.

Greenberg was just the sort of charismatic and clutch superstar to have deservedly held the single-season home run record. Was his home run record stolen by anti-Semitic pitchers and a baseball commissioner who didn't want it broken? Greenberg never claimed any collusion in the years that followed, but I'm not so sure that he simply ran out of gas.

* * * * *

OTHER INSTANCES OF CONSPIRACIES TO PROTECT CHERISHED RECORDS

Daryl Spencer is a former Major League Baseball infielder who played with the Giants, the Cardinals, the Dodgers, and the Reds from 1952 to 1963. One of the few National League teams he did not play for was the Braves. But after he was released in 1963 by the Reds (they had a rookie infielder named Pete Rose in their plans), Spencer found himself employed by the Hankyu Braves—a second-division team in the Japanese League.

Spencer learned a lot in 1964, his first year overseas. He hit thirty-six home runs and drove in ninety-five runs that year, but that was just the beginning. He had a truly special season in 1965. Few expected the thirty-seven-year-old Spencer to challenge the Nankai's catcher, the great home run hitter Katsuya Nomura, for supremacy in Japan's Pacific League (Sadaharu Oh played in the Central League). But Spencer did just that, and more. By the middle of July, Spencer was batting close to .350, with twenty-five home runs. About a month later, Spencer (with a league-leading thirty-three HR) was still hot, and was approached by his interpreter and the batting coach.

According to Robert K. Fitts' 2005 book *Remembering Japanese Baseball: An Oral History of the Game*, Spencer was a victim of a racially-motivated conspiracy. Here is what Spencer told Fitts:

> The batting coach said, "Spencer, you must concentrate on keeping Nomura from winning the Triple Crown." They didn't think Nomura was worthy of the Triple Crown after so many great players had failed to clinch it. I said, "Well, don't worry. I'm going to win the home-run title." Then [the coach] said, "No, no, no. That has already been decided. You will not win the home-run title."

Try to put yourself in Spencer's shoes. You're playing in a foreign land, and you're told to concentrate on winning the batting title, but told in no uncertain terms that you must lose the home run title—despite being ahead at the time by six homers. Spencer was then walked at a rate that would make Barry Bonds blush. When his team went to Tokyo to play the Orions (and Koyama) they walked Spencer eight straight times! Only a frustrated Spencer throwing his bat at the ball prevented even more consecutive bases on balls. Japanese players went on record saying, "Why should we let an American win the home run title?"

Although it appeared that the Nankai Hawks and Tokyo Orions wouldn't give Spencer anything worthy to hit, other teams would pitch carefully but over the plate. After a month-long homer-less drought, Spencer got hot late in the season, hitting three homers in five days and pulling to within three home runs of the slumping Nomura.

The Braves had a doubleheader with the Hawks. In the first game, Spencer walked on four pitches in his first at-bat. In his second at-bat, he went up to the plate with his bat upside down, and they still walked him! It was ridiculous. In the second game, he hit a home run off American Joe Stanka, pulling within two homers of Nomura.

The next day was an off day, and Spencer was taking a one mile trip to the train station on his motorcycle. About a block and a half from his house, a little delivery truck pulled out of a side street and hit him. Spencer suffered a broken leg, and lost any chance at the home run title. Nomura wound up with forty-two homers, and Spencer finished with thirty-eight.

Bob Rives, a member of SABR (Society for American Baseball Research) interviewed Spencer in December of 2005 and January of 2006. He asked Spencer, "Did Nomura or his backers arrange the accident?" "Who knows?" Daryl replied. "I laughed about it later."

*　*　*　*　*

Leron Lee had a similar story. He played in the Major Leagues from 1969–1976, with the Cardinals, the Padres, the Indians, and the Dodgers. Like Spencer, he then went to Japan, where he became one of the most successful foreign players in Japanese baseball history. He played eleven seasons there, and set career records for foreigners in Japan in home runs, RBI, and hits. (Leron is the uncle of Derrick Lee, who won a National League batting crown with the 2005 Chicago Cubs.)

Leron told the story of his attempt at the Triple Crown in Fitts' book. "My first year in Japan, I was in line to win the Triple Crown," he said. "The guy who beat me in batting average was my teammate Michiyo Arito. During the second half of the season, I saw him get about thirty hits that shouldn't have been scored hits."

Lee swears that one of the Japanese papers that year carried a story saying that it would be a disgrace to Japanese baseball if a foreigner won the Triple Crown. Lee wound up leading the League in homers and RBI.

EVIDENCE TO SUPPORT A CONSPIRACY

It seems obvious that the Japanese players had a sense of pride about their baseball, and didn't want their cherished records broken by foreigners. Obviously, Japanese–American baseball relations have gotten better in the last thirty years. Before that, there were conspiracies that were barely disguised.

Sometimes, it's good that our most cherished records are broken by athletes that the public (or other competitors) openly root against. It means that not everything is orchestrated and scripted.

CONCLUSION:

Was NFL legend Sammy Baugh
involved in a gambling scandal?

Well before several New York Giants were approached by gamblers to fix the 1946 NFL Championship Game, there were rumors and accounts of previous attempts by gamblers to fix NFL games. One of the most well-known stories concerned the 1946 Washington Redskins. NFL Commissioner Elmer Layden investigated the possibility that Washington players were consorting with gamblers and betting on games. Here's some background.

On July 8, 1932, a syndicate headed by George Preston Marshall bought the NFL's Boston franchise, the Boston Braves. By 1933, the franchise became known as the Redskins. In February of 1937, Marshall moved the franchise to Washington. That 1937 season was important for other reasons, as it was the first of sixteen years in a Redskins uniform for "Slingin'" Sammy Baugh, the Redskins first round pick from TCU, who some consider the greatest football player of all time. That year, the Redskins won their first-ever NFL title, defeating the Chicago Bears.

The Redskins became an early glamour team of the NFL, playing in the Championship Game four times between 1937 and

1943. They faced the Chicago Bears all four times, beating them in 1937 and 1942, and losing to them in 1940 (by a score of 73–0, an NFL record for margin of victory that stands to this day) and 1943. In the 1943 title game, Baugh suffered a concussion early in the game when he tackled Sid Luckman on a punt return, and the Bears went on to win the title, 41–21.

Baugh came into the league as a single-wing tailback and quickly established himself as not only the league's best and most accurate passer (by far) but also as an outstanding runner, a terrific defensive back, and the best punter in the game. If gamblers did want to fix a game, they could have not done better than to influence Slingin' Sammy.

It's honestly difficult to measure how great a quarterback he was. In 1945, the NFL average for pass completions was 47%. Baugh completed better than 70% of his passes that season. Beginning in 1940, he led the NFL in punting for four straight seasons. He intercepted thirty-one passes as a defensive back. In 1943, Baugh was at the peak of his career, leading the NFL in passing while picking off more than one pass per game and averaging nearly forty-six yards per punt. Then there's the oft-told story of Baugh's passing accuracy: The coach would say to him, "When the receiver breaks, Sam, hit him in the eye with the ball," and Sammy would reply, "Which eye?" He's basically the first quarterback able to spot the ball exactly where he wanted.

He was also tough. His teammate (and roommate) and fellow Hall of Famer Wayne Millner described what Baugh was like.

> Naturally, Sam was a prime target for the tough guys. But one day he showed he could handle himself. It was early in the season, and a tackle on another club slugged Sam when he was down. Sam told him to cut it out, but on the next play the tackle gave him the knee. When we got back to the huddle, Sam said, "Don't block that

guy this time. Let him in." We let the tackle into the backfield as Sammy had asked. Sam let him come real close, then cut loose with the ball. It hit that character right between the eyes and knocked him cold.

In 1942, the Redskins finished 10–1 and won the NFL Championship, defeating the Bears 14–6 in the Championship Game. Their only loss came against the New York Giants in the second week of the season. They ran off nine straight victories to end the season, by an average margin of victory greater than thirteen points. They began the 1943 season 6–0–1, outscoring their first seven opponents by 198–65 (or nineteen points per game). In their next game, however, the Redskins lost 27–14 at home to the Pittsburgh-Philadelphia Steagles (the Steelers and Eagles had combined to make the Steagles because of the war). The week after, the Redskins fell to the Giants 14–10. The team that had gone 15–0–1 over two seasons had suddenly gone 0–2, and needed a victory in their season finale against the Giants on December 12, to avoid falling into a playoff against the Giants, with the winner meeting the Bears in Chicago for the League Championship.

Throughout this period, there were whispers that turned into loud rumblings. Following the loss to the Giants, articles appeared in the newspapers that hinted at a fix. On December 8, 1943, the Associated Press reported the following:

> Pro football in general and the champion Washington Redskins in particular set out to clear the air of rumors that gamblers had something to do with some of the surprising upsets this season. NFL officials brushed away reports that players associated with gamblers, calling it "pool hall gossip." Nevertheless, the league served notice that any [legitimate] evidence would be appreciated so that the guilty parties could be thrown out of the sport for life.

The NFL and Washington management reported that inquiries had been conducted earlier in the season, and that no evidence of game fixing had turned up. Owner Marshall reported that "anyone who says a Redskins player has been betting on professional football is a liar," and he offered a $5,000 reward for proof of the contrary.

The Redskins were looked at as heavy favorites to defeat both the Steagles and the Giants. Both games were in Washington, where the Redskins hadn't lost since September of '42.

On December 9, the United Press Staff Correspondent Jack Cuddy wrote, "Our only criticism of the current pro football fricassee is this: Commissioner Elmer Layden and owner George Preston Marshall should not have recognized the scandal-shouters with their protesting denials. They should have let the bookies stew in their own deficit juices—in their own evil-smelling telephone booths."

Cuddy's opinion was that the great tempest was raised by bookmakers, who invested lots of money into games which resulted in great upsets. On November 14, the Bears beat the Giants 56–7. The next week, the Redskins defeated those same Bears. That would have made Washington the obvious choice to destroy New York, but the Giants upset the Skins, 14–10. It was the first game all season in which Sammy Baugh didn't throw a touchdown pass. According to Cuddy, "Coach Steve Owen of the Giants let Sammy Baugh pass at will, but kept his receivers protected like so many convent girls." Don Imus couldn't have said it any worse, but it was a different time.

And with the sportswriters both flowery and naive, the National Football League could issue anything they wanted, and not be challenged.

On December 15, 1943, Harry Sheer, a sportswriter for the *Chicago Daily News*, wrote that Commissioner Layden was tricked into the admission that an investigation was under way by an editor from the *Washington Times-Herald*. The Washington editor warned Commissioner Layden that a rival paper was publishing the story and in order to be fair to all newspapers, he would like to know any information. A check later proved that the rival paper did not have the story and had no intention of printing any. "George Strickler, National Football League public relations director, denied today that any 'special investigation' was in progress concerning rumors that league players were associating with gamblers," wrote Sheer, adding that the *Washington Times-Herald*, which published the story of the probe, had "misrepresented" its information to NFL Commissioner Elmer Layden, and had "misquoted" him.

The Redskins lost their third straight game, and second straight to the New York Giants, by a score of 31–7, on December 12. That set up an Eastern Title playoff game in New York on December 19 between the Giants and Redskins. This time, Washington defeated the Giants 28–0, and advanced to play in Chicago the next week for the NFL title.

Layden said he did not find the "slightest bit" of evidence of collusion between gamblers and anyone connected with professional football. "The penalty for betting is expulsion from the league, and it will be enforced swiftly and vigorously," Layden said.

Redskins owner George Preston Marshall asked D.C. police chief Edward J. Kelly to investigate the rumors. Kelly said his men could find no evidence that any Redskins player had been "frequenting gambling houses or liquor bars." And the rumors soon died out.

My Opinion

Let's think about the ways to properly fix a team game. First, you take a heavily favored team, really prohibitive favorites like the Redskins would have been against the Steagles and the Giants. If a star like Sammy Baugh was involved in the fix, the conspiracy could have been limited to just the gamblers and one or two players. Baugh controlled everything for the Redskins, on offense, defense, and special teams.

It's not like Baugh was a millionaire, either. He fought frequently with Marshall over salary, having to do vaudeville stage shows in the off-season (in which he would throw footballs to the balcony, where his receiver, Millner, was to pull in the receptions) to make ends meet. Baugh, like all pro athletes of the time, had no leverage in contract talks. One year he created leverage with owner Marshall by threatening to retire from football to play shortstop for the St. Louis Cardinals.

So, the players weren't rich. The team probably had so much confidence that they thought they could turn the switch and win whenever they needed to. These were the ingredients for a conspiracy, where gamblers and players altered outcomes of games. In the more than six decades after the 1943 Redskins, in this age of microphones and cell phones and camera phones and monitoring of players, it would be downright impossible to fix NFL games by getting to individual players. Players would be crazy to raise eyebrows under these watchful times. That's not to say that eyebrows weren't raised over more recent NFL games, but the suspicions about fixes usually fell on owners, coaches, and referees.

But back in the 1940s, things were different. I can understand how players would have been tempted to throw games, or at least shave points. There were no injury reports. Baugh, who hardly played in the November 21, 1943, game against the Bears, could have pulled himself from the game at any time.

I believe there was a conspiracy. Denials by Marshall and Layden were too pat, and too smug. Newspapers could not have "misrepresented" information to the NFL and the public. The fact that the paper began an investigation, and then just a few days later shut it down, with the NFL publicly putting all rumors to bed, leads me to believe that someone got paid off.

In researching this period of Redskins and Bears history, I came across a great bit of gamesmanship. In fact, it's one of the best acts of gamesmanship I can think of. It speaks to the great rivalry, and what lengths teams would go through to win.

In the 1940 season, George Halas and Luke Johnsos helped perfect the telephone-from-the-press-box trick. Luke had watched an exhibition game between the Bears and the Dodgers from the press box, and noted a Brooklyn Dodgers weakness. He wrote a note, got the attention of a Bears messenger, and the note was carried to Coach Halas on the bench. Minutes later, Johnsos saw something else, and needed to get another note to Halas. They decided to connect a set of phones from an upper press box seat to the bench (today, of course, it's standard for every team to have coordinators watch the game from the press-box view). A few years later, when the Bears lost to the Redskins, Johnsos received a telegram from Lee Jeanes, the President of the Green Bay Packers. The telegram read, "What is wrong, telephone out of order?" Washington Redskins owner George Preston Marshall had stationed the Redskins band behind the Chicago Bears bench and had rigged a phone from his box to the bandleader. Every time Marshall saw Johnsos pick up the phone at a critical time, he'd order the band to play its noisiest number.

CONCLUSION:

Did John McGraw conspire to fix games and World Series?

In the early 1900s, Major League Baseball was similar to the National Football League of the late 1960s. The National League was the senior circuit, proud and boastful of its place in the game, miles ahead of the new American League (just like NFL teams were proud and lordly over their American Football League counterparts). The first World Series had occurred when owners of the two pennant winning teams met following the 1903 season. There would be no World Series the following year, however, as the New York Giants refused any part in a series. The Giants at that time were managed by John McGraw, known as "Little Napoleon."

Some said the Giants refused to participate in the World Series because for much of the 1904 season, the American League was led by the New York Highlanders. Regardless of whether the opponent was the Highlanders or the Boston Red Sox—the team that had defeated the Pirates in the 1903 World Series—McGraw had an intense hatred of A.L. President Ban Johnson. But McGraw (more powerful than the owner of the team) felt that his team had little to gain by playing the A.L. champ—but plenty to lose. The

New York Giants won the pennant again in 1905, but this time they agreed to play the American League champion Philadelphia Athletics. Why did McGraw suddenly welcome the format of a World Series? Could he have received some information before the Series started that would have comforted (or benefited) him?

Reports from the time say that gamblers approached Rube Waddell, the star Philadelphia Athletics pitcher, and offered him $17,000 to miss the World Series against the Giants. Wadell did miss the Series, giving the excuse that he had hurt his arm when he tripped over a suitcase. The Giants won the Series, but Horace Fogel (a sportswriter from Philadelphia, and the leading baseball authority in Philadelphia at the time) said that Waddell was stiffed, only receiving $500 from the fixers. Waddell, who passed away in 1914, was one of the great pitchers in history, and was enshrined in the Baseball Hall of Fame as a Veterans Committee pick in 1946. But reports have suggested that he may have been mentally challenged, and has also been described as an alcoholic. But the official story of why he missed the 1905 World Series was that he hurt his shoulder late in the season, horsing around on a train platform.

It is never good for a team when a pitcher who won twenty-seven games, had a 1.48 ERA, and seventy-five more strikeouts than the next closest pitcher in the league horses around on a train platform and misses the World Series. Ray Robinson's book *Matty: An American Hero* (1993) suggests that rumors were rampant that Rube had been bribed by gamblers to sit out the Series. "In the last days of the season, [Philadelphia manager Connie] Mack even accused Waddell of malingering," Robinson wrote. "Rube's response was that he was pitching in pain for more than a month. 'It would be worse for the team if I pitched. That would be better for the gamblers, wouldn't it? I'm no crook.'"

Crook or not, Rube didn't pitch, and the Giants won the World Series. The whole era was filled with shady characters, and players who were disloyal to their team and the game for their entire careers. One of the players with little integrity for the game was "Prince" Hal Chase, who would meet up with McGraw in later years.

Although the 1912 National League race wasn't close (the Giants won the pennant by ten games), Horage Fogel was banned for life by the National League after making allegations that St. Louis manager Roger Bresnahan (a former Giant) and other former New York players had thrown the season so that the Giants could win. (In 1909, Fogel had been the frontman for a group that purchased the Philadelphia Phillies, and rose to team president before his banishment.)

On one hand, to think the New York Giants needed help from the 63–90 Cardinals to win the pennant is absurd. The Phillies finished thirty games out. Fogel could have made one too many drunken statements. However, if you're keeping score at home, think about this: There was reason to be suspicious of dealings to help McGraw's Giants in 1905. And there was reason to be suspicious of dealings to help McGraw's Giants in 1912. And, incredibly, there was reason to be suspicious of dealings to help McGraw's Giants in 1919. This isn't a conspiracy theory, it's a word problem for high school math students!

My Opinion

Here's why I'm suspicious that John McGraw conspired with Hal Chase to fix and throw games.

The very first manager of the New York Yankees (then called the Highlanders) was a man named Clark Griffith. According to Arthur Cummings in a series of 1924 newspaper articles entitled *What Made Ballplayers Great?*, it was in 1905 that Griffith first laid eyes on a first baseman named Hal Chase. "I don't know how well he can hit," Griffith apparently said, "but it won't make a lot of difference. There is the greatest fielding first baseman I have ever seen in my life." Griffith said that after watching Chase practice for all of one hour. (Remember, this in an era where the bunt was a main offensive weapon.)

Chase became New York's first baseman, and turned out to be a legendary figure in baseball history. Apparently, no first baseman ever ran in on bunts and made force outs at second or third base before Chase. "Prince Hal" was considered the very best defensive first baseman of his time, and he was a proficient batter as well. Miller Huggins, who managed the Yankees from 1918–1929, said in the early 1920s, "If it were possible to include Hal Chase, there could never be any question as to who would be the grand all-American first baseman of all time." Huggins brought up Lou Gehrig to play first base for the Yankees in 1923, and that best-ever tag on Chase didn't last long. But Chase played fifteen years in the Major Leagues, despite a history of betting on games, laying down to lose on purpose, and fixing games. There had to be a conspiracy that allowed him to play as long as he did.

In a syndicated column for the *International News Service* in February of 1916, sportswriter Frank G. Menke wrote, "Probably no player ever was idolized more than Chase. Probably none, outside of Cobb, Christy Mathewson, and Honus Wagner, ever were lauded from one end of the land to the other as was Chase. In the early years of the Yankees, Chase was the sensation of the American League."

Bill James wrote that Chase was accused of "laying down"— not making an honest effort to win games—for the first time in 1908. Chase denied the charges, and jumped his contract with New York to play in a west coast league. Although suspended, he applied for reinstatement, paid a $200 fine, and was eligible to play the 1909 season. In *The Bill James Historical Baseball Abstract*, James writes that Chase was presented with a loving cup when he rejoined New York in May of 1909. It represented a sure sign that all was forgiven, or at least that the club hoped that Chase would play his hardest and remain loyal.

Chase was again accused of throwing a game by New York manager George Stallings in 1910. That year, he missed twenty-four games, often mysteriously. He wanted his manager fired so badly that he tried to lose games on purpose, or so Stallings thought. The owner supported the player, and Chase replaced Stallings as manager for the final fourteen games of the 1910 season. Making Chase the manager made sense for a few different reasons. It made the talented player try harder (to improve his mark as a manager), and also kept him planted in one place (rather than headed back west to the Pacific League).

After one season, Chase was replaced as manager but kept as a player. Because he refused to take himself or his duties seriously, Chase passed up the opportunity to be the manager for many years.

Yankees manager (the Highlanders became known officially as the Yankees in 1913) Frank Chance, nicknamed "The Peerless Leader," suspected Prince Hal of throwing games in the summer of 1913. Some think what Chase did was arrive at first base a step late for a throw from an infielder. For a great defensive player, he was never a good target. Infielders threw to an empty bag. No other first baseman played as deep or as far off the bag as Chase did. Only the most suspicious of men would dare accuse Chase of not getting to the bag on time. But most fans and media members believed at the time that, at the least, Chase had "laid down" on the job.

Chance simply would not stand for Chase's indifference. He had to go. One newspaper account wrote that " [Chase] displayed toward Chance a disposition like that of a pampered child toward its governess." Chance took a chance and was able to chase Chase off the team. The Yankees traded the first baseman to Charles Comiskey's White Sox in return for two average ballplayers.

On July 23, 1913, Chase proved that like a leopard, he couldn't change his spots. That day he committed four errors in one game, arousing suspicion in the stands. By the next season, Chase got into arguments with White Sox owner Comiskey over his contract. He jumped the White Sox, and signed to play with Buffalo in the newly-formed Federal League. Most of the other big American League stars (like Walter Johnson and Ty Cobb) were given raises to stay with their teams. The White Sox, with the help of American League president Ban Johnson, fought in the courts to prevent Chase from jumping teams. It was said that the White Sox were fighting not to keep Chase, but rather to prevent him from playing elsewhere. By now, people wanted to run this character out of the game. The courts ruled that Prince Hal was able to play in Buffalo in the new Federal League. The league folded after the 1915 season, as most of the owners got what they wanted—the ability to buy shares in established Major League clubs.

In February of 1916, Chase was looking for a job back in Major League Baseball. "There is no baseball 'blacklist,'" wrote sports-writer Frank G. Menke at the time, "but there is a gentleman's agreement." Most of the American League clubs—having seen Chase up close for many years—stayed away, but the Cincinnati Reds picked him up for the 1916 season. Most talented and troubled ballplayers wind up with an opportunity like this: the chance to kick-start a disappointing team and refurbish the player's own image. The Reds were coming off a fifth-place finish in 1915, and the thirty-three-year-old Chase led the NL in batting with a .339 average.

Although Chase had a tremendous 1916 season, the Reds were still floundering in the middle of June. In an effort to salvage their season, the Reds traded with the New York Giants, acquiring the great pitcher Christy Mathewson (essentially in return for middle infielder Buck Herzog), and naming him manager.

On August 9, 1918, Chase was suspended from the Reds without pay for the remainder of the season. Chase told the press the reason. "Let's not beat around the bush," he said. "I'm accused of betting on ballgames and trying to get a pitcher to throw a game for money." Chase, of course, denied everything.

The National League finally had a hearing on the matter in January of 1919. Pitcher Jimmy Ring, a Reds teammate, testified that in 1917, he was brought in from the bullpen with the score tied and two runners on base. As he was warming up, Chase came over from first base and said, "I've got some money bet on this game, kid. There's something in it for you if you lose."

Ring said he told Chase to forget about him trying to lose, but he wound up losing the game anyway. The next day, Chase dropped a $50 bill in his lap. Ring told his manager, Mathewson, almost immediately. Mathewson suspended Chase, and Chase sued the team for back pay.

The evidence against Chase appears overwhelming. Although Mathewson was overseas in Europe, fighting in World War I, he sent his testimony in an affidavit. Besides the corroborating stories from Ring and Mathewson, a Giants pitcher named Pol Perritt said that Chase had asked him before a doubleheader which game he was going to start. Chase had apparently told him, "I wish you would tip me off, because if I know which game you'll pitch, and can connect with a certain party, you will have nothing to fear." Perritt also said that Chase boasted that he had won $500 after a 1918 game, and testified in the hearing that he had told his manager John McGraw about this. There was even more damning testimony. But McGraw's testimony apparently helped Chase, and Mathewson (no fan of Chase) was fighting a war on the other side of the Atlantic. It seems incredible, but John Heydler, president of the National League, found the evidence against Chase insufficient to warrant expulsion. But why would "Little Napoleon" help Chase, a noted fixer of games, to stay in baseball?

Two weeks after the trial, Chase was traded to the New York Giants for two players. Chase went right from the Reds to McGraw's Giants! How convenient! In 1919, Chase played for the Giants until he hurt his wrist and missed most of the last month, as the team was battling the Reds for the National League pennant.

Chase's career in the majors ended after that 1919 season. Soon after that, a player named Lee Magee threw even more dirt on Chase's baseball grave, saying that Chase fixed games when Magee played for Chase and the Reds in 1918.

My Opinion

The whole era was filled with underworld figures that fixed, threatened to fix, or influenced many more people than the small handful we're led to believe. Even revered moral figures of the day like Christy Mathewson had to "play ball" and work with guys like Chase.

John McGraw was not the religious, moral man that Mathewson was. He was interested in winning, at all costs. If this meant looking the other way when gamblers accosted members of his team—or refusing to testify truthfully in regards to a noted cheater and gambler—I can't put it past him.

Although there were rules against gambling on games, it was much harder to throw players out of baseball before Judge Landis came on the scene in the 1920s. Chase was allowed to flourish, and was given repeated chances in New York (despite indifferent play, accusations, and even jumping the team to play on the west coast in another league for a spell), in Chicago (despite breaking his contract and signing with the Federal League), and in Cincinnati (despite teammates going to management with reports that Chase bet on games).

What kind of sport could put up with a player like that—so obviously gifted defensively, but one who led the league in errors no less than seven times?

Why was McGraw never questioned about signing Chase in 1919? McGraw was given a pass over and over again. He was bigger than the game. In his era, McGraw earns only four Oswalds, but in a later era, he would ring up the maximum number of five.

CONCLUSION:

Did the NFL conspire in the mid-1980s to monopolize professional football?

On April 1, 2007, two media giants squared off in a pay-per-view extravaganza entitled "Battle of the Billionaires" as part of World Wrestling Entertainment's annual Wrestlemania event. Donald Trump's designated professional wrestler, Bobby Lashley, defeated Vince McMahon's wrestler, Umaga, and as a result Lashley and Trump were allowed to shave the head of losing billionaire McMahon. That would be the latest, but far from the first time that real estate king Donald Trump took on the heads of professional sports.

In the spring and summer of 1986, Trump was the powerful owner of the New Jersey Generals in the fledgling United States Football League. He decided to take on the National Football League in several different ways. First, he spearheaded the movement for the United States Football League, which played its games in the spring, to move to a fall schedule, offering direct competition with the NFL. He then took the league on in the courts, charging that the NFL tried to illegally monopolize pro football. Interestingly, in the early 2000s, it was McMahon who tried to take on the NFL by creating the XFL as a spring league. He didn't have any more success than Trump.

The United States Football League, for those who are too young or don't remember, was far from a gimmicky, entertainment-based league like the XFL. Instead, it was more like the American Basketball Association (a rival pro basketball league that eventually merged its four teams into the NBA). The USFL lasted three seasons, and lost somewhere between $150 and $200 million.

The USFL started in 1982 with a plan to keep salaries and costs down. In May of that year, the League signed a network television contract with ABC and a cable television contract with ESPN (then separate entities) which guaranteed each team roughly $1.1 million per year in revenue. The USFL hired established NFL coaches like George Allen, Chuck Fairbanks, and John Ralston, and the owners settled in late August of 1982 on a $1.8 million salary cap per team, using a thirty-eight-man roster. $1.3 million was allotted to sign thirty-eight players and a ten-player developmental squad, and $500,000 was allotted to sign two "star" players that did not count against the cap.

It sounded like a solid plan then, and still does. The NFL was in labor strife, following a 1982 players strike. USFL teams sought leases to play in NFL stadiums like Soldier Field, Giants Stadium, and Veterans Stadium. In the very first spring season, average attendance for all USFL games was 24,000. It was then, in August of 1983, that Donald Trump bought the New Jersey Generals. By January, Trump was calling for his fellow USFL owners (only one of whom had made money in 1982) to switch to a fall schedule and compete directly with the big boys. In February of 1984, Michael Porter, a Harvard business professor, wrote a document called "The USFL versus the NFL" (which in hindsight could have been called, "How to Destroy the USFL"), and delivered it to sixty-five members of the NFL management council. The USFL would use this document to justify their antitrust case (unlike baseball, the NFL had no anti-trust exemption). In August, the USFL owners would agree with Trump, and announce that after the 1985 season, they would move to a fall schedule.

On October 18, 1984, the USFL filed their antitrust suit against the NFL. This was a real gamble, taking on the NFL. USFL executives were swayed by the swagger of Trump and Chicago Blitz co-owner Eddie Einhorn. Michael MacCambridge's 2004 *America's Game* quotes former Philadelphia Stars and present Kansas City Chiefs General Manager Carl Peterson as saying, "They absolutely were convinced that this move would either precipitate an acquisition of some USFL teams into the NFL or we would have an antitrust case . . . because they controlled basically all the networks at the time, and that we would win hands down."

It took from October of 1984 to July of 1986 for the case to make it through all the courts. The USFL had a lot to juggle in those two years. They had to spend a ton of money to make their product competitive (and to appease their broadcast partners). In some cases, they had to work out new stadium deals, since NFL teams would be occupying their stadiums in the fall. In short, the USFL was springing leaks all over the place.

Once the USFL folded, NFL teams signed close to 200 USFL players, including future Hall of Famers Reggie White and Jim Kelly. The players and coaches (Jim Mora and Marv Levy, for examples) and general managers (Carl Peterson, Bruce Allen, and Bill Polian) of the USFL became key figures in NFL history in the late 1980s, 1990s, and into the present decade. The NFL even adapted some of the USFL rules, including instant replays and the use of the two-point conversion.

The USFL attempted to get the jury to believe New Jersey Generals owner Trump, who testified in July of 1986 that NFL Commissioner Pete Rozelle had offered him an expansion franchise in the established league if he dropped the lawsuit. Trump told the jury that Rozelle also promised him a franchise if Trump would influence the USFL to keep its spring schedule and not bring suit. Rozelle denied ever offering Trump a franchise, under any terms. Rozelle said that Trump had said he had the responsibility of bringing on the lawsuit, "but I don't want to do these things. I want an expansion team in New York in the National Football League." Rozelle testified that he explained to Trump that day why an expansion team in New York wouldn't work with network television deals. But Trump had a real estate mentality (location, location, location), and must have believed that three NFL teams in the New York market could work.

The jury basically had to believe either Trump or Rozelle. Trump's story, that the NFL tried to "divide and conquer" by wooing Trump and dangling an offer to get into the NFL, seemed to have some merit. But Rozelle's side of the story, that Trump offered to get out of the USFL and sell the Generals to some stiff in exchange for membership in Rozelle's group, seemed more likely to be true. In MacCambridge's book, he credits Rozelle's successor Paul Tagliabue with steering the NFL away from settling out of court. In Tagliabue's mind, you couldn't encourage fly-by-night leagues to be created, in the hope of walking away with a lot of money.

That makes a lot of sense to me. Tagliabue did an awful lot right in his seventeen years as Commissioner of the NFL. It makes sense that he would have offered up sound judgment to the league as a lawyer for the league in the years prior.

EVIDENCE AGAINST A CONSPIRACY

In John Fortunato's book, *The Legacy of Pete Rozelle*, the author gives Rozelle's account of the antitrust suit brought against him.

> The failures [of the USFL] included abandoning the initial strategy of building loyalty through playing in the spring and quickly escalated the cost of doing business

by signing prominent players. The USFL's failures culminated in a hasty move to a fall schedule with the hopes of merging some of its teams into the NFL. . . . The jury thus concluded that the networks freely chose not to purchase the USFL, and that the NFL was trying to achieve through the courts what it could not achieve in the marketplace.

EVIDENCE TO SUPPORT A CONSPIRACY

In his 1987 book, *Trump: The Art of the Deal*, Donald wrote that the USFL had problems playing its games in the spring, and that they didn't present a first-class product. When Trump bought the New Jersey Generals, he was intent on spending money to sign top players and coaches, in order to create a legitimate competitor for NFL fans and TV dollars. Trump's aggressiveness in signing NFL-caliber players like Heisman Trophy winner Herschel Walker nudged his fellow USFL owners to do the same. Steve Young, a future Hall of Fame quarterback, signed up right out of college with the Los Angeles Express. Trump signed Heisman star Doug Flutie. In all, USFL teams signed close to half of the top college players they went after. Trump absolutely believed that the NFL did everything they could—legally and illegally—to monopolize professional football.

Howard Cosell, despite being employed by ABC (then the network that gave a spring television contract to the USFL), testified for the USFL, believing that the NFL was engaged in a monopoly. Cosell wrote in *What's Wrong with Sports* (1991), "You don't have to be a genius to recognize that Pete Rozelle and the entire NFL were very upset with ABC for giving the USFL a television contract during its first three spring seasons. Yet [ABC News and Sports President Roon] Arledge denied that Rozelle or anyone else from the NFL ever expressed a negative reaction to the network's decision. Who's kidding whom?" Cosell went on to write that he testified that Arledge told him that Rozelle was all over him for sustaining the USFL.

Trump wrote, "It was obvious to me that the NFL was putting enormous pressure on the networks not to do business with us [the USFL] in the fall—particularly on ABC, with whom we already had a contract for the spring."

In February of 1986, the USFL reduced its number of teams from fourteen to eight, in an effort to consolidate costs. The League had one remaining hope, which was to convince the six jurors that the NFL had operated illegally. Trump was the only USFL owner to testify. Howard Cosell and Raiders owner and league agitator Al Davis also testified for the USFL. The NFL was able to score points with the jurors because Trump was painted (as he put it in his book) as "a vicious, greedy, Machiavellian billionaire, intent only on serving my selfish ends at everyone else's expense."

On July 29, 1986, the NFL was ruled to have violated antitrust laws by conspiring to monopolize pro football, and that they did illegally damage the USFL. They were found guilty on one of the nine counts, anyway. But even The Donald doesn't get everything he wants. The USFL was seeking $440 million in damages (which could have been trebled). What they were awarded was $1, trebled to $3. They won, but they lost. The rebel league had hoped to receive enough money to keep their league alive, and force the NFL owners to treat them as honest competitors. On August 1, the USFL owners voted to suspend the 1986 season.

How did the NFL escape without paying for their conspiracy? In Trump's 1987 book, he wrote that a juror named Miriam Sanchez had "favored giving us damages of $300 million, but said that she'd misunderstood the mechanism for doing so. 'I didn't understand the instructions, so I had to put my faith in the judge, hoping he would give the USFL more money.'"

Cosell wrote in 1991 that Sanchez said there was a hung jury. "Ms. Sanchez said openly—and this is key—that the jury chose to set damages at $1 because they were unsure about how high the damages should be, and they wanted Judge Peter K. Leisure to set the damages for them. Judge Leisure had the right to do this, but to the delight of the NFL, he refused."

In Fortunato's book on Rozelle, he writes, "One juror, Miriam Sanchez, described the award verdict as a compromise. She said, "One dollar is all we could do, or we'd have [had] a hung jury."

So, it appears that three of the six jurors adjudicating the case favored giving the USFL money, which would have kept the league in business. At the very least, the history of the NFL would have been different, if Sanchez could have swayed one of the other three opposing jurors. As it turned out, it seemed a thankless task portraying the exceedingly wealthy Trump as the poor man's underdog. So the jury ruled that there was a conspiracy, with the NFL engaging in a monopoly, but that they deserved only a slap on the wrist.

Two decades have passed, and it appears that both sides had their points. Trump was correct about the move from the spring to the fall. The Arena Football League has existed for more than twenty years, operating in the NFL's off-season, and it has never gotten a fraction of the television ratings or advertising money that the NFL gets. It has sent a handful of players to the NFL—most notably Kurt Warner, who won a pair of MVPs and a Super Bowl with the Rams—but was mainly seen as a minor football league (and financial problems forced it to suspend operations). Maybe fans are burnt out with football by February. Everything has a season, and football has the fall. Baseball is not as popular as the NFL these days, but Major League Baseball in the spring and summer sure beats football—especially football that isn't top-notch.

Trump was also correct that the NFL was monopolistic by having contracts with all the television networks. Ironically, the addition of a fourth network, Fox, would give the NFL something better than a monopoly in future television negotiations. It gave them leverage, with the prospect of one network always being left out.

Trump was further correct that leagues needed first-class stars to succeed. Fans will tune in to new leagues with exciting rules for curiosity, but they will stay only with top competition.

Rozelle was right in that the USFL didn't have deep enough pockets to sustain itself, and should have built up its franchises with solid spring seasons. He was probably also correct in saying that the two men who testified against the NFL, Davis and Cosell, had personal reasons for doing so.

The USFL didn't have a bunch of Trumps to trump the NFL. What television network was going to bankroll a league with just a few good teams and a handful of superstars? The USFL strategy, in football terms, was to throw a deep pass on third-and-long and hope for a flag. Well, they managed to draw the flag, but it wasn't a spot foul that would result in the long gain that was needed.

MY OPINION

It was once possible for upstart leagues to compete directly with the NFL (the American Football League), the NBA (the American Basketball Association), and the NHL (the World Hockey Association), but by the mid-1980s, that time had passed. The NFL was big by the 1960s, but it was more powerful than all but a handful of superpower nations by the 1980s. Of course they monopolized pro football, and tried to limit their competition. But did they do so illegally, or was it simply a case in which the NFL was so big that it didn't need to resort to anything under-handed and didn't need to make threats to networks? The mere thought of a television network operating without the NFL was enough to keep everyone in line.

The NFL won this case, in every way. It became the sports league more powerful than probably all the others put together.

The NFL deserves to take bows in becoming so powerful. They took steps to generate revenue sharing long before other leagues. The NFL also took active steps twenty years ago in the areas of steroids and substance abuse. New NFL Commissioner Roger Goodell is making a point of coming down hard on the league's knuckleheads, who repeatedly get in trouble with the law. And in a sport that has more wagering on it than any other, it has stayed clear of any scandals involving referees.

CONCLUSION:

Shoeless Joe Jackson kept out
of Baseball Hall of Fame

In the early 1900s, baseball had no commissioner. According to an article on the official site of Major League Baseball titled, "The Commissionership: A Historical Perspective," there was, instead of a single commissioner, a National Commission, a three-man body (the two league presidents and an owner) endowed with supervisory control of professional baseball. This commission was granted the power to interpret the terms and rules of baseball, as well as the ability to enact and enforce fines and suspensions. One of the three men on the committee from 1903–1920 was Cincinnati Reds owner August Herrman. This was like having a Fantasy League owner also serve as commissioner, as one of the commissioners had a vested interest in one of the teams he was making rulings on. Following the 1919 World Series, in which eight members of the White Sox allegedly took bribes from gamblers to intentionally lose, the National League proposed to eliminate the National Commission and replace it with one leader. On January 12, 1921, the position of baseball commissioner was created with the ratification of the new Major League Agreement.

Judge Kenesaw Mountain Landis was elected as the game's first commissioner. He banned all eight White Sox players, including the legendary "Shoeless" Joe Jackson.

Jackson, whose career was cut short at the age of thirty, was one of the greatest hitters in baseball history. Born in 1889, he never learned to read or write, having been put to work sweeping floors in a mill at the age of six. The fact that he was uneducated would hurt him dearly in his baseball years.

White Sox owner Charles Comiskey bought Jackson's contract from the Cleveland Indians late in the 1915 season. The move paid dividends, as Jackson led the 1917 White Sox to a World Series championship. World War I limited Jackson to just seventeen games in the war-shortened 1918 season. Jackson didn't enter the army, though, as he was the sole supporter of his wife, mother, and brother. Instead, he accepted draft exemption and spent most of the year working in a ship-building plant. His employer, Comiskey, sent him a contract for $6,000 for the 1919 season, despite calling him a coward, in published remarks, for not fighting overseas. The entire White Sox team had a payroll of only $85,000, which was so low that there was much bitterness between Comiskey and the players. Second baseman Eddie Collins made $15,000 that season, by far the most of any player on the team. Pitcher Eddie Cicotte made only $5,000 and another hurler, Lefty Williams, made just $3,000. Despite their meager salaries, Cicotte won twenty-nine games and Williams twenty-three more in the 140-game season of 1919.

It is little wonder that Collins was not approached by gamblers to fix the World Series, for several reasons. First, he made the most money on the team. Second, he was sharp. The eight players indicted for fixing the 1919 World Series (Eddie Cicotte, Happy Felsch, Chick Gandhil, Swede Risberg, Fred McMullin, Buck Weaver, Lefty Williams, and Jackson) were all uneducated, and therefore prone to being taken advantage of.

Chick Gandhil, the White Sox first baseman, made the initial contact with gamblers, which got the ball rolling. Eddie Cicotte, who had received $10,000 before the first game of the World Series, let the gamblers know the fix was on by hitting the very first batter he faced. He was knocked out of the game in the fourth inning of Game One. In Game Four, Cicotte committed a pair of suspicious fielding errors. The World Series was a best-of-nine series then, and Cicotte won Game Seven to cut the Reds' lead to 4–3. The gambling syndicate must have gotten nervous, and it was later revealed that Lefty Williams was told that his wife's life would be in danger if he didn't lose Game Eight. Williams saved a life by getting knocked out in the first inning of Game Eight. Risberg, the shortstop, did his part and more. He committed four errors in the World Series, and batted just .080. Weaver and Jackson both played well. Weaver took no money, but like Jackson, knew too much.

In the middle of the World Series, Lefty Williams came into Jackson's room at the Lexington Hotel and threw an envelope with $5,000 in it down on the ground. (This is information from Jackson's grand jury testimony.) Williams apparently told Joe that the conspirators had told the gamblers that Jackson would play crooked, too. It makes sense that they would have wanted the .351 hitting outfielder to cooperate. Jackson told Williams that he didn't want the money, and that he was going to go to the owner and inform him of the fix. Williams, however, left Jackson's room, with the envelope with the $5,000 still on the floor. After the fourth game, Jackson went to ringleader Gandil and told him that he wasn't going to be in on any fix. Jackson testified that he told Gandil that he was going inform Comiskey of what was going on. But when Jackson went to Comiskey's office, Comiskey refused to see him, and Joe was sent home after waiting several hours. This leads me to believe that either Comiskey was part of the fix, or he wanted the whole thing swept under the rug.

The underdog Cincinnati Reds won the 1919 World Series five games to three. There were rampant rumors of the series being fixed. Comiskey, at this point, was trying to cover it up. When Harry Grabiner, an executive with the White Sox, was sent to Jackson's off-season home to negotiate a contract for 1920, Jackson brought up the fix and the bribe, but was told to keep the money. (At this point, it was to Comiskey's advantage for any hint of a fix to disappear, or his franchise players would be gone and the value of his team would dissipate). A grand jury was formed to clean up baseball in September of 1920 and would eventually indict eight of the White Sox players. They were all banned from organized baseball for life by Judge Landis, who was brought in to clean up the game, in one of his first acts as commissioner.

Cicotte implicated the others. The wire stories reported on September 28, 1920, that "Joe Jackson visited the office of attorney Alfred Austrian, counsel for the White Sox, with manager Kid Gleason, shortly after Cicotte had appeared before the inquisitors. It was reported that Jackson was preparing a statement . . . similar to one that Cicotte made to the grand jury." Historians have written that Jackson volunteered to tell what he knew. He told Austrian he was innocent, but was pressured to confess involvement or face greater danger from the grand jury and angry gamblers. Austrian "tricked" Jackson into signing a waiver of immunity. In 1989, Donald Gropman, Jackson's biographer, told Mike Decourcy (of the Scripps Howard News Service), "It was incumbent on Austrian to destroy Jackson's credibility. Comiskey was covering his behind." (Comiskey couldn't let on that Jackson had tried to come to him about the fix, and had tried to return the money.) Poor Jackson didn't even have proper legal advice. Despite the fact that the White Sox players were acquitted, they were all barred from baseball for life by the new commissioner.

In 1924, Jackson sued Comiskey for back wages, and in that trial Joe asserted that he had refused to take money and had tried to tell Comiskey about the fix. Jackson didn't make deliberate errors, or attempt to make outs while batting. His role—perhaps unwittingly—was merely having his name attached to the group of teammates who took money for throwing the World Series. This second jury cleared Jackson of his alleged role in the fix.

I understand why Kennesaw Mountain Landis had to come into office, and ban Shoeless Joe. But why didn't he ever go back and clear his name, especially since he was cleared by a jury of his peers?

When Judge Landis banned Jackson, he wrote the following:

> Regardless of the verdict of juries, no player that throws a ball game; no player that undertakes or promises to throw a ball game; no player that sits in a conference with a bunch of crooked players and gamblers where the ways and means of throwing games are planned and discussed and does not promptly tell his club about it, will ever play professional baseball. . . . Of course, I don't know that any of these men will apply for reinstatement, but if they do, the above are at least a few of the rules that will be enforced. Just keep in mind, regardless of the verdict of juries, baseball is entirely competent to protect itself against crooks, both inside and outside the game.

In the introduction to Donald Gropman's 1979 book, *Say It Ain't So, Joe! The True Story of Shoeless Joe Jackson and the 1919 World Series*, Alan Dershowitz, a Harvard Law School professor, wrote, "Former Baseball Commissioner A.B. Happy Chandler has gotten behind efforts to clear Jackson's name. 'I never in my life believed him to be guilty of a single thing,' said the man who was privy to the secret files of the Major Leagues."

And why hasn't any commissioner since Landis lifted the life-time ban? After Pete Rose was banned from baseball in 1989, the Baseball Hall of Fame ruled that any player banned from the game was ineligible for induction into the Hall. That rule, put in place to spare Major League Baseball the embarrassment of enshrining Rose, closed the door on any chance Jackson had to be inducted—long after his death—into the Hall of Fame.

Clearly there was a conspiracy to throw the 1919 World Series. It involved gamblers, star players for the White Sox, and others who knew too much. It was proven that conspirators in the "Black Sox" scandal took money to fix the Series. But while this conspiracy is well known and has been chronicled at length, there were probably other World Series of that era that were also fixed. The 1919 Series involved too many gamblers, and way too many players for it to have gone off without a hitch. The plan was overly ambitious. Indeed, there were whispers and rumors that the 1920 World Series could have been fixed, as well.

The more interesting conspiracy to me concerns the lifetime ban of Shoeless Joe. Jackson was by far the best player on the White Sox. He admitted to knowing about the fix, and testified that he was against the plot, and wanted no part of it. Even when Joe threatened that he was going to go to Charles Comiskey with information, the other players said the fix would go down anyway. Ultimately, the uneducated Jackson took $5,000 to keep quiet. Who knows? He might have stayed quiet about the fix because he was afraid for his life. We'll never know. There were so many contradictions. Joe didn't know who to believe, or who to trust. At first, owner Comiskey pretended to protect his players, but later wanted nothing to do with them. Comiskey bullied Jackson into signing and confessing things. At first, Jackson voluntarily appeared before the grand jury and made a confession in which he named his co-conspirators. He later retracted his confession, which, as it happened, was among the documents later stolen from grand jury files. What a mess! Jackson certainly didn't play like he was fixing on losing the World Series. He didn't commit even one error, batted .375, and hit the only home run in the

Series. He swore that he was not involved in any of the planning meetings, and was acquitted in a court of law.

When Joe Jackson died in 1951, the United Press obituary quoted Jackson as being bitter at Landis. "Landis said if the courts declared me not guilty, he'd stand by me. He didn't keep his word."

The proper definition of conspiracy is an agreement between two or more persons to commit a wrongful act. In this case, the wrongful act is not exonerating one of the mythical figures in baseball history. Jackson truly was one of the greatest hitters of all time. Expelled from baseball at the age of thirty, his numbers would have exploded in the 1920s, as they did for almost all other batters. He paid a heavy price for little more than being in the wrong place at the wrong time. In my opinion, he paid too big a price. The punishment was not worthy of the crime. He lacked the savvy to deal with unsavory propositions, and allowed himself to trust the wrong authority figures. Two or three wrongs don't make a right, but they do set a precedent. If there are members of Baseball's Hall of Fame that conspired with gamblers to throw games from the same era as Jackson—and there are—then Jackson's name should be cleared. This is not the same as keeping the lifetime ban on Pete Rose. Jackson was not a Major League manager, betting on his team to win (and not betting on his team on other days) while making personnel and pitching decisions. Rose, unlike Jackson, had excellent legal representation. Jackson's options were limited. After trying to sue Landis for back pay in 1923—and convincing a jury he was owed money—a judge reversed the decision on the basis of contradictions. The judge ruled that Jackson had committed perjury, and ordered him jailed for a couple of days. After that, Jackson—not even allowed to play sandlot baseball or manage a Minor League team—never applied for reinstatement.

There is no denying that Joe Jackson knew about the fix. He was an obvious choice to be approached, and was told that it was going to happen with or without his help. He had $5,000 thrown at his feet—and reluctantly kept it. He knew too much, and was thrown, to employ a modern phrase, "under the bus," paying an extremely heavy price. He was used by his fellow players, as a name to entice the gamblers. He was used by his owner. He was used by the new commissioner as a symbol for the cleansing of the game. For all we know, Joe could have "picked his spots" in fixing one or two of the games. Maybe he was more street-smart than modern historians give him credit for. Then again, maybe not.

All things considered, Shoeless Joe Jackson should be in the Hall of Fame. His lifetime ban should have been lifted when he died, and no less than eight different commissioners have had a chance to lift the ban and did not. That the ban has not been lifted by now raises some eyebrows with me. This is one conspiracy theory that clearly isn't motivated by money. No one stands to gain financially, which makes it even more puzzling.

Jackson never agreed to the fix, although he kept the money. He was punished greatly in his lifetime. Unlike Rose, Jackson couldn't make a living from signing his name on memorabilia. Not being able to sign his name (even if someone was willing to pay him for it), and not being able to play or manage any organized baseball team, Jackson made more money pressing pants than he ever did in baseball.

Commissioner Bud Selig can look at the record books of his beloved game and find them littered with great playesrs who did unsavory things and embarrassed the game. In Jackson's case, it is time to clear his name. He belongs on the same "Field of Dreams" with all the other Hall of Famers.

Conclusion:

U.S. Olympic basketball team gets cheated out of the gold in 1972

The twelve members of the 1972 United States national basketball team won a hard-fought gold medal, but they had only seconds to celebrate their crowning moment before it was snatched away from them in what was undoubtedly the most controversial finish in international basketball history. In the grand scheme of things, the fact that the players and coaches were cheated by a conspiracy involving the Soviet team and its coaches, Olympic officials, and members of the International Federation of Amateur Basketball (FIBA) pales in comparison to the tragic events of those same games. But still, the conspiracy remains.

The slaughter of eleven Israeli athletes by the terrorist group Black September (part of the Palestine Liberation Organization, formed a few years prior from the remnants of an Arab force routed in Jordan), was the tragedy of those Munich Games. The terrorists stormed through the lax German security—which was intentionally minimal on the part of the hosts, to make a different impression on the world than the one it imparted at the 1936 Berlin Olympics—took eleven Israelis, and demanded that the

Israeli government free 236 Palestinian prisoners. The terrorists immediately murdered two Israeli athletes who resisted in the athletes' village, and the remaining nine were taken as hostages. The hostages would die later, after a rescue attempt when the terrorists were attempting to extradite a flight to Cairo. For many, the most lasting image from the Munich Games will always be the German tanks sealing off the athletes' village, while police took up rooftop positions.

Many people felt at that point that the games should have been suspended and not completed. However, the head of the International Olympic Committee, Avery Brundage, allowed the Games to resume after only twenty-four hours. Although the Games continued, many of the athletes couldn't wait for them to end.

The United States didn't do exceptionally well in those Olympics, with the exception of swimmer Mark Spitz. Outside of Spitz, the United States athletes were snakebit in 1972. A track coach had the wrong start times of two world record-holding sprinters who were both overwhelming favorites for medals. An American named Rick DeMont had a great chance at gold in the 1,500 meter freestyle, but he failed a drug test when doctors neglected to clear his asthma medication and he was therefore denied the opportunity to compete.

The initial controversy at those Games didn't concern the United States at all, however. Rather, it concerned South Africa. In 1968, Rhodesia and South Africa had been barred from the Olympics for their practice of apartheid racial discrimination. While South Africa was still out by 1972, Rhodesia had been reinstated in 1971 by the IOC. Incredibly, the day before the Opening Ceremonies, the IOC bowed to the pressure from the African countries surrounding white-ruled Rhodesia (within a few years, it would no longer be British and ruled by whites, and it would be called Zimbabwe). Brundage was so incensed by having to bow to the African nations that he alluded to it even in his memorial service to honor the Israelis—describing the Rhodesian expulsion and the death of the Israeli hostages as "two savage attacks" on the Olympics.

I do not equate the death of the Israelis with the disappointments of Americans who failed to win a gold medal due to a mix-up in the starting times, or equate it to the judges of Communist-bloc nations voting to deny American athletes a hard-fought victory. But this book is about sports conspiracy theories. And the story of a basketball team who would ultimately win, and then win again, and then finally lose the same game—that belongs in a book about sports conspiracies.

Although there were a lot of great college basketball coaches to choose from in 1972, the United States Olympic coach was Hank Iba. It seems strange today that the U.S. would have bypassed Dean Smith, John Wooden, and all the great coaches in the prime of their careers for the then sixty-nine-year-old Iba. However, the old coach was a strict disciplinarian who had won college championships in the mid-1940s. He had been the United States national coach in 1964 and 1968, and had led his country to a pair of Olympic gold medals.

Many of the top United States players in the 1971–1972 season elected not to try out for the team—including UCLA center Bill Walton, the best player in the country. Walton was evasive in his reasons over the years. At one time, he said it was because he didn't want to be exposed to negative coaching. Another theory was that he was making a political statement, due to U.S. involvement in Vietnam. Regardless, Walton's absence didn't cost the United States a gold medal. Hey, four years earlier Iba had won a gold medal without the services of UCLA center Kareem Abdul Jabbar. The fact of the matter was that it usually didn't matter which twelve college players were selected. Since basketball became an Olympic sport in 1936, the United States had never lost a game. They had never even came close to losing one.

Iba's team had won the gold medal game against the Soviet Union in 1964 by a score of 73–59. In Mexico City four years later, the United States defeated Yugoslavia for the gold medal game by a score of 65–50.

The team that Iba assembled in 1972 was far from the "Dream Team" that the 1960 team had been. Instead, the United States had a young team which hadn't ever played together, unlike the Soviets, who had many of their players back from the 1968 bronze-medal squad. The Soviets were much older than their American counterparts, more than five years older per man.

Even before the gold medal game, the United States had their problems. Brazil, rated number two in the 1972 Olympic tournament, gave the United States all they could handle. The United States led by a point with 6:50 remaining, and then Doug Collins from Illinois State scored seven points in about ninety seconds to give the U.S. some breathing room. The U.S. team eventually won by a score of 61–54. At that point, writers were writing that the other teams—particularly Russia and Brazil—had players that could play with the Americans, but not the depth.

The U.S. amateurs had the players who would turn out to be the top two picks from the 1973 NBA draft—Collins and six-foot-eight Jim Brewer (from the University of Minnesota). The United States didn't just have one talented center, they had two. Tom Burleson was the third overall pick in the 1974 NBA draft, and the seven-foot-four center played in the NBA for seven years. Tom McMillen was a six-foot-eleven center that would go on to be the ninth pick in the 1974 draft, and play eleven seasons in the NBA before becoming a congressman.

Because of McMillen and Burleson, one can understand why Iba elected not to run teams off the court. His teams walked it up more than the players liked. In the semifinals, the United States had no trouble with Italy, while the Soviets came from behind to defeat Cuba 67–61 in their semifinal game. It set up the two super-powers going against each other, with the United States trying to go 64–0 with eight gold medals in basketball.

The gold medal game pitted world, as well as basketball, rivals. The U.S. team started the game in a hole, with the Soviets scoring the first seven points. By halftime, the score was 26–21, in favor of the USSR. The Russians led by as many as ten points early in the second half. With just under thirteen minutes remaining in the gold medal game, the American's leading scorer and rebounder, Dwight Jones, and Soviet reserve Dvorni Edeshko were both ejected from the game after a loose ball scuffle. Seconds later, the U.S. suffered another setback when Jim Brewer suffered a concussion after being knocked to the floor. The U.S. still trailed by eight points, with six minutes to go. It is a cliché, but the Americans never quit. Guard Kevin Joyce got hot. In the final forty-five seconds, Jim Forbes hit a huge shot, McMillian blocked a shot, and Collins made his potential game-winning steal. The Soviets were ahead 49–48 when Doug Collins intercepted a pass and drove in for the potential game-winning hoop. He was given a hard foul, with his Soviet opponent making sure that Collins would have to earn the points at the free-throw line. Doug was groggy getting up, and Iba wasn't even sure if Collins would be able to shoot. Collins made two of the most pressure-packed free throws of all time, giving the United States their very first lead with only three seconds remaining.

McMillan was assigned to guard the out-of-bounds opponent with the ball. The Soviets threw a desperation pass which was deflected, and the United States won the game. The young U.S. amateurs were celebrating their hard-fought victory, when they noticed confusion at the scorer's table. Referee Renato Righetto of Brazil noted the disturbance and called an administrative timeout. The Soviet coach was claiming that he had called a timeout following Collins' first shot. The horn had indeed gone off just as Collins released his second free throw. The German officials at the scorer's table apparently forgot to tell the game officials about the coach's timeout request following the Collins' first free-throw. The USSR was awarded the time-out. When play resumed, they inbounded the ball and time ran out. Give the gold to the boys in the red, white, and blue, right? Not so fast.

An Olympic official in the stands, Great Britain's R. William Jones, who had no jurisdiction in the game (but was the Secretary-General of FIBA, the governing head of international basketball), was instructing the scorer to reset the clock to *three seconds, not one*, giving the Soviets another chance to win the game. Again, the United States defended the in-bounds pass. This time, the pass was short, and the United States had won the game again. Only it *still* wasn't over! The official decided that the clock had been improperly reset. This time, there was bedlam on the court. Iba and his assistants were arguing fiercely at the scorer's table, to no avail.

There was mass confusion on the court. Aleksandr Belov shoved Joyce and Forbes out of the way, caught the inbounds pass and scored an easy lay-up. This time, it was really over. USSR 51, U.S. 50 was the final. One of two officials working the game—the Brazilian Righetto—refused to certify the score. The medal ceremony was postponed while FIBA heard the U.S. appeal.

R. William Jones appointed Ferenc Hepp of Hungary to be chairman of the FIBA jury of appeals committee. The vote was 3–2, with representatives of the Communist bloc countries of Hungary, Poland, and Cuba voting for the Soviets. Judges from Italy and Puerto Rico voted for the United States. It was quite a surprising vote.

The U.S. team voted not to accept their silver medals, and have never backed away from that stance.

EVIDENCE TO SUPPORT A CONSPIRACY

It certainly appeared that the Soviets were going to get as many chances as they needed to score those last two points. If you're looking for conspirators, start with Jones, who lived in Munich, and did everything possible to ensure the gold went to the Soviets. Include the ref that didn't call an offensive foul on Belov as he scored the game-winning field goal as well (although, try making that call in any game!). Other conspirators included the committee which ignored the video evidence and ruled against the U.S., and the IOC, which sat through a desperation protest from the United States and did nothing to rectify the situation.

MY OPINION

This was a game that the United States was not allowed to win. They couldn't put away the Soviets by a substantial margin early in the game, and would be later criticized at home for not running the Soviets off the court. Iba played a slow-down game, and that played into the Soviets' hands. Some questioned why the 7'4" Burleson wasn't in the game for the final seconds.

I wish coach Iba could have taken his team off the court and not come out for the second and third passes by the Soviets. The coaching staff could have sized up the situation, decided that the game was over, and let the chips fall where they may.

Barring that, I wish that a compromise had been formed in the appeals process, perhaps even allowing the two teams to play the entire game over. That, to me, would have been the only fair way to settle things.

*   *   *   *   *

OTHER OLYMPIC SHENANIGANS
1908 Men's 400-meter Final in London

This was one of the most controversial events in Olympic history, and nearly led to a walkout by the entire American squad. Four athletes, including three Americans (John Taylor, W.C. Robbins, and J.C. Carpenter) qualified for the final in the 400 meter. The favorite was London-born Wyndham Halswelle, who had set an Olympic record in the semi-final. There were not assigned lanes or a staggered start.

Guess what happened? Coming into the home stretch, Halswelle attempted to make his move on the outside, but Carpenter ran wide and kept the hometown hero from taking the lead. British officials immediately called foul. Before the race was even finished, they broke the tape and pulled Taylor off the track before he could come in first. The Americans exploded, as you can imagine. Olympic officials studied the footprints of the runners and ruled that American Carpenter had deliberately cut off Halswelle. The American was disqualified, and the race was scheduled to be re-run two days later, this time with strings laid out to divide lanes. Robbins and Taylor pulled out in protest, leaving Halswelle running around the track in a no-contest, to become the only track and field athlete ever to win a gold medal unchallenged.

The 1972 U.S. basketball team should have taken a page from the 1908 U.S. track team and not gone back onto the court to replay the game's final seconds. By the way, that 1908 men's 400-meter had ramifications: the judging and supervision of events was taken away from the host country and given to the international federations. But the question remains, was it gamesmanship by the Americans, or a conspiracy by the British officials?

1992 Unified Weightlifting Team

Then there's the story of the short-lived "Unified Team." The IOC couldn't have the USSR compete in the Olympics after the 1988 Games, what with the Soviet Union having broken up into fifteen independent nations. Estonia, Latvia, and Lithuania all competed independently in Barcelona in 1992, but the other twelve ex-Soviet republics entered as a combined squad, known as the "Unified Team." The head coach of the Unified Weightlifting

Team, Russian Vassily Alekseyev, passed up overwhelming favorite Altymurat Orazdurdiyev of Turkmenistan in the light-heavyweight division. Ibragim Samadov, a Russian, was also on the Unified Team. Fifteen minutes before the official weigh-in, Alekseyev informed Orazdurdiyev that he would not be allowed to compete because he would "get in the way" of Samadov. Orazdurdiyev pleaded with his coach and even offered to lose to Samadov and settle for a silver medal, but Alekseyev, himself a former Olympic champion, ignored him.

Ibragim Samadov competed ahead of his more deserving team-mate Orazdurdiyev, but didn't come home with any kind of medal, mainly because he was a sore loser. One of the other weightlifters competing was Pyrros Dimas, who had competed for Albania until 1990. In February of 1991, Dimas slipped across the border into Greece and was granted Greek citizenship. Samadov lifted the same 370 total KG that Dimas and Poland's Krzysztof Siemion managed, but lost to both in a tie-breaker based on body weight. The crowd had cheered on Dimas, and had heckled Samadov. As Samadov was about to be handed his bronze medal on the podium, he refused to lean forward to allow the medal to be put around his neck. He then left the podium. The walkout was considered a slap in the face by the Olympic officials, who disqualified Samadov, and kicked him out of the Olympic Village. Samadov wrote a letter the next day to the International Weightlifting president, explaining that he wasn't feeling well, and that is why he left the podium. The excuse didn't wash.

1976 East German Swimmers

The East German women won eleven of thirteen races in 1976, with Kornelia Ender winning four gold medals. But it turned out the East German women were ahead of the curve in using performance-enhancing drugs. And to be fair, North Americans were soon in on the trick, with Canadian sprinter Ben Johnson getting caught in 1988 after winning the 100-meter. He tested positive for the anabolic steroid stanozolol. Unless these athletes were whipping up potions in their dorms, there was a conspiracy of sorts that enabled them to get the drugs. You don't have to have a conspiracy to cheat, but it certainly helps.

CONCLUSION:

Olympic gold medalist in women's 100-meter hides a secret

Most of the conspiracies and lies that people had to keep secret were for a short time. Perhaps Tris Speaker had to worry about having fixed a game during the 1919 season for seven years, since he knew there was a paper trail and evidence of his involvement. But seven years is still just seven years. It's not a lifetime. Perhaps the members of the 1951 New York Giants conspired to hide their secret sign stealing for fifty years. Eventually, it was revealed. There was one athlete who competed for so long and so well that she was enshrined in her sport's Hall of Fame. However, that person had to keep a secret that would have destroyed reputations and possibly caused her accomplishments to be wiped from the record books. That athlete had to bring in at least one other person to help ensure the secret. You bet it was a conspiracy. And Stella Walsh would have gone to the grave with her secret, had she not been gunned down by a stray bullet at the age of sixty-nine near her home in Cleveland, Ohio.

The list of Olympic champions in the women's 100-meter race is filled with some of the greatest female athletes of all time, including Betty Cuthbert, Wilma Rudolph, Evelyn Ashford, Florence Griffith-Joyner, Gail Devers, and Marion Jones. A few may have cheated, possibly getting help from Bay Area lab chemists to alter their bodies, but none had a story like 1936 gold medalist Stella Walsh.

Walsh, born in Poland in April of 1911, moved to the United States when she was less than one year old. She grew up in Cleveland, Ohio, and the little girl born Stanislawa Walasievicz became known as Stella Walsh. By 1927, when she was sixteen, she had earned a spot on the American Olympic track and field team. However, since she had been born in Poland, she wasn't an American citizen, and could not apply for citizenship until 1932, when she turned twenty-one. Walsh began to run for the Polish national athletic team. She was one of the most well-known female athletes in the late 1920s, winning sprints and long jumps in both America and Poland.

In the 1932 Olympic games, she represented Poland. She matched the then-world record times in both the heats and the semi-finals of the 100-meter race. She also competed in the discus throw, finishing sixth. These games, held in Los Angeles, were the same games where Babe Didrickson made a name for herself, becoming the greatest female athlete in the world. While Walsh was setting new records in the 100-meter, Didrickson won two gold medals (in the eighty-meter hurdles and the javelin toss) and a silver medal in the high jump.

Walsh returned to Poland following the games, and was one of the most popular people in the country for a number of years. In the 1936 Olympic games in Berlin she was beaten out for the gold medal by U.S. track star Helen Stephens. Walsh came in second, running the race in 11.7 seconds. Stella almost got her groove back, when Stephens had to submit to a genital inspection to prove that she was a woman. German doctors proved Stephens was a female, and the fastest one in the world.

That would prove considerably ironic, as it was Stella Walsh who was concealing male genitalia. But that wouldn't be discovered for decades.

Get this: Also at the 1936 Olympic games, German Hermann Ratjen, a member of the Hitler Youth, taped up his genitals and entered the Olympic games as "Dora." (We only know the truth about Ratjen because he confessed to this in 1957, claiming that Nazi officials put him up to it.) He was obviously not the perfect Aryan specimen, as he couldn't even place for a medal among the women. Ratjen finished fourth in the women's high jump. My point is this: Wanting to win gold medals led certain athletes to hide their private parts. Some people were suspected, and some were tested. Some were caught. And some were not.

Walsh moved back to the United States and continued to compete as an amateur. In 1947, she applied for and received American citizenship, and married boxer Neil Olson. Walsh and Olson were married for only a few months, but she used his last name for the rest of her life. Olson was obviously in on her deception, and what he got out of it remains his secret.

On June 13, 1963, Walsh competed in a track meet at the age of fifty-two. Sportswriter Oscar Fraley wrote this for UPI:

> Stella Walsh must stand out as one of the two greatest women athletes of all time. The other, of course, would the late Mildred "Babe" Didrickson Zaharias. The Babe was something pretty special . . . but Stella is a marvel in her own right, too.
>
> For Miss Walsh won the 1932 Olympic 100m run, and four years later, despite a pulled leg muscle, came in second. She won forty-one National AAU Championships in the 100-yard dash, 220-yard dash, broad jump, discuss throw, and basketball throw. Even Stella doesn't know how many records she set or held. The closest guess

would have to be 100, and it can be estimated that she won more than 1,100 events.

Five times Stella was the National AAU pentathlon champion, from 1950–1954. And now she's competing at the age of 52.

Just in case you're panting at the mere thought of it, Stella provides this formula for physical fitness: Regular morning calisthenics. A careful diet which avoids fried foods and taboo pastries, and plenty of sleep at regular hours.

Of course, it probably didn't hurt to be a man competing against women. Walsh was inducted into the U.S. Track and Field Hall of Fame in 1975.

Walsh was a bystander during an armed robbery in Cleveland on December 4, 1980. She was killed instantly by a stray bullet. The *New York Times* reported in January of 1981 in an Associated Press story, "Stella Walsh, who won a gold medal and several silver medals in track competing as a woman, had male sex organs, according to an autopsy. The report also said that Miss Walsh had no female sex organs."

Well, then the *Associated Press* found her husband, and his story was published in all the newspapers on February 12, 1981, with a headline reading: "Stella Walsh's Husband 'Disgusted' By Publicity."

Harry Olson said his late wife's name had been slandered. "I don't see what Cleveland is doing and what sadistic satisfaction the city is getting out of all this," Olson said in a telephone interview from Northridge, California. "Where does the city government get the right to persecute someone? It appears Nazi Germany is right here in the U.S. and alive and well in Cleveland. If Cleveland weren't so bankrupt, I'd sue the city for slander."

Sure you would, Harry. That's exactly the kind of tough talk people expect of a co-conspirator.

This 1981 Associated Press story reported that Olson married Miss Walsh in 1956, but lived with her only a few months. Walsh considered herself single at the time of her death, and her autopsy reported her as "divorced."

Olson, the 1981 AP story says, met Walsh through friends when she was living in California, and he rarely saw her because of her heavy competing schedule in basketball and track. He said he never received any notification that he was divorced, and was under the impression that they were still married at the time of her death.

It is my contention that this is the perfect sports conspiracy. It is the ultimate cover-up.

CONCLUSION:

Did UNLV throw the 1991 NCAA semi-final game vs. Duke?

Looking back with the perspective afforded by history, it's hard to imagine a time when Mike Krzyzewski's Duke University Blue Devils could be considered a major underdog in a game of consequence. Over the course of twenty-eight years at the end of the bench in Durham, Krzyzewski has built the Blue Devils into one of the true powers of college basketball. His 833 wins, 3 national titles, 10 Final Fours (third most in history), 11 Atlantic Coast Conference Championships, and 71 NCAA tournament victories (an NCAA-record) have cemented Coach K's place among the greatest coaches in history. But in 1991, when his Blue Devils' entry into the Final Four marked their fourth consecutive trip to the game's ultimate showcase, they had yet to return to Durham as champions. In order to do that, they'd have to first find a way to beat one of the greatest teams the college game had ever seen in the national semifinal.

When Jerry Tarkanian's University of Nevada, Las Vegas Runnin' Rebels arrived at Indianapolis' Hoosier Dome for the 1991 NCAA Final Four, they did so as overwhelming favorites to repeat as National Champions of the college basketball world. After all, UNLV hadn't lost a game in more than thirteen months, a span of forty-five games. They had won thirty-four times that season by an average margin of 27.3 points, scoring an average of 98.3 points in those victories. The Runnin' Rebels also returned four of their five starters from the previous season's championship roster, including Larry Johnson, the recipient of all three National Player of the Year Awards in 1991 (the Naismith Award, the John R. Wooden Award, and the Oscar Robertson Trophy), and Stacy Augmon (nicknamed Plastic Man), who that year took home the Henry Iba Corinthian Award (presented to the nation's top defensive player) for the third consecutive season.

The Runnin' Rebels were justifiably confident heading into their semi-final matchup against Duke, a team they had humiliated in the previous season's championship game by thirty points (a record for margin of victory in a championship game that stands to this day). Duke had put together an impressive season in 1991, winning thirty games against just seven losses, but after losing three of their top four scorers from the previous season's runner-up squad to graduation, few observers gave the Blue Devils much of a shot to beat Johnson, Augmon, and Co. And with good reason.

Johnson was, without exaggeration, one of the most dominant college players of his or any era. A junior college transfer from tiny Odessa College, Johnson, an athletic power forward known for his ferocious dunks and physical style of play, was listed at 6'7" in the UNLV media guide. In truth, however, he was likely several inches shorter. Like Charles Barkley before him, Johnson played bigger than his size, attacking the basket aggressively, going after rebounds with great tenacity, and regularly defending opponents significantly larger than him. As a senior in 1991, Johnson averaged 22.7 points per game, 11.2 rebounds per game, shot 66.2% from the field, and was named to the first team All-America squad for the second straight year. In June, the Charlotte Hornets made him the first overall pick in the 1991 NBA Draft. He was joined at the top of the first round by teammates Augmon (#9 to Atlanta) and point guard Greg Anthony, (#12 to New York). Center George Ackles was also drafted that year, going twenty-ninth overall to the Miami Heat.

In short, the Runnin' Rebels were stacked. But despite this star power, some skeptics in the national media attempted to downplay their dominance heading into the Big Dance by citing the weak competition they faced in the Big West Conference. But in addition to their 18–0 conference record against also-rans like San Jose State, Long Beach State, and UC Santa Barbara (the last team to beat the Rebels before their streak began), UNLV also posted impressive wins in 1991 against eventual tournament teams Michigan State (95–75), Florida State (101–69), and the University of Arkansas (112–105 at Fayetteville), which, at the time of the game, was the nation's second-ranked team.

"That bunch with Larry Johnson and Anderson Hunt just manhandled you," former Arkansas Head Coach Nolan Richardson said years later. "They were men playing with boys. I think [UNLV] is the best team I've ever seen. I'm not sure anyone else is even close."

After easily dispatching of the University of Montana, 99–65, in the tournament's opening round, Tarkanian's Rebels faced what was perceived by many to be their most serious threat when they faced John Thompson's Georgetown University Hoyas in round two. Georgetown possessed the twin towers of Alonzo Mourning and Dikembe Mutombo, and the defensive presence of the 6'10" Mourning and 7'2" Mutombo helped contribute to UNLV shooting just 37% from the field, their worst shooting performance all season. Though the Rebels outlasted Georgetown and escaped with a 62–54 victory, it was only the second time that season that they had been held to a margin of victory below ten points.

Once past Thompson's Hoyas, it was supposed to be easy sailing to a second consecutive title for UNLV. No team had repeated as champions since John Wooden's UCLA team won the last of its record seven consecutive titles in 1973 (UCLA would hold this distinction until Billy Donovan's Florida squad captured back-to-back titles in 2006–07). Moreover, no team had finished a complete season undefeated since Bob Knight's Indiana Hoosiers managed the feat back in 1976. But all that was expected to change, and when the Runnin' Rebels bested a very good University of Utah team, 83–66, and a Terry Dehere–led Seton Hall team, 77–65, in the West regional final in Seattle, few believed they would be challenged in Indianapolis.

Duke's berth in the 1991 Final Four was somewhat of a surprise. Though they were a #2 seed and were the regular season champions of the ACC (an unofficial title), their stunning twenty-two-point loss at the hands of the archrival North Carolina Tar Heels (a team they had beaten twice in the regular season) in the conference tournament championship led many to question whether the 1990–91 Blue Devils had what it took to win on the big stage. Though led by second-team All-America selection Christian Laettner and sturdy point guard Bobby Hurley (son of the legendary high school coach Bob Hurley, Sr. of St. Anthony's in Jersey City, New Jersey), the losses of graduating seniors Alaa Abdelnaby, Phil Henderson, and Robert Brickey, who together combined to account for just under half of the points the entire Blue Devils team scored in 1989–90, was palpable. While the 1990–91 team was bolstered by the addition of freshman Grant Hill, he had yet to become the dynamic player he'd prove to be in future campaigns. And though Duke's roster boasted five players averaging double-digit scoring averages, they seemed to lack the toughness and grit required to compete with a team like UNLV. On paper, it looked like an epic mismatch.

Fortunately for the Blue Devils and their fans, championships aren't decided on paper. Let the record show that Duke defeated UNLV, 79–77, and then captured their first national title two nights later by beating Kansas, 72–65. The semifinal victory is considered by many to be one of the greatest upsets in modern sports history (ESPN *Page 2* readers voted it the fourth greatest upset ever in a 2001 poll behind only the 1980 Miracle on Ice, Buster Douglas' unlikely knockout of Mike Tyson in Tokyo, and wrestler Rulon Gardner's defeat of the seemingly invincible Alexander Karelin at the 2000 Olympic Games in Sydney). But for years, incredulous fans and members of the media have cast doubt of the validity of Duke's incredible upset. An analysis of the game's final minutes and some rather damning photographic evidence suggests that the shocking victory may have been the result of UNLV shaving points or, worse, conspiring with gamblers to throw the game.

Breakdown of final two-and-a-half minutes of the game

UNLV's uncharacteristically sloppy play and poor defending over the final two-and-a-half minutes of the game is what first draws suspicion of a fix. Here's the play-by-play:

2:32: UNLV center George Ackles tips in his own shot, capping a 6-0 Runnin' Rebels run. UNLV leads 76–71.

2:15: Bobby Hurley comes down court, pulls up, and sinks a three. With Anthony having fouled out at the 3:51 mark, Hurley is not particularly well-defended on the play. Duke is now down two, 76–74, at the 2:15 mark.

1:24: UNLV is called for a 45-second shot-clock violation. Duke ball.

1:02: Inexplicably, Brian Davis is poorly guarded on the in-bounds pass from half-court. He is permitted to drive the baseline and reaches the basket before he is finally encountered by Johnson, who fouls Davis as he sinks a short layup. Davis completes the three-point play, giving Duke a one-point edge at 77–76.

0:49: Augmon continues his miserable game by missing a short jumper in the lane. Augmon, who had averaged 16.5 points during the season, is held to just six points (3 for 10 shooting).

0:49: Johnson, whose thirteen points are also well below his season average, grabs the offensive rebound and is fouled by Grant Hill. Johnson misses both free throws but Duke is called for a lane violation on the second, giving Johnson another chance. He converts, tying the score at 77.

0:15: Working for a good shot, Duke takes thirty-four seconds off the clock before Thomas Hill takes and misses a short jump shot. Laettner grabs the offensive rebound and is fouled by reserve forward Evric Gray.

0:12: After UNLV calls a timeout, Laettner makes both free throws to give Duke a two-point lead at 79–77.

0:12: UNLV calls another timeout and Tarkanian draws up a final play. Larry Johnson somehow ends up handling the ball on the wing and finds himself with an open look at the basket from three-point range. Inconceivably, he passes up on the shot and skips a pass back to Anderson Hunt who throws up a desperation three-point shot with time expiring. The shot bounces hard off the back of the iron, Hurley grabs the rebound, and time expires. Duke wins.

EVIDENCE TO SUPPORT A CONSPIRACY

If UNLV's poor performance down the stretch of the game wasn't enough to suggest the likelihood of a fix, A.D. Hopkins of the *Las Vegas Review-Journal* reported on May 26, 1991, that three UNLV players, Moses Scurry, Anderson Hunt, and David Butler had been entertained at the home of Richie "The Fixer" Perry, a twice-convicted sports-event fixer who had figured in both the fixing of harness races at the Roosevelt and Yonkers racetracks in New York in 1974 and the Boston College basketball point shaving scandal of 1978–79. At the time of the publication of the

Review-Journal article, Perry was under consideration by Nevada state gaming investigators for inclusion in the state's "Black Book," the list of individuals prohibited by law from entering Nevada casinos. Perry was also a key figure in an ongoing NCAA investigation of the UNLV basketball program, which had become a popular target during Tarkanian's years in Las Vegas. Because of violations stemming from the improper recruitment of New York playground phenom Lloyd Daniels in 1986 (in which Perry figured prominently), the Runnin' Rebels had already been placed on probation and had been banned from postseason play in 1991–92, before Hopkins' report was published.

What made the article so credible was that it included photographs, including one now legendary shot of the three UNLV players sitting in a hot tub with Perry. Another shot showed the three players playing basketball with Perry on Perry's home court. Though it was impossible to verify, the photos were believed to have been taken in the fall of 1989, before UNLV's first championship run.

A few months before that, in April of 1989, Ted Gup and Brian Doyle of *Time* magazine reported in an article titled "Playing to Win in Vegas" that Butler and Scurry accepted money and a free lunch from Perry at Caesar's Palace the previous fall. Other reports indicated that Perry had often been seen at UNLV games sitting in seats originally provided to the coach. Perry had also been seen at the 1991 Final Four sitting in floor-level seats allotted to NCAA coaches, though there was no way to determine whether or not those seats had been given to Tarkanian.

Further evidence of a fix was revealed in February of 1992 when the *Las Vegas Review-Journal* reported that a federal investigation had been launched in an attempt to determine whether or not UNLV shaved points in games during the 1990–91 season, including the Final Four loss to Duke. The report also indicated that the authorities had inquired about surveillance tapes at Trump

Plaza hotel in Atlantic City that may contain visual evidence of Augmon associating with Perry shortly after the loss.

Though he vehemently denied any involvement with Perry or any other gamblers, Tarkanian resigned as head coach of the Runnin' Rebels in March of 1992, citing an inability to recruit in the wake of the scandal.

EVIDENCE AGAINST A CONSPIRACY

The most compelling argument against the existence of a fixed game is that in 1991, before the rise of online sportsbooks, there was no way to legally bet on the game. Because of the law that prohibits the sportsbooks of Nevada casinos from taking bets or posting lines on events or games involving Nevada teams (put in place to avoid game fixes), there was no official line on the semi-final game (reports vary on the issue, but it is generally agreed that the illegal line on the game was six and seven points). Bookmakers in the UK, where sports gambling is legal, have never paid much attention to the NCAA basketball tournament and there is no evidence that the 1991 tournament marked an exception. That left all of the action to illegal bookmaking operations, most of which are mob run.

Perry had a documented relationship with the Lucchese crime family dating back to his race fixing in New York in the 1970s, but none of the investigations turned up any evidence of Perry or any of the UNLV players associating with mobsters in 1991. It seems unlikely that players like Johnson and Augmon (who combined for only nineteen points in the loss) would risk associating with mobsters for a payday that would pale in comparison to the one awaiting them in the NBA (as previously mentioned, both were selected within the first nine picks of the 1991 NBA Draft).

UNLV players like guard Anderson Hunt, who was not destined to become an NBA lottery pick (in fact, he was undrafted) might seem like a more likely candidate to shave points. After all, Hunt was one of the three players pictured in the infamous hot tub photo. But that argument falls apart when one takes a look at the game's box score and sees that Hunt led all scorers that night with twenty-nine points. Knowing the likely repercussions he'd face for crossing the mob, it is unlikely that Hunt (who shot 11 for 20 from the field, including 4 for 11 from behind the arc) would have been part of any fix.

Box Score
DUKE 79, UNLV 77

	FG–A	3G–A	FT–A	RO	RD	RT	F	TP	AS	TP	BK	ST	MN
UNLV													
4 Johnson, Larry	5–10	0–2	3–4	5	8	13	3	13	2	3	2	1	39
23 Gray, Evric	1–2	0–0	0–0	0	1	1	2	2	0	3	0	0	14
44 Ackles, George	3–6	0–0	1–2	2	3	5	4	7	0	0	1	0	25
32 Augmon, Stacey	3–10	0–0	0–1	5	3	8	2	6	2	4	1	2	39
24 Spencer, Elmore	0–2	0–0	1–2	1	2	3	2	1	1	0	0	0	9
12 Hunt, Anderson	11–20	4–11	3–5	1	3	4	0	29	2	1	0	1	39
50 Anthony, Greg	8–18	2–2	1–1	3	2	5	5	19	6	1	0	3	35
TEAM	31–68	6–15	9–15	18	22	40	18	77	13	12	4	7	200

	FG-A	3G-A	FT-A	RO	RD	RT	F	TP	AS	TP	BK	ST	MN
DUKE													
34 Palmer, Crawford	0–0	0–0	0–0	0	1	1	1	0	0	0	0	0	6
23 Davis, Brian	6–12	0–0	3–4	1	3	4	1	15	1	1	0	1	21
5 McCaffrey, Bill	2–3	0–0	1–2	0	0	0	1	5	2	0	0	0	14
12 Hill, Thomas	2–6	0–0	2–2	0	2	2	2	6	1	0	1	1	22
21 Lang, Antonio	0–0	0–0	0–0	0	0	0	0	0	0	0	1	0	2
22 Koubek, Greg	1–6	0–3	0–0	0	1	1	1	2	3	1	1	0	22
32 Laettner, Christian	9–14	1–1	9–11	3	4	7	2	28	2	4	1	1	40
11 Hurley, Bobby	4–7	3–4	1–1	0	2	2	3	12	7	3	0	2	40
33 Hill, Grant	5–8	0–0	1–1	0	5	5	2	11	5	5	0	1	33
TEAM	**29–56**	**4–8**	**17–21**	**7**	**19**	**26**	**13**	**79**	**21**	**14**	**4**	**6**	**200**

TECHNICAL FOULS: Johnson (UNLV)

ATTENDANCE: 47,100

OFFICIALS: John Clougherty, Tom O'Neill, Ted Valentine

Another argument against the fix is the spectacle of the game. Most of history's more notable college basketball point-shaving scandals (CCNY, Boston College, Arizona State, Northwestern) have occurred far from the national spotlight. Usually the fixed games are the ones the fixers don't think anyone's paying attention to, because the games generally don't attract national interest and, in turn, suspicion. Clearly it's easier to shave points in a mid-January game between Northwestern and, say, Iowa than in one of the most-watched college basketball games in history. With a national television audience watching, and a national media analyzing, irregularities in game play are much more likely to be noticed. Fixers aren't looking to attract that kind of attention.

Tarkanian, not surprisingly, was and is the most vocal defender of his players. Asked about the possibility of a fix a few years later, he said, "No one would have [accused us of throwing that game] if we weren't from Las Vegas. Every March there are upsets—Bucknell over Kansas, George Mason over Connecticut—but when it occurs no one says Kansas or Connecticut was throwing the game. Like the mob couldn't get to a player at a school outside of Las Vegas. We lost to Duke, a team with three lottery picks and a great coach who goes on to win consecutive national championships, and people questioned whether we threw the game? It's unbelievable."

Tarkanian also claimed that until the *Time* magazine piece ran he only knew Perry as "Sam" and believed he was in the "commodities business." In a 2008 column he wrote for the *Las Vegas Sun*, Tarkanian again addressed the infamous hot tub photo, saying, "We didn't know who [Perry] was. I didn't. Moses said as a young kid Perry would buy him shoes and bring groceries to the family. I don't blame Moses. Nothing wrong with that. Moses said Perry talked to him about getting his grades up and doing what's right. A writer in Dallas came up with that Richard "The Fixer" Perry stuff. I told guys to stay away."

To add a further sordid wrinkle to the whole ordeal, Tarkanian leveled a rather serious allegation that the photo of his players in the hot tub with Perry had been leaked to the *Journal-Review* by

Dennis Finfrock, UNLV's interim athletic director at the time, at the behest of University President Robert Maxson. This claim, however, was never substantiated.

My Opinion

It's hard for me to believe that the UNLV players didn't throw this game. "They keep trying to find a reason why we lost to Duke," Stacey Augmon told the *Las Vegas Review-Journal* shortly after the game. "But we just lost, period."

Sorry, Plastic Man, but I just don't buy it. And it's not just the hot tub photos that have me convinced.

Sure, the photos are damning. But they themselves aren't proof of a conspiracy. Of the three UNLV players pictured in the photos, only Anderson Hunt played in the loss to Duke. And as I mentioned, his twenty-nine points led all scorers. To me, the most damning evidence can be found by watching the final twelve seconds of the game. They're on YouTube if you're curious.

Tarkanian had called a timeout following Laettner's second free throw, conceivably to design a play. But when play resumed, the in-bounds pass came in to Johnson, a power forward not known for his ball-handling skills. Instead of passing, Johnson carries the ball up-court. He pulls up around the three-point line on the right side, at about a forty-five degree angle to the basket. Laettner comes out on him, mindful, I'm sure, of Johnson's ability to drive to the basket, and does not defend aggressively. As Johnson takes a clear look at the basket with seven seconds remaining, Laettner raises his arms but does not leave his feet, careful not to foul the shooter. Johnson, however, decides not to take the shot, instead pulling the ball down and passing it out to Hunt with about four seconds remaining. Defended well by Hurley with help from Laettner, Hunt's desperation shot at the buzzer is off the mark. The long rebound is gathered by Hurley, and Duke is victorious.

Today, eighteen years later, I still don't understand why Johnson didn't take the shot when he had the open look. Some have argued that after missing the mark on both of his three-point attempts earlier in the game, Johnson lacked confidence in his outside shot and therefore decided to give the ball up to Hunt, a much better three-point shooter. But while Johnson was far from a Reggie Miller-like sharpshooter from distance, anybody who remembers his miracle four-point play vs. Indiana in the 1999 Eastern Conference Finals knows that Johnson had the ability to knock down the three-ball. He shot 34.9% from three-point range as a collegian (30 of 86) and 33% as a pro (414 of 1,259 including the playoffs), decent percentages for a power forward, so despite Hunt's hot hand it is unlikely that's the reason Johnson passed up on an open look at the basket. Plus, if there was one thing Larry Johnson never lacked, it was confidence.

Put yourself in Johnson's shoes for a moment. Imagine that you're the consensus national player of the year. A two-time first team All-American. You have a clean look at the basket. The national championship is on the line. There's seven seconds on the clock. Don't you take the shot? Of course you do. Anderson Hunt may be the better shooter from distance, but if you're playing to win the game there's no way you pass the ball there. No way. Sorry, Tark.

CONCLUSION:

Was Cal Ripken's 2001 All-Star Game home run a set-up?

When "Iron Man" Cal Ripken, Jr. of the Baltimore Orioles announced in June, 2001, that he would be retiring from baseball at the end of that season, the rest of the year became a farewell tour of sorts for the decorated twenty-one-year veteran. The highlight of this tour was unquestionably the All-Star Game, held that year at Seattle's Safeco Field.

While Ripken's career accomplishments made his eventual election to the National Baseball Hall of Fame in 2007 a no-brainer, some questioned whether his selection to the 2001 Midsummer Classic (his nineteenth in a row) was warranted. Playing in a record 2,632 consecutive games over seventeen seasons had taken a toll on Ripken, and in his last few years in the majors his offensive production declined significantly. In 2001 he'd post the worst statistical season of his career, and at the All-Star break Ripken was batting just .240 with four home runs, twenty-eight runs batted, in seven doubles in and a dreadful OPS (on base plus slugging) percentage of .594. By comparison, fellow third baseman Eric Chavez of the Oakland Athletics was not selected to the

American League squad despite substantially superior numbers (his .245 batting average notwithstanding, Chavez had tallied eleven homers, forty-six RBI, twenty-five doubles, and an OPS of .738 while on his way to earning the first of six consecutive Gold Glove Awards as the league's best defensive third baseman).

Overtaking Anaheim's Troy Glaus and Seattle's David Bell for the starting position in the final week due to a flurry of online voting, Ripken was clearly a sentimental choice for the 2001 AL roster, and it's hard to argue against his inclusion. The Major League Baseball All-Star Game has long been a popularity contest and Ripken was not the first (or last) seemingly undeserving player to be selected. As long as voting is primarily determined by the fans, that's the way it will always be. And I don't have a problem with the fans' desire to see Ripken take his last All-Star hacks in 2001. That's not the point of this chapter, anyway.

This chapter also isn't about the selfless, touching gesture extended to Ripken by Alex Rodriguez, the AL's starting short-stop, in the first inning. Rodriguez had arranged with AL manager Joe Torre to pay tribute to Ripken, his boyhood idol, by switching positions with him and allowing Ripken to play the first inning at the position he had played for 2,216 consecutive games. They switched back to their elected positions at the start of the second inning. While that was a nice touch on the part of a player who could use that kind of good press these days, it was really just the icing on Major League Baseball's PR-baked cake.

The real drama of the evening came in the bottom half of the third inning, when Ripken stepped up to bat for the first time. Upon his introduction by the public address announcer, he was greeted by the fans at Safeco with a standing ovation. This was a classy move on the part of the Seattle fans, considering how it was their guy, Bell, who Ripken's supporters knocked out of the game with their late voting. As if to show his appreciation, Ripken connected with the very first pitch he saw from pitcher Chan Ho Park of the Los Angeles Dodgers—a waist-high fastball—and launched the ball over the left-center field fence. Just forty-five days shy of his forty-first birthday, he became the oldest player to hit an All-Star Game home run. The crowd, sensing that they had just witnessed a genuine moment of baseball history, naturally responded with a second standing ovation.

Emboldened by Ripken's heroics, the American League squad added three more runs and went on to win the game, 4-1. The National League managed only three hits. Ripken, of course, was named the game's MVP, the second time he had earned that honor.

In his postgame press conference, Torre called the home run "unbelievable."

"It was great; it was something special," added Yankees' short-stop Derek Jeter, who also homered in the game.

"It's like a dream come true," Cubs slugger Sammy Sosa said. "It doesn't get better than that as a human being."

It was quite the storybook ending to Ripken's All-Star career and the fawning national media ate it up, writing saccharine, overblown columns extolling Ripken's importance, irrevocable virtue, and shining example to America's youth. Here, the sports radio hosts opined, was a man we could believe in. Set our clocks by. Trust, even. The last of a dying breed. ESPN, never one to shy away from hyperbole, went as far as to rank Ripken's homer the fifty-sixth most memorable sporting moment of the past twenty-five years, ranking it ahead of such indelible baseball moments as Luis Gonzalez' World Series–winning base hit off of the Yankees' Mariano Rivera later that same year and George Brett's infamous pine tar home run.

But not everyone was buying it; especially those who had watched repeated replays of the home run. The moment was so perfect that some have had the audacity to question whether or not it was on the level. Park, some suggested, appeared to have grooved the pitch.

Could that be so?

EVIDENCE SUPPORTING A CONSPIRACY

It's important to note that none of those who have questioned the authenticity of Ripken's final All-Star Game home run have implied that Ripken himself was in on the fix. He was far too proud and honorable a player (and man) to agree to such a thing. What the conspiracy theorists have suggested is that Park was instructed, whether by NL manager Bobby Valentine or by Commissioner Selig, to toss ole Cal a meatball.

Park, who was making his first (and only) All-Star appearance, didn't exactly throw a meatball, though. A meatball traveling ninety-two miles per hour would likely disintegrate before reaching home plate. But what was questionable about Park's delivery was the location of the pitch. Even an average Major League hitter can hit a poorly located pitch thrown at that velocity. And Park's fastball not only came in to Ripken waist high, but right down the middle and without movement. It was straight as an arrow, and right in Ripken's wheelhouse. All Ripken needed to do, the theorists conjectured, was make contact. Simple as that.

One reason why Selig or Valentine (or perhaps Park himself) may have decided to give Ripken such a nice parting gift is that in those days the outcome of the game meant very little. Since 2003, the winner of the All-Star Game has determined which league's representative is awarded home field advantage in the World Series. In 2001, though, it was still just an exhibition. And since most of the gate receipts go to the Major League Baseball Players Association (MLPA) pension fund and not to the players (though their expenses are covered), it's not like the participants are competing for much more than pride (individual contract bonuses notwithstanding).

As the first Korean-born player to play in an All-Star Game, Park was representing an entire country and may therefore have had a greater sense of pride than his teammates. But he also had a knack for surrendering some historic long balls. After all, Park was not only the guy who once famously gave up two grand slams in one inning to the same player (Fernando Tatis), but he's also the guy who served up Barry Bonds' record-breaking seventy-first (and seventy-second) home run just two months after his "gift" to Ripken.

Speaking of Bonds (and the aforementioned Sosa), some have argued that shining the spotlight on a guy like Ripken, who had become symbol for all that was good and pure in baseball, may have been an attempt by Major League Baseball to direct fan (and media) attention away from how cartoonishly large its players were getting using performance-enhancing drugs. After all, this was 2001, the year three National Leaguers—Bonds, Sosa, and Arizona's Luis Gonzalez—combined to slug 194 round-trippers. Gonzalez, a slight 6'2", 180 lb. outfielder, had averaged just 16.4 home runs per season over the previous ten campaigns. Surprisingly, only one of Gonzalez's fifty-seven home runs in 2001 was surrendered by Park.

EVIDENCE AGAINST A CONSPIRACY

The strongest evidence against this conspiracy is the nature of baseball. It is often said that hitting a round ball with a round bat is the hardest thing to do in all of sports. Even if that's a debatable point, one thing that isn't debatable is that Ripken still had to connect and hit the home run even if Park did groove one for him.

Asked by the *San Francisco Chronicle*'s John Shea about the possibility of Park teeing one up, catcher Mike Piazza, who called the pitch Ripken knocked out of the park, expressed his doubt. "It was a strike," Piazza said. "Major-league hitters hit strikes. Even if you groove one, there's still a chance the batter's not going to hit it out. He could pop it up, roll it over. I read some pretty amazing things that people conjured up."

Commenting on the likelihood of the conspiracy in a column for ESPN.com's *Page 2*, Jim Caple wrote, "Bud Selig being capable of orchestrating anything more involved than the Beer Barrel Polka? Please." Ironically, this column came a year before Selig's awful and much-criticized decision to declare the 2002 All-Star Game, contested in his home park in Milwaukee, an eleven-inning tie after both teams had run out of available relief pitchers. In a later column, Caple wrote that the conspiracy theory surrounding Ripken's feat was "hokey," adding, that the homer "was just Cal, rising to the occasion as usual. Just as when he homered in the game he tied Lou Gehrig's playing streak. Just as he homered the next night when he broke Gehrig's record. Just as he so often did during his twenty-year career."

My Opinion

While there is little evidence to support the accusation that Commissioner Selig himself instructed Park to groove one to Ripken, it bears mentioning that Bobby Valentine, the National League's manager who once snuck back into the Mets dugout donning a fake moustache after being ejected, was not above resorting to dramatic shenanigans. Still, considering how Valentine and Ripken had no professional connection to each other, it seems unlikely that he would have ordered Park to put one on a platter for him.

I'm inclined to agree with Piazza on this one. Even if Park did groove the pitch, too many different things could have happened. Ripken could have fouled it off. He could have hit a line drive right at someone. He could have simply hit a sharp ground ball up the middle. And if any of those things had happened, we wouldn't be talking about a conspiracy today.

Park, himself, has never acknowledged that he had grooved the pitch. "It was an amazing moment," he said in the post-game press conference, presumably through a translator. "The first pitch I ever threw in an All-Star Game was the last home run for Mr. Ripken. It's a big gift for him. It made him MVP, that's pretty good."

An interesting choice of words, sure, but this conspiracy theory just doesn't hold up to scrutiny.

CONCLUSION:

#28&29

Two conspiracy theories in one! Did the New England Patriots, with an assist from the NFL, cheat their way to a dynasty?

With their three Super Bowl titles, four conference championships, six division titles, and .718 winning percentage (102–41) this millennium, it's hard to argue against the New England Patriots being the team of the decade in the National Football League (though fans of the Pittsburgh Steelers might disagree). But in 2000, Bill Belichick's first season as the Patriots' head coach, they were just another middle-of-the-road NFL team struggling their way through a miserable 5–11 season. Their sixth-round pick that year, a young quarterback out of the University of Michigan named Tom Brady, began the season fourth on their depth chart behind the entrenched starter, Drew Bledsoe, and backups John Friesz and Michael Bishop. Not one player from the Patriots' 2000 squad was selected for the Pro Bowl, and when they began the 2001 season with consecutive defeats and lost Bledsoe to injury, it looked like the Patriots were in for another losing season. Nobody could have predicted that this was a team on the verge of a dynasty.

So what happened?

For starters, Brady happened. Subbing for Bledsoe, a former three-time Pro Bowl selection, the unheralded and untested Brady seized the opportunity given to him and led the Patriots to victories in eleven of the team's final fourteen games in 2001, including seven out of eight to end the regular season.

Next, the defense improved vastly under Belichick and Defensive Coordinator Romeo Crennel. The same unit that had surrendered 338 points in 2000, reduced that total to 272 in 2001, holding their opponents to seventeen points or less in fourteen of the nineteen games they played—the playoffs included.

Speaking of the 2001 playoffs, it was there that the Patriots received a little, um, help from the refs.

And there's also that minor detail about their coaches illegally spying on their opponents.

Oh, and did I mention that the NFL rigged the whole thing to boost national morale?

I didn't? Well, then I guess I'll need to explain myself. And the only way to do that is to start with the night the Patriot Dynasty was born.

#28: The Tuck Rule Game

On the evening of January 19, 2002, I was sitting with my then girlfriend (now wife) in Grassroots Tavern on St. Mark's Place in New York City, drinking beer and casually watching the football game being shown on the television above the bar. It had only been a week since my beloved New York Giants let a twenty-four-point second-half lead slip away out in San Francisco, and I didn't have much of a stomach for football. But the game, which was being contested in a blinding snowstorm at Foxboro Stadium outside of Boston, was compelling. There's just something about football in the snow that gets me every time, and considering how this was the playoffs, and a close game, I was drawn in despite my lack of rooting interest.

Late in the fourth quarter, the Oakland Raiders clung to a 13–10 lead over New England. With 1:50 left on the clock, and having just crossed midfield, Brady dropped back to pass. He pump-faked, then pulled the ball down. As he did so, he was crushed by cornerback Charles Woodson, who had blitzed untouched off left end. The impact of Woodson's blow knocked the ball out of Brady's hands and to the ground, where it was recovered by Raiders linebacker Greg Biekert.

Both teams reacted as if it were a fumble. The Raiders were celebrating, knowing that the Patriots had no timeouts left, and therefore couldn't stop them from running out the clock. The Patriots players, including Brady, walked off the field dejectedly. None of them seemed to be petitioning for a video review.

"Game over," I said to my girlfriend. "Let's go."

We exited the bar and headed out into the cold New York night.

"Attaboy, Charlie Woodson," I said to myself. It had been a career-defining moment, and I felt happy for Woodson who, like Brady, was a former classmate of mine at Michigan. It wasn't until I got home an hour or so later that I learned the fumble didn't count, and the Patriots had *won the game*. When I heard the news on the radio, I couldn't believe it.

As it turned out, in my haste to exit the bar, I had missed the replay booth signal referee Walt Coleman to review the play which, in the final two minutes, is the replay official's call to make. I quickly turned on the TV and flipped to ESPN, whose analysts were dissecting the play. The replay, which they showed roughly 7,000 times (give or take a few thousand), clearly showed that Brady had begun his throwing motion but, sensing the charging Woodson, lowered his throwing arm and clutched the ball *with both hands* in a last-second attempt to "tuck" away or protect the football. Brady seemed to have halted his throwing motion *before* becoming separated from the ball, but he never completed the tucking action. Still, it sure looked like a fumble to me.

Subsequent highlights revealed that as I had been ignorantly waiting for an uptown 6 train, a hush had fallen over the anxious, capacity Foxboro crowd. With the Patriots' entire season riding on the call, one could have heard the snowflakes falling as Coleman walked to the middle of the field and confidently announced, "After reviewing the play, the quarterback's arm . . . was coming forward. It is an incomplete pass."

I beg your pardon? The quarterback's arm was doing *what*? Were we just watching the same replay?

Apparently we were. While under the hood, Coleman had seen enough to reverse his own call, later explaining that the play fell under the purview of Rule 3, Section 21, Article 2, Note 2 of the NFL rulebook, which states:

> *When a Team A player is holding the ball to pass it forward, any intentional forward movement of his arm starts a forward pass, even if the player loses possession of the ball as he is attempting to tuck it back toward his body. Also, if the player has tucked the ball into his body and then loses possession, it is a fumble.*

Much to the delight of the Patriots and their fans, the interpretation of this strange "Tuck Rule" caused the call on the field to be reversed. Brady, given new life, quickly completed a first-down pass to wide receiver David Patten that put placekicker Adam Vinatieri in a position to attempt a forty-five-yard, game-tying field goal. Without a timeout, the Patriots did not have the luxury of clearing the spot for Vinatieri, but he got the kick off cleanly and somehow managed to boot the ball through both the snowflakes and the uprights to send the game into overtime. The poor Raiders never saw the ball again. Brady completed all six of his passes to start the extra session, and with 8:29 remaining, Vinatieri connected yet again on a twenty-three-yard, game-winning kick. Incredible.

Incredible, that is, for the Patriots. In the locker room after the game, the Raiders expressed the overwhelming opinion that they had been robbed.

"[The call] never should have been overturned," said an angry Woodson. "Ball came out. Game over."

"I feel like we had one taken away from us," said the usually reserved Jerry Rice.

"We didn't lose this game," added linebacker William Thomas. "It was stolen from us."

Jon Gruden, the Raiders' head coach at the time, fumed in his post-game press conference. "It was obvious," Gruden said through his trademark scowl. "I thought it was a fumble. But the officials thought otherwise. You can never count on anything in the NFL."

Standing by his call, Coleman explained it to the media. "When I got over to the replay monitor and looked, it was obvious that Brady's arm was coming forward," he said. "He was trying to tuck the ball, and they just knocked it out of his hand. His hand was coming forward, which makes it an incomplete pass. He has to get it all the way tucked back in order for it to be a fumble."

Mike Pereira, the NFL's vice president of officiating, also stood behind Coleman's call, as did then Commissioner Paul Tagliabue in the days that followed. The Patriots won the next week in Pittsburgh to reach the Super Bowl for only the third time in franchise history, then pulled off one of the biggest upsets in pro football history one week later by knocking off the high-scoring and heavily-favored (by fourteen points) St. Louis Rams in the big game—again on a last-second Vinatieri field goal. And just like that, the Brady legend was born and the New England dynasty was underway. They never looked back.

So what makes this a conspiracy as opposed to just a really questionable call? Well, according to some conspiracy theorists (not all of whom are Raiders fans), the NFL may have had a vested interest in seeing the Patriots prevail.

EVIDENCE SUPPORTING A CONSPIRACY

As a New York Giants season-ticket holder and passionate fan of pro football, I've watched hundreds, if not thousands, of football games in my life. And the first time I had ever heard the phrase "Tuck Rule" was the evening of January 19, 2002. Sure, I'd seen plenty of calls overturned because of a quarterback's arm moving forward—that's well-worn territory—but until that night I had never seen a quarterback stop his throwing motion, put his non-throwing hand on the ball, lose the ball, and not have it called a fumble. It was almost like the officials came up with the rule on the spot. But don't just take my word for it. I may have seen a lot of games, but I'm a fan, not an expert.

Tom Flores, however, *is* an expert. By 2001, Flores had spent close to forty years in pro football as a player, coach, and broadcaster, winning two Super Bowls as head coach of the Raiders. Working this game for San Francisco's KSFO (560 AM) alongside play-by-play man Greg Papa, Flores expressed astonishment at Coleman's call.

"Oh no!" Flores shouted from the broadcast booth. "I don't believe that," adding, "I'm just surprised. I'm just surprised because Walt Coleman overturned *his own call.*"

If a guy like Flores, who had spent most of his life in football, and who had reached the pinnacle of his profession, could be surprised by Coleman's bizarre reversal, then maybe (just maybe) there's something more to it than meets the eye. Granted, Flores was hardly an impartial observer in this scenario, but it's also doubtful that his reaction in the booth that night wasn't genuine. It was a call informed by forty years of pro football experience. It was also a call echoed by color man Phil Simms, a former NFL quarterback of fourteen seasons, who had a similar reaction in the CBS television booth that night while calling the game with his partner, Greg Gumbel. And the next day, while calling the play-by-play for the Baltimore–Pittsburgh divisional game, CBS's venerable Dick Enberg quipped "How can you call a pass incomplete when the man doesn't want to throw the ball?"

If you were to ask Al Davis, the cantankerous 80-year-old owner of the Raiders, he'd likely tell you it's because the league has been out to get him for years. Decades. In fact, Davis has been feuding with NFL management going back to the days before the AFL–NFL merger which, for the record, he opposed (and was not party to). Known for his litigiousness as much as for his relentless "commitment to excellence" (the man once tried to sue the Carolina Panthers because their uniform colors included both silver and black, which Davis argued infringed on the Raiders' brand) the self-styled "maverick" had long been a thorn in the side of NFL Commissioner Pete Rozelle and later his successor, Paul Tagliabue.

In 1980, when Davis attempted to move the Raiders from Oakland to Los Angeles, Rozelle had him blocked by a court injunction. In retaliation, Davis filed an anti-trust lawsuit against the NFL, and in June of 1982, a federal district court ruled in Davis' favor. Davis was also the only NFL owner who supported the fledgling United States Football League (or USFL) when its members filed an anti-trust suit of their own against the NFL in 1986 (see chapter #22). And after playing in Los Angeles from 1982 to 1994 (and winning a championship in 1983), Davis moved the Raiders back to Oakland in 1995 and again sued the league, this time claiming that the NFL deliberately sabotaged his effort to have a new, luxury box-lined stadium built in nearby Irwindale.

This is all to say that Al Davis is no friend of the league, and that the league is no friend of Al Davis. I'd like to be able to say that they've managed to peacefully coexist, but that's not true. Instead, they coexist despite what can best be described as open resentment. And in moments like these, with a national television audience watching and a so-called team of destiny's season on the line, it wasn't completely out of the question for him to suggest that someone on-high influenced Coleman to overturn his call.

Asked about the call by a perilous interviewer some time later, Davis said,

> It's my opinion—the opinion of almost everybody in the world—that the play was a fumble [and] should have been called a fumble. That someone would reverse it without conclusive, indisputable, visual evidence is just unbelievable. To this day we don't know what happened. We don't know who made the call. I know who made the call *verbally*, but I don't know who *made* the call, what was said amongst the replay guy upstairs and the official downstairs. I don't know who else was in the booth. I know of things that were done with the networks [in the past]. I know that the head of officials is still out there trying to spin it, that we had a tuck rule, and that it was really not a fumble. I mean, it's ridiculous.

Ridiculous, indeed.

EVIDENCE AGAINST A CONSPIRACY

Defenders of Walt Coleman, such as Mike Pereira, point to a literal interpretation of Rule 3, Section 21, Article 2, Note 2.

"The rule is very specific," Pereira told the *Washington Post*'s Mike Maske in a 2005 interview after a similar call had been made in a game between the Washington Redskins and the Denver Broncos. "We have to make our decision based on the rule. Intent doesn't factor into the rule. Does the ball come out after [the quarterback's] arm is going forward and before he tucks the ball back into his body? If so, then it's an incomplete pass."

"Under the rule, a quarterback's throwing motion begins when he raises the ball in his hand and begins to move his arm forward," Maske explained further. "That motion doesn't end until the quarterback tucks the ball back against his body, making him a runner. If the ball comes loose any time in between, it's an incomplete pass, not a fumble. Only if the quarterback reloads— and raises the ball again to start a new throwing motion—can he fumble, as long as the ball is knocked loose before his arm begins to move forward again."

Under that complicated interpretation, Coleman's call certainly makes more sense than it did in the heat of the moment. But to me, the most compelling argument against the Tuck Rule conspiracy theory (beyond dismissing Davis as a paranoiac) is also the simplest: right or wrong, the call itself didn't decide the game. After the ball was spotted, the Patriots were still outside of Vinatieri's range. And furthermore, they were still playing on a snow-blanketed field in blizzard-like conditions. The Patriots had no timeouts remaining, and had to rely on Brady, an inexperienced second-year player who had yet to show more than flashes of his future greatness, to carry the team toward a realistically makeable field-goal attempt. Though he had played college ball in the northern climes of Ann Arbor, Michigan, the California native had never before played in conditions like these. Who had? But Brady still needed to make a first down to keep the chains moving. And once he managed to complete the pass to Patten, the Patriots still needed to get to the line and execute the kick before time expired. Vinatieri, of course, still had to make the field goal. This was all just to tie the game, mind you. Overtime was another story entirely.

Barring the extreme unlikelihood that Walt Coleman was in possession of a two-headed coin, it seems impossible that the refs could have fixed the overtime coin toss. This means that as the visiting team, the Raiders could have conceivably won the toss, elected to receive, and driven for the game-winning score. This, of course, didn't happen, as it was Brady who drove his team to that winning score. But the Pats still had to execute on the drive. And in conditions like those, anything could have happened. Another fumble. A tipped pass. An interception. A bad snap. A botched hold. A shanked kick. Anything.

Granted, the winning drive was made a bit easier by the dramatic shift in momentum caused by Coleman's reversal.

"It was like a vacuum that just sucked the life out of all of us," Raiders Pro Bowl tackle Lincoln Kennedy told NFL Films. "From that point on, we just weren't the same team. We no longer had that swagger. We no longer believed we were the better team. I knew after that [call] that we were not going to win this game."

But even so, the Patriots still had to win two more games before they'd be crowned champions. One bad call in the divisional round does not a champion make, and Pittsburgh's Heinz Field, where the Pats had to play the following week, is one of the toughest places to win in all of sports. Add to that the knowledge that St. Louis, their opponent in the Super Bowl, was a fourteen-point favorite and had won the title just two years before. All those things considered, the likelihood of a fix seem miniscule.

But sticking it to Al Davis may not have been the only reason, ridiculous or otherwise, that the league may have wanted the Patriots to advance in the 2001 playoffs and beyond. One theory, which spread like wildfire across the Internet in the weeks after the Super Bowl, but failed to gain traction from mainstream news sources (with good reason), was that the Bush administration, in the immediate wake of the tragedies of September 11, 2001, conspired with NFL executives to use the New England Patriots as a propagandistic symbol in a covert attempt to foster passionate support of "patriotic" ideals. Some, including creative posters to the forums at abovetopsecret.com—a popular conspiracy website—went as far as to suggest that the government wanted the Patriots in the first Super Bowl after 9/11 because their presence would help generate public support for the impending war in Iraq and toleration of forthcoming egregious abuses of personal freedoms under the Patriot Act.

I know, I know. It's a ludicrous theory. Depending on your sensibilities, it might even be an offensive one. I will not argue that point. But before you dismiss it completely, or start calling me names or egg my house, consider the league's (and the government's) reaction to the revelations made public in 2007 that Bill Belichick's staff had been illegally videotaping its opponents for years.

#29: SPYGATE

On September 9, 2007, the first truly credible and damning evidence of a Patriot conspiracy was brought to light when an NFL security official, tipped off by New York Jets security, confiscated a video camera and videotape from Matt Estrella, a Patriots video assistant who had been caught illegally taping the signals of Jets defensive coaches during the season opener at Giants Stadium. This incident and the resulting controversy have since come to be known, rather infamously, as "Spygate."

A former assistant under Belichick from 2000–2005, then Jets Head Coach Eric Mangini possessed an insider's knowledge of the Patriots' covert surveillance tactics and, according to reports, shared what he knew with members of the Jets' organization when first arriving in New York in 2006. It took the Jets a while to catch the rival Patriots in the act, but once they did, the Patriots were exposed as cheats. The story that unfolded afterward cast serious doubt not only on Belichick's integrity and the origin of the Patriots' success dating back to their first championship season, but also on the NFL's knowledge of (and possible role in covering up) their deceit.

According to a report by Jets beat reporter Rich Cimini in the *New York Daily News*, Estrella was caught videotaping hand signals from the Jets' defensive coaches on the sideline. Stopped by stadium security as he tried to enter the visitors' locker room shortly before halftime, a contentious confrontation ensued. Representatives from league security, Jets security, and Patriots security were all summoned, as were New Jersey state troopers, who were called in as a precaution to prevent the situation, which had grown heated, from escalating out of control. League security confiscated Estrella's camera and tapes and forwarded them to the league office.

Four days later, before he had even had a chance to review the tapes, Commissioner Roger Goodell ruled that the Patriots had indeed violated league rules. He fined Belichick $500,000, the maximum penalty allowed under NFL bylaws for violating league policy. He also levied a $250,000 fine against the Patriots themselves, and took away a conditional 2008 draft selection (a first-round pick if the Pats made the 2007 playoffs, or second- and third-round picks if they did not qualify for the postseason). Belichick, however, was not suspended as a result of his actions.

"This episode represents a calculated and deliberate attempt to avoid longstanding rules designed to encourage fair play and promote honest competition on the playing field," Goodell wrote in a letter to the Patriots.

"I specifically considered whether to impose a suspension on Coach Belichick. I have determined not to do so, largely because I believe that the discipline I am imposing of a maximum fine and forfeiture of a first-round draft choice, or multiple draft choices, is in fact more significant and long-lasting, and therefore more effective, than a suspension."

As part of the league's investigation, the Patriots were required to turn over all existing notes and tapes that related to the recording of opponents' defensive signals. The Patriots complied with this demand, turning over six tapes which Goodell initially said were from the 2007 preseason and late 2006. He also said that the league confiscated some notes. After the league reviewed the materials, they quickly (and rather curiously) chose to destroy them.

On February 1, 2008, just two days before the undefeated Patriots were due to meet the New York Giants in Super Bowl XLII, Republican Senator Arlen Specter of Pennsylvania publicly criticized Goodell's bizarre decision to destroy the materials.

"The American people are entitled to be sure about the integrity of the game," Specter said. "It's analogous to the CIA destruction of tapes. Or any time you have records destroyed."

Citing a September 14, 2007, ESPN report in which Belichick had admitted to taping signals going back as far as 2000 (his first season as the Patriots' head coach) Specter, the ranking member on the Senate Judiciary Committee, requested a meeting with Goodell. The commissioner, who said in a press conference on the same day Specter issued his criticisms that there was "no indication that [taping] benefited [the Patriots] in any of the Super Bowl victories," agreed to the meeting despite previous plans to travel to Hawaii in advance of the Pro Bowl.

According to a phone interview Specter gave the *New York Times*' John Branch afterwards, Goodell revealed in their meeting that the confiscated notes actually dated back as far as 2000 and that the materials had been destroyed, of all places, in Foxborough, Massachusetts, where the Patriots' offices are located. Goodell's explanation for destroying the materials—mainly that there was no use for them—didn't wash with Specter, and he left the meeting unsatisfied.

"There are red flags all over the field," Specter told Branch. "There are many matters which have not been explained. And the commissioner is stonewalling."

Further complicating the issue was a *Boston Herald* report that claimed an unnamed source, later revealed to be former Patriots video assistant Matt Walsh, held evidence that the Patriots had videotaped the St. Louis Rams' walk-through practice prior to Super Bowl XXXVI in February 2002.

The report was later proven to be false and the *Herald* issued an apology for the story. But Walsh, who had been fired by the Patriots after the 2002 season, was truly in possession of other tapes, and expressed a willingness to share them with Goodell if he were granted immunity. After an agreement was negotiated, Walsh sent eight videotapes containing opponents coaches' signals from the 2000 through 2002 seasons, and then met with Goodell on May 13, 2008. In this meeting, Walsh reportedly told Goodell that he and other Patriots employees were present at the Rams' walk-through to set up video equipment for the game, but that no tape of the walk-through was made.

Specter also met with Walsh and continued his public cry for an independent investigation. On May 15, 2008, Senator Ted Kennedy of Massachusetts, who also sits on the Senate Judiciary Committee, remarked that "with the war in Iraq raging on, gasoline prices closing in on $4 a gallon, and Americans losing their homes at record rates to foreclosure, the United States Senate should be focusing on the real problems that Americans are struggling with." This sentiment was echoed by Senator Lindsey Graham of South Carolina, as well as by certain members of the media who suggested that Specter's interest in the matter stemmed from the Patriots having an 8–1 record against his home state's teams in the Spygate era, including victories over both teams in the 2004 postseason.

After that, there was little Specter could do to push the issue. In a June 16, 2008, interview with the *Philadelphia Daily News* he said that he "had gone as far as [he] could" with the matter, and would not pursue a senate hearing.

EVIDENCE SUPPORTING A CONSPIRACY

Certain aspects of the Spygate controversy cannot be debated. First and foremost is the incontrovertible fact that the Patriots did cheat, and that they were caught in the act.

The rule states:

> *Any use by any club at any time, from the start to the finish of any game in which such club is a partici-pant, of any communications or information-gathering equipment, other than Polaroid-type cameras or field telephones, shall be prohibited, including without limitation videotape machines, telephone tapping, or bugging devices, or any other form of electronic devices that might aid a team during the playing of a game.*

Belichick went on record to say that he didn't flout the rule, but instead only misinterpreted it, assuming that it only applied to the use of film in the same game in which it was collected. But I don't see much room for misinterpretation here. The fact of the matter is that Belichick likely knew exactly what he was doing, and if it wasn't useful to him (or integral to his team's success) he wouldn't have been doing it since 2000 (and quite possibly before). So let's consider that part of the conspiracy theory a closed case.

What's more interesting to me is the league's role in this madness, as well as, potentially, the officials'. Like Specter, I don't quite understand why Goodell would have the material destroyed unless he feared the repercussions of a potential leak.

If the Patriots used illegally gathered knowledge of opponents' defensive signals and also received help from the referees (a convincing YouTube video reveals that two weeks after the absurdity of the "Tuck Rule Game," the Patriots benefited from 150 yards of uncalled penalties in Super Bowl XXXVI) to establish and sustain their dynasty, then perhaps the league destroyed the materials to protect its legacy and to maintain the trust of their broadcast partners, corporate sponsors, and the American public (gamblers included).

EVIDENCE AGAINST A CONSPIRACY

Not surprisingly, the exceedingly tight-lipped Belichick didn't comment at all on the Spygate allegations until two weeks after his Patriots had lost to the Giants in Super Bowl XLII. And when he finally spoke, he did little more than deny and deflect.

"My interpretation was that you can't utilize anything to assist you during that game," Belichick said. "What our camera guys do is clearly not allowed to be used during the game and has never been used during that game that it was shot. I respect the integrity of the game and always have and always will. I regret that any of this . . . has in any way brought that into question or discussion or debate. The decision was made by the commissioner, the practice was immediately stopped, and we're not doing it.

"I take responsibility for it," he continued. "Even though I felt there was a gray area in the rule and I misinterpreted the rule, that was my mistake and we've been penalized for it. I apologize to everybody that is involved—the league, the other teams, the fans, our team—for the amount of conversation and dialogue that it's caused."

This explanation and pseudo-apology are the only real defense of the Patriots to be made. Patriots General Manager Scott Pioli and owner Robert Kraft issued similar statements, each indicating that they just wanted to move on. For the purposes of this chapter reaching a conclusion, I'll grant them their wish.

As for Goodell, he has continued to defend his baffling decision to destroy the evidence, saying that he has "nothing to hide" and that destroying it was the right thing to do to keep it out of enemy hands.

My Opinion

With all due respect to Al Davis, who had been curiously burned by the refs in big games before (see: Reception, Immaculate), I'm going to have to chalk the Tuck Rule fiasco up to bad officiating, or rather the interpretation of a bad rule. Not a conspiracy. As horrendous as it was, it was still just one call in one non-championship game, and it didn't decide anything in and of itself. Raiders fans are just going to have to let that one go. Eventually.

I'm also going to rule out any connection between the Patriots' success and the Bush administration. It's a seductive if entirely ludicrous theory, but there's no evidence of any kind to support it other than the coincidence of the team's name. Besides, Bush's record in professional sports does not indicate an aptitude for successful administration. Baseball's Texas Rangers never reached the postseason in the five seasons he served as their managing general partner and traded away slugger Sammy Sosa shortly after he arrived on the scene. His last year with the Rangers, 1994, was (and is) the only year since 1904 in which no World Series was played.

Spygate, however, is another story altogether. Despite Belichick's statements to the contrary, I believe that he and his coaches willfully and knowingly cheated. I also believe that Commissioner Goodell made an effort to conceal the extent of

Belichick's transgressions and destroyed the tapes because they revealed significantly more than what had been reported to the public.

The league, with the help of an adoring media, had helped build the Patriots into the model franchise of the NFL. In the salary cap era, the Pats had managed to win three championships (and four conference titles) by stressing team over individual achievement, yet in doing so, saw their MVP quarterback develop into the face of the league (and Stetson). By beating St. Louis in Super Bowl XXXVI, the underdog Pats had lifted the spirit of a nation still reeling from tragedy, uniting us all through a common, patriotic ideal. Then they won again. And again. And they did it—they'd like you to believe—the right way. So how could the league come out and admit that it was all a hoax? How could they and their network partners continue to sell all those pickup trucks and cases of beer, not to mention rhinestone-studded Tom Brady jerseys, if it were all proven to be a lie?

Goodell made a point to draw attention toward his quick and decisive action in fining Belichick and the Patriots those exorbitant, unprecedented sums. But doing it so quickly, without even knowing the full extent of their transgressions, leads this writer to believe that Goodell actually knew a lot more, and was afraid of where a real investigation into the matter might lead. His proclamations about maintaining the integrity of the game were, therefore, in the words of Shakespeare, those of "an idiot, full of sound and fury, signifying nothing." Just like Senator Specter, I'm not buying it.

Obviously, I have no way of knowing how much Goodell or his predecessor, Paul Tagliabue, actually knew about the extent of the Patriots' covert activities. But I will contend that Goodell's too-quick decision to levy fines and his inability to provide a reasonable answer for the destruction of the evidence suggests the very real possibility of a cover-up.

Hundreds of billions of dollars are spent each year on NFL broadcast rights, licensed merchandise sales, and ticket sales. This is not even to mention the billions that are spent, legally and illegally, gambling on what is generally perceived to be a fairly contested game. In order to keep that cash cow producing sweet, green (unpasteurized) milk, Commissioner Goodell had no choice but to protect those interests at any cost. He could not let it be revealed that the league's model franchise cheated, because there's no stuffing that cat back into the bag once it's out.

And really, what other choice did Goodell have but to cover up? Could he have stripped the Patriots of their three Lombardi trophies and awarded them to the teams they had beaten in those Super Bowls? How would he justify that decision to the teams the Patriots had vanquished in the earlier playoff rounds? And would he have had to refund whatever money was spent by the networks, fans, and Nevada sportsbooks on games where it had been proven that one team had been cheating? The ramifications of that sort of scandal would be enough to take down the league, and Goodell knew it. So he told Belichick to fall on his sword so we could all live happily ever after. Well, all of us except Al Davis.

CONCLUSION(S):

ON THE TUCK RULE CONSPIRACY THEORY:

ON THE SPYGATE CONSPIRACY THEORY, INCLUDING COMMISSIONER GOODELL'S ROLE IN A COVER-UP:

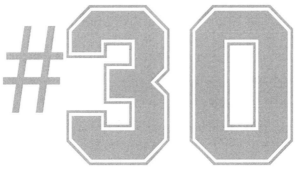

Did Chinese Olympic hero Liu Xiang fake an injury in the 2008 Beijing Games?

If you were to query a cross-section of average American sports fans, chances are most of them wouldn't recognize the name Liu Xiang. Despite winning the Olympic gold medal in the 110-meter hurdles in the 2004 Athens games, and setting the world record in the event two years later at the IAAF Super Grand Prix in Lausanne, Switzerland, Liu hasn't quite penetrated the American consciousness.

In his native China, however, the 26-year-old Liu is a household name, as popular and celebrated as heroes like Michael Jordan and Tiger Woods are stateside. His image appears spread across advertising billboards throughout the country, the result of his numerous, lucrative endorsement deals with nineteen different brands, including major international corporations like Nike, Coca-Cola, Visa, and Cadillac. A 2007 *Forbes* magazine article estimated Liu's annual endorsement income to be in the range of $23 million dollars ($9 million more than basketball superstar Yao Ming), and his legs are reported to have been insured for $14.6 million by Chinese insurance giant Ping An.

His victory in Athens was the first by a Chinese track athlete in an international competition, and it didn't take long for him to become a symbol of the country's national pride. Referring to his gold medal triumph in the moments after the race, Liu told reporters in Athens that his performance "changes the opinion that Asian countries don't get good results in sprint races. I want to prove to all the world that Asians can run very fast." With those words, Liu became the hero of 1.3 billion people.

After proving himself on the track not only in Athens, but also in Lausanne, Liu was the obvious choice to be the face of the 2008 Beijing Olympics, by far China's greatest hope for a track and field medal. Liu represented the new China, an athlete that had confidently shattered the stereotype that track and field could only be dominated by western athletes. His breakthrough was as significant for the Chinese people as Jackie Robinson's had been for black Americans.

The expectations heaped upon Liu's shoulders for another gold medal was immense, the prevailing sentiment throughout the nation being that anything less than another gold medal would be a failure. This was highlighted in a 2007 press conference when Liu's coach Sun Haiping said, "Leaders told us that if Liu Xiang could not win the gold medal in Beijing, all of his achievements before will be meaningless." As if that weren't pressure enough, confidence in Liu's impending victory reached its absurd peak when, a few weeks before the games, Madame Tussaud's wax museum in Shanghai (Liu's hometown) unveiled a model of Liu dressed in his Beijing Olympic uniform, adorned with a wax gold medal. A bronze statue of Liu had already been erected in Shanghai in 2005.

Unfortunately for Liu and the Chinese people, victory on the track was not assured. The demands of Liu's hectic appearance schedule (in promotion of both the games and the various products he endorses) threw a wrench in his training. Then, in late May, tightness in his hamstring forced Liu to pull out of the Reebok Grand Prix in New York. A week later, he was disqualified after twice false-starting in the Prefontaine Classic in Eugene, Oregon. As the Beijing games neared, it was clear that Liu was not in top form. The best time he had posted in 2008 was 13.18 seconds, a full three-tenths of a second off his world record time, and only the thirteenth best time posted on the world stage that year.

The pressure on Liu only intensified when Cuba's Dayron Robles, his chief rival, broke his world record (by .01 of a second) just a few months before the Beijing Games. But as expectations multiplied, Chinese officials insisted Liu was coping with it well. "He withstands the pressure like no other athlete can," said Feng Shuyong, the Chinese national track coach. "His psychological powers are great."

In what was assumed to be a concentrated effort to improve his conditioning and regain his top form for Beijing, Liu spent the final months leading into the Games training in virtual seclusion. This caused concerned Chinese fans to wonder about the severity of Liu's hamstring injury, a curiosity that became magnified when, at the opening ceremonies, Liu was conspicuously absent. According to official reports from Chinese state media, Liu had missed the ceremonies to conserve his strength and energy. Liu did not join the Olympic Village until eight days later, and it wasn't until August 17—the day before he was scheduled to appear in the qualifying heats—that Liu first appeared inside the Bird's Nest (the nickname for Beijing's Olympic stadium).

With wild rumors swirling around the Internet about Liu's condition, Sun told reporters in Beijing one week before the qualifying heats that Liu was "very close to his best form." Liu himself had been quoted in a report published in *South Cities News* on July 25 saying that he was not injured, but the rumors persisted, especially on the Internet.

On Monday, August 18, a near-capacity crowd gathered inside the Bird's Nest to catch a glimpse of China's national sporting hero. Liu arrived on the track wearing only one shoe, and NBC's cameras caught him struggling in the warm-up area. After attempting a few hurdles before the start of the race, those same cameras caught Liu grimacing in pain. It was obvious that he was injured, perhaps seriously, but he still lined up with the rest of the field for the start of the race.

Once in the starting blocks, Liu slapped at his right Achilles tendon, trying to loosen it up. With a pained expression spread across his face, he rose with his competitors to the set position, then took off at the sound of the gun. Liu only made it a few steps before he pulled up in agony. A false start had been called, yet instead of heading back to the starting blocks, Liu removed the tags from his hips and walked gingerly off the track. Just like that, his Olympics was over. The crowd was shocked, left in stunned silence as they began to realize that their hero would not be able to defend his title. The rest of the field then completed the race without him, but not before an estimated 60% of the crowd left the stadium, according to a report in the *Epoch Times*. Sadly, four years after capturing gold, Liu never even made it to the first hurdle in Beijing.

Many of the fans remaining in the Bird's Nest began to cry. They had waited for four years to see their hero triumph on home soil, and now it was over before it had even begun. The hopes of an entire nation were dashed in an instant.

In the press conference following the race, Feng explained that Liu's Achilles tendon, which has plagued the superstar throughout his career, had suddenly flared up again two days before the race. "The injury on his Achilles tendon deteriorated last Saturday in training," Feng said. "He was still confident of sprinting. We didn't realize it was so serious and [that it] would cause the problem of today. That's why we didn't want to tell our people that he could not compete. It was with the greatest and strongest will that he wanted to compete and he tried a few times to run. And then obviously we saw the pain in his face. Liu Xiang would not withdraw unless the pain was unbearable and he had no other way out."

Sun wept uncontrollably when he took to the microphone, apologizing for Liu through his tears. "He has been keeping fighting and fighting until the last moment," said an emotional Sun, who had been a father figure for Liu since the hurdler left home at age fifteen to train with him.

The next day, China Central Television (CCTV) aired an interview with a somber Liu in which he said, according to a translation, "I feel sorry. I could do nothing but pull out of the race. I didn't feel right when I was warming up. I knew my foot would fail me. It felt painful when I was just jogging. I wanted to hang on, but I couldn't. It was unbearable. If I had finished the race, I would have risked my tendon. I could not describe my feeling at that moment."

Perhaps not, but that didn't stop a whole lot of people from speculating wildly on the *real* reason behind Liu's withdrawal.

Evidence to Support a Conspiracy

Within minutes of Liu's hobbling off the track, an estimated 8,000 Chinese citizens flooded the Internet with their opinions on his dramatic withdrawal. A great many of the posts expressed heartfelt sympathy and disappointment, but many others expressed outrage. Some blamed government officials, who had placed unreasonable pressure on Liu to win repeat gold in Beijing. Others pointed fingers at Liu's corporate sponsors, who distracted him from his purpose in preparing to compete. Some questioned Liu's mental state, suggesting he had withdrawn because he had been psyched out by Robles. And some conspiracy theorists took things a step farther, suggesting that Liu had accepted bribes from the Chinese mafia not to compete so that they could collect on large bets spread around the sportsbooks of Las Vegas and Macau.

One post to the Chinese language forum sina.com.hk, however, attracted the most attention. Under the alias "NikeInsider," the poster made the shocking claim of first-hand knowledge that Liu had been forced to withdraw from the race by his sponsors at Nike.

Alleging to be a Nike employee, "NikeInsider" wrote that once corporate executives in the United States and China realized Liu could not win gold in Beijing, they agreed to orchestrate his withdrawal under the pretext of injury so that Liu could "save face" and Nike could minimize the financial losses that would surely result from his defeat on the track.

"If Liu Xiang cannot defend his title (or even win any medal)," the poster wrote, "then his value would definitely shrink and we would receive no return on the vast sum that we invested in him as spokesperson."

A remarkable example of the far-reaching influence and impact of the Internet on the shaping of public opinion, news of the post spread rapidly and become a major, international news story within hours. Online chatter regarding possible conspiracy reached such a level in the immediate wake of Liu's withdrawal that Chinese censors removed all postings on the subject from Internet forums. China's Central Propaganda Department also issued a bulletin to Chinese media in which they forbade reporters from criticizing Liu or speculating as to the reasons behind his withdrawal. It also instructed them to follow the party line as presented in Feng and Sun's press conference, which was that Liu remained a national hero regardless of his withdrawal.

The day after NikeInsider's post appeared, Nike issued a forceful denial of the rumors in a statement they emailed to the American Foreign Press.

"The posting is a malicious rumor, and has not only misled netizens, but also seriously damages the company's reputation," the statement read. "We have immediately asked relevant government departments to investigate those that started the rumor."

By then, though, there was little Nike could do except go into damage control.

EVIDENCE AGAINST A CONSPIRACY

If seeing is believing, and a picture tells a thousand words, then the video of the event is the strongest argument against this conspiracy. Watching replays of Liu's time on the track, it's nearly impossible to imagine that he was faking the injury. Actually, it was quite the contrary. Liu looked like an athlete bravely trying to fight through the pain, acutely aware of the significance of the moment. While he may be a smooth corporate pitchman able to sell a Cadillac or a pair of sneakers, he is not an actor. In fact, he had been discouraged from acting in movies after his triumph in Athens. And I certainly didn't see a faker on the track that day. Neither did NBC's Tom Hammond, who covered the event for American television, nor the CCTV anchorwoman who, overcome by the emotion of the moment, needed a moment to compose herself.

It's also unlikely that an athlete like Liu, who had reached the pinnacle of his sport, would be willing to throw away four years of intense training for an opportunity to, as the reports said, save face, or worse, earn a payday. While it's true that Liu stood to gain a lot more money in future endorsement opportunities by winning a second gold medal, he had a lot more to lose if he was discovered to be deceiving the world. As a symbol of the virtue of the Chinese athlete, he had more to live up to than his record on the track.

If Feng is to be believed, and Liu truly possessed great psychological powers, then it's doubtful that Liu would be psyched out by Robles' success on the track. If anything, Robles' success would motivate Liu to train harder, strive more, and rise to the challenge Robles presented. That determination is in the nature of champion athletes, and it's integral to their success. Champion athletes don't fold when the going gets tough, which is what makes them champions in the first place.

The rumors of Liu's involvement with the Chinese mafia have never been substantiated.

My Opinion

At the risk of sounding like a xenophobe, I'll concede that it's difficult to put anything past the Chinese government. I say this because of all the reports out of Beijing by western journalists covering the Games that spoke of the repression of information and the control the communist regime exerted over the games. I say this because it was proven that they had a pretty little nine-year-old girl lip synch her performance during the opening ceremonies while the real singer, who was deemed to be less physically attractive, sang off camera. I say this because they demand that their athletes sacrifice half of their earnings to government and sports authorities within China, and because they knowingly allowed an underage female gymnast to compete on their gold medal–winning team in Beijing.

It is no secret that the Chinese government looks after its own interests first, but even so, I can't believe they instructed their national sporting hero to fake an injury to spare the country the shame and disappointment of losing.

If anything, I believe they urged Liu to compete despite his injury, that they asked him to bite the bullet, run through the pain, and risk his long-term health for the honor of his country. A late attempt to rehab the injury and get him ready to compete would explain why Liu trained in seclusion, missed the opening ceremonies, and didn't appear in the Olympic Village until two days before he was scheduled to run. It also explains why there was no official report of Liu's injury prior to his withdrawal.

In American sports, we call that a "game-time decision." An athlete arrives at the stadium on game day and gives it a go in pre-game warm-ups. If his body holds up, and he shows that he can withstand the pain, the athlete will go ahead and play. If he can't, he won't. In this case, Liu gave it a go but could not bear the pain in his Achilles.

If the government is to blame for anything here, it is the suppression of information regarding the injury. With reports of "spotty attendance" in the Games' early-round competitions, Chinese officials were certainly aware that a race without Liu would negatively affect the gate at the Bird's Nest for the qualifying heats. Tickets for the 110-meter finals were already selling for ten to twenty times their face value in anticipation of Liu's historic triumph, according to reports. Therefore, it is my opinion that they did everything they could to ensure the capacity crowd that Liu's appearance guaranteed.

The Nike conspiracy, however, seems the most unlikely. After the sweatshop scandals of the 1990s, Nike already had a less-than-stellar reputation in the Far East, and the last thing they needed, if they wanted to continue extending their brand throughout Asia, was for it to come out that they forced China's Olympic hero to lay down so they could protect their investment in him. That would be a public relations disaster from which they could never recover.

Add to that the lesson Nike undoubtedly learned from Reebok's failed campaign leading up to the 1992 Barcelona Games. The promotion, which included a costly Super Bowl ad, asked, "Who will be the world's greatest athlete? Dan or Dave? To be settled in Barcelona." The ad featured two American decathletes, Dan O'Brien and Dave Johnson, both of whom were favored to medal in Spain. The only problem was that O'Brien failed to qualify for the Olympics. After having already committed millions of dollars to the campaign, Reebok was left scrambling for a new angle.

Following Reebok's disastrous campaign, sponsors have been careful not to put all their eggs in one basket. And as much as Nike may have wanted Liu to recapture gold, they used his great disappointment as an opportunity to honor him anyway. In a full-page color ad on the back of *China Daily* in the days following his withdrawal, they ran a color headshot of Liu with the following words printed alongside it:

Love Competition
Love Risking Your Pride
Love Winning It Back
Love Giving It Everything You've Got
Love the Glory
Love the Pain
Love Sport Even When It Breaks Your Heart

CONCLUSION:

SUMMARY

5 Oswalds:

1) Chapter 3   Major League Baseball owners collude (poorly) in the mid–1980s against free agents

2) Chapter 9   Alan Eagleson conspires with hockey owners to keep salaries down in the NHL

3) Chapter 1   Unwritten gentleman's agreement prevents baseball from integrating until 1947

4) Chapter 2   NBA has quota system for black players in its early years

5) Chapter 15   Everyone closes their eyes to the growing steroid problem in baseball in mid–1990s

6) Chapter 12   Ty Cobb and Tris Speaker bet on (and possibly fix) games, yet stay in baseball

7) Chapter 25   Olympic gold medalist in the Women's 100 meters hides a secret for decades

4 Oswalds:

1) Chapter 4   At least one of the Liston–Ali fights are fixed

2) Chapter 14   Cheaters in baseball steal signs, throw illegal pitches, and steal pennants

3) Chapter 7   Someone keeps Isiah Thomas off the 1992 Olympic Dream Team in Barcelona

4) Chapter 24   Conspiracy snatches the gold medal from the 1972 U.S. Olympic basketball team

5) Chapter 18   Unwritten agreement not to sign Japanese ballplayers after 1965 (until Hideo Nomo)

6) Chapter 21   Manager John McGraw conspires to fix baseball games in the early 1900s

7) Chapter 29   Bill Belichick and the Patriots illegally tape opponents' defensive signals

3 Oswalds:

1) Chapter 11 Pete Rose has a secret agreement with Bart Giamatti

2) Chapter 10 The 1946 NFL Championship Game between Bears and Giants is fixed

3) Chapter 16 Dennis Rodman and Peter Vecsey are kept out of the Basketball Hall of Fame

4) Chapter 23 Shoeless Joe Jackson is kept out of the Baseball Hall of Fame and is never exonerated

5) Chapter 8   Michael Jordan's 1993 "retirement"

6) Chapter 19 Hank Greenberg isn't pitched to because of his religion

7) Chapter 26 UNLV throws 1991 NCAA Semi–final vs. Duke

2 Oswalds:

1) Chapter 22 NFL squashes the competing USFL in the mid–1980s

2) Chapter 17 Funny business at the Kentucky Derby

3) Chapter 20 Sammy Baugh is part of an NFL gambling scandal to fix games in the 1940s

1 Oswald:

1) Chapter 7   Super Bowl III is fixed; possibly by Don Shula and/or Carroll Rosenbloom

2) Chapter 5   NBA sends Patrick Ewing to the Knicks in the league's first draft lottery

3) Chapter 13 Auto races that are too good to be true

4) Chapter 27 Cal Ripken's 2001 All–Star Game home run a set–up

5) Chapter 28 NFL referees hand New England a victory with Tuck Rule call during the 2001 playoffs

6) Chapter 30 Hurdler Liu Xiang fakes injury in 2008 Beijing Olympics

ACKNOWLEDGMENTS

My wife, Amy Kalb, brings to mind the lyrics of an old song by The Band. "*Up on cripple creek, she sends me. If I spring a leak, she mends me. I don't have to speak, she defends me . . .*" I don't know how I deserve that treatment, but my kids and I sure are the better for it. Amy is perfect. Well, she's not *perfect*. A perfect wife would be a *Honeymooners* aficionado, not an *I Love Lucy* devotee. A perfect wife wouldn't complain that it poured buckets of rain on her throughout Super Bowl XLI in Miami. A perfect wife wouldn't *occasionally* complain about my insistence to watch Howard Stern on–demand late at night, every night. Then again, I'm so far from perfect that I'm the wrong one to do any complaining.

Lenny and Phyllis Kalb are wonderful parents that truly make a difference in the world. Lenny, by teaching boating safety and finding jobs for hundreds and hundreds of people through the years, has made the world a far better place for so many. Phyllis has brought together diverse lecture subjects for book discussions, concerts, and town meetings at the South Orange library for more than two decades. As for their contributions to this particular book, they have an abject hatred for lying and liars and cover–ups.

How lucky am I? I own a baseball glove and a ball, and I have sons to play catch with. A man doesn't need much more than that. I know I don't. I have several passions, and each of my kids has grabbed hold of one that I'm able to share. Wyatt is the sports announcer and/or talk–show host for the next generation. His life, like mine, has been blessed by our love for sports, and we're bonded by a devotion to a certain baseball team in pinstripes. Heath loves playing and watching all sports, but there is no greater NBA fan at any age (he's only seven). My stepson Jordan is a fine athlete who has embraced football, and has the will and the skill to excel at it. And Alissa, with realistic dreams of being a screenwriter or playwright, loves New York City, and devours the *New York Post* each morning. I will be a lucky and rich man if I am able to negotiate any of their future contracts. Heath also would want me to mention our beautiful chocolate lab. The dog has provided Heath and his siblings with daily love and security; and me with the ability to recall the more than 300 passwords needed for my daily life.

My brother David and sister Randi are huge parts of my life, no matter how busy all of us get. They are compassionate and loyal, and better siblings to me than I am to them. My in–laws Irving and Barbara not only buy my books, but also actually read them (c'mon, say it: "So they're the ones," you're thinking). They are solidly in my corner, as are my aunt and uncle, Barbara and Jimmy DeNoble. There are a pair of supporting brothers–in–law (Billy Edelman and Roy Levinson), and a pair of sisters–in–law (Susan Kalb and Eilene Levinson, both of whom recently went back to school to earn Masters' degrees). And then there's my team of nephews and nieces, including Sammy, Danny, Jacob, Sara, Jessica, and Lindsay.

Mark Weinstein is my editor, and the reason that you're reading this book. He's the best kind of sports fan—he's passionate and intelligent and he knows so much about a lot of different sports. Carol Mann must dread each and every one of my phone calls. Thanks to a great agent. Jim Gallagher led me in the right direction regarding Japanese ballplayers. I was so lucky to be able to work with him beginning in 2000 at the Sydney Olympics. Phil Harmon read several chapters of mine, as I pestered him with first–hand accounts of the 1946 NFL Championship Game. Of course, he was only in elementary school at the time, but he should have taken notes, figuring the information would come in handy one day. There are my friends and colleagues at NBC

Sports—I am so lucky to have a chance to work with men like Dick Ebersol and Tommy Roy and Sam Flood and Joe Geshue. The Peacock has been like a second family to me, and I have to mention longtime associations with Cathy Crowther, Arnie Marshe, and Gil Capps.

Dennis D'Agastino is a sports historian and author who happens to be married to Helene Elliott, who is enshrined in the Hockey Hall of Fame. Thanks to both for setting this hockey puck straight. Howie Deneroff would have made a great investigative journalist. Instead, he chose to be the best radio producer and executive I know. I can't thank my manic friend enough for support, phone numbers, and his memory. Brian Tuohy is a thoughtful and provocative author that I came across on the Internet. I contacted him and got his permission to share some of his musings with my audience. Thanks again, Brian. I work with great colleagues at HBO Sports, including Rick Bernstein, Brian Hyland, and the ever–caffeinated Peter King. And then there is the great Cris Collinsworth, whom I can't say enough good things about.

John McCarthy has been a friend long enough for me to consider him family. Thanks to Dave and Ruth and Maris and Rachel Harmon for letting us into their ski house each winter and for letting us into their hearts. Thanks to Lisa Kalb, who shared many earlier important moments in my life. There are plenty of conspiracy theories about my close friend Steve Horn. Before you sleep tight, Mr. and Mrs. America, remember this: Horn probably does have something on each and every one of you.

SOURCES

BOOKS

Araton, Harvey; Keteyan, Armen and Dardis., Martin F. *Money Players: Days and Nights Inside the New NBA.* Atria Publishing, 1997.

Ashe, Arthur. *A Hard Road to Glory: A History of the African–American Athlete, 1919–1945.* Warner Books, 1988.

Asinof, Eliot. *Eight Men Out.* Holt and Rhinehart, 1963.

Barber, Red. *1947: When All Hell Broke Loose in Baseball.* Da Capo Press, 1982.

Brodowsky, Pamela K. and Philbin, Tom. *Two Minutes to Glory: The Official History of the Kentucky Derby.* Collins Publishing, 2007.

Bryant, Howard. *Juicing the Game: Drugs, Power, and the Fight for the Soul of Major League Baseball.* Plume Publishing, 2006.

Canseco, Jose. *Juiced: Wild Times, Rampant 'Roids, Smash Hits and How Baseball Got Big.* William Morrow, 2005.

Carroll, Bob, Gershman, Michael, Neft, David, Thorn, John, eds. *Total Football II: The Official Encyclopedia of the National Football League.* Harper Collins, 1999.

Chamberlain, Wilt. *Wilt: Just Like Any Other 7 Foot Black Millionaire Who Lives Next Door.* Macmillan Publishing, 1973.

Cobb, Ty and Stump, Al. *My Life in Baseball: The True Record.* Bison Books, 1993.

Cosell, Howard. *Cosell.* Playboy Press, 1973.

Cosell, Howard and Whitfield, Shelby. *What's Wrong With Sports?* Easton Press, 1991.

D'Agastino, Dennis. *Garden Glory: An Oral History of the New York Knicks.* Triumph Books, 2003.

Daly, Chuck and Sachare, Alex. *America's Dream Team: The Quest for Olympic Gold.* Turner Publishing Inc, 1992.

Davis, Jeff. *Papa Bear: The Life and Legacy of George Halas.* McGraw–Hill, 2004.

Fainaru–Wada, Mark and Williams, Lance. *Game of Shadows: Barry Bonds, BALCO, and the Steroid Scandal that Rocked Professional Sports.* Gotham Publishing, 2005.

Fitts, Robert K. *Remembering Japanese Baseball: An Oral History of the Game.* Southern Illinois University Press, 2005.

Fortunato, John. *Commissioner: The Legacy of Pete Rozelle.* Taylor Trade Publishing, 2006.

Frommer, Harvey. *Shoeless Joe and Ragtime Baseball.* Taylor Publishing Company, 1992.

Gay, Timothy M. *Tris Speaker: The Rough and Tumble Life of a Baseball Legend.* University of Nebraska Press, 2006.

Greene, Bob. *Rebound: The Odyssey of Michael Jordan*. Viking Adult, 1995.

Gropman, Donald. *Say it Ain't So, Joe! The Story of Shoeless Joe Jackson*. Little, Brown Publishing, 1979.

Ham, Eldon. *Larceny and Old Leather: The Mischievous Legacy of Major League Baseball*. Academy Chicago Publishers, 2005.

Hinton, Ed. *Daytona: From the Birth of Speed to the Death of the Man in Black*. Warner Books, 2001.

Houston, William and David Shoalts. *Eagleson: The Fall of a Hockey Czar*. McGraw–Hill, 1993.

Jackson, Phil and Delehanty, Hugh. *Sacred Hoops: Spiritual Lessons of a Hardwood Warrior*. Hyperion Books, 1995.

James, Bill. *The Baseball Book 1990*. Villard Press, 1990.

James, Bill. *The Bill James Historical Baseball Abstract*. Villard Books, 1986.

Jones, K.C. and Warner, Jack. *Rebound: The Autobiography of K.C. Jones and an Inside Look at the Champion Boston Celtics*. Quinlan Press, 1986.

Kalb, Elliott. *Who's Better, Who's Best in Baseball?* McGraw–Hill, 2005.

Kalb, Elliott. *Who's Better, Who's Best in Basketball?*. McGraw–Hill, 2003.

Lally, Richard. *Bombers: An Oral History of the New York Yankees*. Three Rivers Press, 2003.

MacCambridge, Michael. *America's Game: The Epic Story of How Pro Football Captured a Nation*. Random House, 2004.

McMillen, Tom and Coggins, Paul. *Out of Bounds: How the American Sport Establishment is Being Driven by Greed, Hypocricy—and What Needs to Be Done About It*. Simon and Schuster, 1992.

Miller, Jeff. *Going Long: The Wild 10–Year Saga of the Renegade American Football League in the Words of Those Who Lived It*. Contemporary Books, 2003.

Murray, Jim. *The Autobiography of the Pulitzer Prize Winning Sports Columnist*. Macmillian Publishing, 1993.

Myler, Thomas and Sugar, Bert Randolph. *The Sweet Science Goes Sour: How Scandal Brought Boxing to its Knees*. Greystone Books, 2006.

O'Neil, Terry. *The Game Behind the Game: High Stakes, High Pressures in Television Sports*. Harper and Row, 1989.

Parrish, Bernie. *They Call it a Game*. The Dial Press, 1971.

Perkinson, Gary and Michael J. McCormick. *The 1996 Midsummer Classic*. Major League Baseball Properties, 1996.

Povich, Shirley and Solomon, George, Povich Lynn, Povich Maury, and Povich David, eds. *All Those Mornings...at the Post*. Public Affairs, 2005.

Prager, Joshua. *Echoing the Green: The Untold Story of Bobby Thomson, Ralph Branca, and the Shot Heard 'Round the World.* Pantheon Books, 2006.

Ritter, Lawrence S. *The Glory of their Times: The Story of Baseball Told by the Men Who Played It.* MacMillan Publishing Company, 1970.

Robertson, Oscar. *The Big O: My Life, My Times, My Game.* Rodale Books, 2003.

Robinson, Ray. *Mattie: An American Hero.* Oxford University Press, 1993.

Rose, Pete and Rick Hill. *My Prison Without Bars.* Rodale Press, 2004.

Rose, Pete and Roger Kahn. *Pete Rose: My Story.* MacMillan Publishing, 1989.

Schaap, Dick. *Flashing Before My Eyes: 50 Years of Headlines, Deadlines, and Punchlines.* William Morrow Publishing, 2001.

Shecter, Leonard. *The Jocks.* Paperback Library Edition, 1970.

Stump, Al. *Cobb: A Biography.* Algonquin Books of Chapel Hill, 1994.

Taylor, John. *The Rivalry: Bill Russell, Wilt Chamberlain, and the Golden Age of Basketball.* Ballantine Books, 2006.

Torres, Jose. *Sting Like a Bee: The Muhammad Ali Story.* Abelard–Schuman, 1971.

Trump, Donald and Schwartz, Tony. *Trump: The Art of the Deal.* Ballantine Books, 1987.

Vincent, Fay. *The Last Commissioner: A Baseball Valentine.* Simon and Schuster, 2002.

Wallechinksky, David. *Sports Illustrated presents The Complete Book of the Summer Olympics 1996 Edition.* Little, Brown, and Company, 1996.

Weiss, Don and Day, Chuck. *The Making of the Super Bowl: The Inside Story of the World's Greatest Sporting Event.* McGraw–Hill, 2003.

Whiting, Robert. *The Samurai Way of Baseball: The Impact of Ichiro and the New Wave from Japan.* Grand Central Publishing, 2005.

Wolf, David. *Foul: The Connie Hawkins Story.* Holt, Rinehart, 1972.

REFERENCE

Official NBA Guide *Official NBA Guide 2006–2007 Edition.* Sporting News Books, 2007.

Official 2006 National Football League Record and Fact Book. Compiled by NFL Communications Department and Seymour Siwoff, Elias Sports Bureau, 2006.

Super Bowl by the Numbers: A Statistical History of Games I–XXX. National Football League. Produced by NFL Properties Publishing Group, 1997.

The Best American Sports Writing of the Century. Edited by David Halberstam. Houghton Mifflin Publishing, 1999.

The Original 2005 Thoroughbred Times Racing Almanac. By the Staff of Thoroughbred Times, 2005.

1987 American League Red Book. The American League of Professional Baseball Clubs. Published by The Sporting News Publishing Co.

1987 National League Green Book. The National League of Professional Baseball Clubs. Published by The Sporting News Publishing Co.

WEBSITES

nba.com
mlb.com
disinfo.com
footballresearch.com
nfl.com
baseball–reference.com
newspaperarchives.com
sportslawnews.com

INDEX